Young Catholics
in the United States and Canada

A Report to the Knights of Columbus

YOUNG CATHOLICS

A Report to the Knights of Columbus

Joan L. Fee

Andrew M. Greeley

William C. McCready

Teresa A. Sullivan

Center for the Study of American Pluralism
National Opinion Research Center
University of Chicago
March, 1980

Sadlier

Los Angeles   New York   Chicago

Library of Congress Catalog Card Number: 81-0310

ISBN: 0-8215-9875-9

To
Peter H. Rossi
without his encouragement and support
this tradition would not have begun.

Printed in the United States of America

Published by William H. Sadlier, Inc., 11 Park Place, New York, New York 10007

Contents

Acknowledgements

This study could not have been successfully completed without the participation and cooperation of a great many people. We gratefully acknowledge the support and assistance of all of them, while assuming ourselves the responsibility for what is written here.

We are grateful to the Knights of Columbus (especially to the Supreme Knight, Virgil Dechant, and to the board of directors) for being the first organization within the Catholic Church to see the need for this research, and to pursue that need with diligence, persistence and the financial resources sufficient to make the project a reality.

There were others in various Church offices who worked equally hard to enable this study to be accomplished. Among those we especially thank are the Most Rev. Joseph L. Bernardin, Archbishop of Cincinnati, the Most Rev. Charles P. Greco, Bishop Emeritus of Alexandria, Louisiana, and Rev. John F. Meyers, President of the National Catholic Educational Association.

Our colleagues at the National Opinion Research Center (NORC) provided guidance and stimulation. Especially helpful were our director, Norman Bradburn, Profs. James Coleman, D. Garth Taylor, and J. David Greenstone. The data collection and preparation were ably supervised by Senior Survey Director Paul Sheatsley, with the assistance of Shirley Knight and Ruth Kellam. The sample was designed by Prof. Martin Frankel, NORC's Technical Director.

In addition, members of the NORC technical operations staff performed many crucial and valuable tasks which enabled the project to achieve a high degree of scientific success. Dan McGuire and David Cook were responsible for much of the required specialized programming, and Kristine Yasutake supervised the data cleaning and data processing functions. The coding of the survey was supervised by Edward Schuldt. Special thanks is extended to Karin Steinbrenner, the Director of Data Processing for NORC, who designed the automated receipt control system used for this study.

Members of the Center for the Study of American Pluralism who assisted with the analysis portion of the project were Gary Byram and Elizabeth Borowitz. The administrative personnel of the

Center, Mary Kotecki and Robert Holst, supervised the preparation of the report and made it possible for eveyone else to coordinate their various activities.

The Canadian survey was directed by Victor Tremblay and Pierre Bouchard of the University of Montreal's Centre de Sondage.

Introduction

This project began as an outgrowth of the 1974 study of the educational effects of Catholic schools done at NORC and published in *Catholic Schools in a Declining Church* (Greeley, McCready & McCourt, 1974.) A major question remaining after that study was whether the situation of religious decline which had been documented in the adult population would be true also for those younger Catholics. A second question was whether recent innovations in Catholic education changed the impact which Catholic schools have had on their graduates.

Very quickly, this current project began to take on a much more comprehensive scope than merely being an extension of the previous one. The Knights of Columbus expressed their interest in supporting a study of young people which would include research on their attitudes toward religious vocations, Catholic fraternal societies and a variety of other topics which were important to the ongoing policy discussions within the Church today.

In addition, the Center for the Study of American Pluralism at NORC has been involved for many years in studying ethnic and religious diversity in the United States. A major portion of this effort has concentrated on developing sociological analysis of the changes occurring within the Catholic population and the research has been summarized in *The American Catholic: A Social Portrait* (Greeley, 1977).

The result of these converging events was that funding became available from the Knights of Columbus to do a major sociological survey of the Catholic population between the ages of 14 and 29, in both the United States and Canada. The National Opinion Research Center at the University of Chicago and the Centre de Sondage at the University of Montreal collected the data (1398 cases from the United States and 782 cases from Canada). The research team at NORC analyzed the data and wrote the final report.

Chapter One is divided into two parts, one dealing with the description of youthful religiosity and the other with an analysis of these data. Our respondents provided us with a complex look at the way in which young Catholics order their religious lives. They are quite likely to remain close to God and appear to have a strong sense of religion, but they are neither particularly close to nor respectful of the teaching authority of the Catholic Church. We demonstrate, in part two, that the parish is the most important element in bonding young people to the Church, and that a vibrant parish life appears to be the best influence the Church can have on young religious lives.

In Chapter Two we discuss the reasons why those young Catholics who have left the Church have done so. About 15 percent of the sampled population no longer identify themselves as Catholics and the primary reason seems to be that they came from family situations which did not support their religious growth. Their religious imagination is lacking in the warm imagery which sustains other young Catholics, and to some extent they are more likely than others to be in religiously mixed marriages that tend to have a deleterious effect on their continued religious identification.

A central component of our analysis is contained in Chapter Three in which we document a religious and marital rebound during the first decade of marriage for young Catholic adults. Church attendance and marital satisfaction, which decline in the years immediately following marriage, begin to climb up again in the latter part of the first decade. Ours is not the only research which has confirmed this "rebound" effect, and in fact a recent Gallup report notes a similar resurgence of devotion for young Catholics, but not for young Protestants. As can be seen in the table below there is a sharp decline in weekly church attendance for Catholics in their early and middle twenties, from 41 percent to 30 percent, and then a sharp rebound to 52 percent in the early thirties. (This 11 percent decline and 22 percent increase are both statistically significant.) The comparable rebound curve for Protestants is a decline of four percentage points and then a rebound of seven points. This Catholic rebound effect has been observed in three different data sets: the General Social Survey from NORC, the Knights of Columbus study of young Catholics, and the Gallup data reported below.

Weekly Church Attendance By Age
For Catholics And Protestants
(Percent answering "yes," to . . . "Did you go to church last week?")

AGE	CATHOLIC	PROTESTANT
18 to 20	41	34
21 to 24	30	30
25 to 29	37	34
30 to 34	52	37
35 to 39	56	37

In Chapter Four we present a specific example of the way in which the religious imagination operates to create and sustain warm symbolic representations of the heritage of faith. The importance of the Madonna symbol, and the positive warmth and strength of that imagery in the lives of our young respondents, is explored. (A discussion of this phenomenon also appears in *America* magazine for February 23, 1980 under the title, "Mary Survives.")

The fifth and sixth chapters contain materials related to the life cycles of these young people. In Chapter Five we present analytic models describing the impact of religious imagery on people's lives, including its mitigating influence on religious alienation and its supportive effect on the religious rebound noted in the previous chapters.

Chapter Six contains a discussion of the influence of Catholic education on the religious life cycle. We note that the schools appear to be even more important during times of religious transition and turmoil than they appeared to be in the 1974 study, and that this is particularly true when it comes to their effect on the rebound phenomenon at the end of the first decade of marriage. It is precisely those respondents who have had more, rather than less, Catholic education who benefit most from the rebound.

Chapter Seven is devoted to a discussion of the attitudes of young Catholics toward a vocation to the religious life. This analysis concentrates on the reasons why young people seem to be disinclined toward pursuing vocations and considers a variety of possible explanations. Overall the most important reason is that no one ever encouraged them to think about having a vocation. Other attitudinal factors do enter in, but the one component for vital vocations which appears to be critical is supportive encouragement from family members or religious professionals.

In Chapter Eight we look at the attitudes of young Catholics toward various fraternal organizations, including the Knights of Columbus. Not only are the Knights the best known of the organizations, but there are also approximately eight to twelve times as many young people who are presently members, who would be interested in considering future membership. In other words, while there are not a great many young people who are currently members of the Knights of Columbus, there are many, many young Catholic men who would be interested in learning more about the organizations and perhaps eventually joining. The situation for productive recruitment is promising.

Chapter Nine consists of an analysis of the demographic and fertility patterns of young Catholics. We conclude that there is a strong pro-child and pro-family sentiment in this population, but that it is coupled with a moderate level of divorce which ought to

receive considerable pastoral attention in the future.
(Approximately 10 percent of the young married Catholics were
divorced before their tenth year of marriage was over.)

In Chapter Ten we present an analysis of the relationship between
religious and political beliefs for these young respondents. While
there is a moderate connection between religiosity and politics, it
will require further research and study to detail the interaction
completely. However, it does appear as though when people
rebound religiously, they also rebound politically, in the sense that
they return to the party in which they were raised.

Finally we present a concluding chapter in which we summarize
the research findings and make some policy-related suggestions
and recommendations which we hope will be useful additions to
the ongoing discussions currently taking place within the Church.
This project, thanks to the support of the Knights of Columbus, has
been a groundbreaking effort for research within the Church. It
represents the first time Church-related funds have supported
research of this type. These data will be used by scholars and
Church professionals for years to come. Hopefully, it also
represents the beginning of a serious research effort within our
Church which will help us plan for and adapt to and influence the
ever-changing social environment in which we live.

Any research project of this scope is a collaborative effort of the
entire team. However, each member of the team was primarily
responsible for certain chapters. Chapters 1 and 10 were written
by Joan L. Fee; Chapters 2 and 9 by Teresa A. Sullivan; Chapters
3, 4, and 5 by Andrew M. Greeley; and Chapter 7 by William C.
McCready. Chapter 6 was co-written by Andrew M. Greeley and
William C. McCready, and Chapter 8 by Joan L. Fee and Andrew
M. Greeley.

Highlights

1 *Catholics between the ages of 15 and 30 have emerged from the turmoil of the 60s and 70s with a renewed and deeper interest in religion.*

2 *While some young people who have left the Church find a new home in sects or Eastern religions, the majority of the young people who leave the Church do not join a new religion.*

3 *The religious profile of young people indicates that they do indeed pray. The way that they pray gives a good indication of their sense of closeness or distance to God.*

4 *Young adults who disagree with the Church's teachings on certain moral and doctrinal matters feel free to do so without seeing themselves being cut off from the Church.*

5 *A majority of young Catholics rejects the teachings of the Church on such topics as birth control, divorce and remarriage, mercy killing, and abortion in the case of a defective baby. However, on such topics as abortion on demand and homosexual relations, a majority of young Catholics express agreement with the teachings of the Church.*

6 *If young persons are to feel close to the Church, they need good and vibrant experiences of the Church at the parish level. The most important way to develop these experiences comes from good sermons, warm and understanding priests, and available and relevant parish activities for youth.*

Selected comments from Young Catholics
Study Respondents

I believe that over the years the children of my time have come to respect the Church as just a thing your parents did because it was expected. I think a lot of us believe that you can be close to God anywhere. There's no reason why you should have to go to church to do it. They just want your Sunday money.

I studied for the priesthood for five years. I have a degree in theology. I love the Church, my Faith, and my Creator. I left the seminary for one reason only—I felt I needed to have family (especially children) to have a fulfilling life. I am presently a Navy pilot with a good career, good pay, and a good future, but I would leave it all in a minute if the Church would let me become a married priest. I hope this questionnaire is God's way of arriving at this end. I am returning the $2.00 as a contribution to the K. of C.

I used to be an extremely religious person, but when I began to have questions about my faith (as everyone does at some time), I didn't really have anyone that I could talk to about it (except for my non-Catholic friends). If I mentioned it to my Catholic friends, I felt ostracized by their reactions. My mother got angry, and my (religious) teachers (in Catholic school) pushed aside my questions or just didn't understand. I think it would be helpful to have someone kids can talk with about this and be helped.

Chapter 1

Religiosity and Youth

PART 1: Religiosity Among American and Canadian Youth

Today's young Catholics will determine the tapestry of the Catholic Church as it enters the twenty-first century. Recent research on American Catholic attitudes and practices (e.g., Greeley, McCready and McCourt, 1976) shows a dramatic change in the views and behavior of Catholics of all ages over the past decade—decreasing Mass attendance, a tendency to reject the role of the Church as teacher, a decline in vocations. As is true with much social change, young people appear even more actively involved (or in some cases, passively involved) in producing these changes than are their parents and grandparents. Yet, the greatest era of youthful change may be over. Krump (1979) and other youth observers report increasing religious interest among youth on college campus.

This study examines in detail the beliefs and practices of young Catholics and former young Catholics between the ages of 14 and 29. With a *youthful Catholic* case base of roughly 1,400 Americans and nearly 800 Canadians, much larger than that encountered in the usual national survey, we were able to discover the religious and social motivations of young Catholics—where they are religiously and why they are there.

As a beginning, this chapter offers a portrait of American and Canadian youth and the state of their respective religiosity. While the bulk of the report concerns explanations of religious behavior, this chapter establishes where American and Canadian youth stand in terms of religious belief and behavior. A final section of the chapter begins the explanatory process—examining how close young people feel to the Catholic Church and what processes foster closeness.

Religious Practice

To qualify as a respondent for the Young Catholics Study, a person has (1) to be presently a Catholic, to have been raised a Catholic,

3

or to have spent at least ten years as a Catholic, and (2) to fall within the 14-and 29-year-old age guidelines. We begin our sketch of youthful religious practice with the American component of the study. In a later section of the chapter we compare and contrast the American findings with those of young Canadians.

Table 1.1 (page 5) indicates the current religious affiliations of the American respondents in the study and also their religious histories. Of those young people (aged 14 to 29) who were raised Catholic, 18 percent have left the Church. However, if one shears off the younger adolescents (aged 14 to 17) who are less likely to have left their family's religion, the figure jumps to a defection rate of 25 percent for the 18- to 29-year-old group. The majority of those who leave the Church (57 percent) take on no new religion. However, a sizable minority (25 percent) join religions other than the main Protestant or Jewish denominations—smaller sects and Eastern religions. Interestingly, a number of respondents list "agnosticism" as an alternative *religion*.

For every 4.6 young American Catholics who leave the Church, one young person of another religion converts to Catholicism. Table 1.1 reveals that 4 percent of the current Catholic population between 14 and 29 is made up of converts. Most of the converts were formerly Protestant.

We now turn to that segment of the population which presently considers itself Catholic. To form a preliminary religious profile of these Catholic youths we consider (a) their religious participation, (b) their sense of their personal relationship to God, and (c) their religious and moral beliefs.

Religious Participation

Greeley (1979) and Potvin, Hoge, and Nelsen (1976) have detailed a continuing drop in Mass attendance by American Catholic youth since the 1960s. The fresh data gathered for this study indicate that the decline may have bottomed out. Table 1.2 (page 5) illustrates the Mass-attendance rates of young Catholics between the ages of 18 and 29 as reflected in the annual General Social Survey conducted by the National Opinion Research Center. Three time periods are depicted—the years 1972–73, 1974–75, and 1976–77. (Since the General Social Survey represents the American population as a whole, it contains only about one hundred *young* Catholics each year. The combining of two years boosts the case base providing more stable attendance figures.) These attendance rates at three time periods are compared to those of the 18-to 29-year-old group sampled in the Young Catholic Study.

While weekly Mass attendance rates declined for young adults between 1972 and 1977, they seem to have begun to rise again in 1979 nearly equaling the 1974–75 rates. Even more encouraging is

TABLE 1.1

Religious Make-Up and History of American Catholic Youth Study Respondents
(Percent)

A. PRESENT RELIGION

Respondents	(N = 1,259)
Catholic	85
Protestant	3
Jewish	0
Other	4
None	8

B. RELIGIOUS HISTORY

1. Proportions who changed religions:

Raised Catholic,	18% (184) of 14- to 29-year olds
left the Church:	25% (169) of 18- to 29-year olds
Raised non-Catholic,	4% (40) of 14- to 29-year old Catholics
joined Church:	4% (38) of 18- to 29-year old Catholics

2. Direction of change

		(N = 184)
	Protestant	19
Catholic →	Jewish	0
	Other	25
	None	57

	(N = 40)	
Protestant	55	
Jewish	0	→ Catholic
Other	15	
None	30	

TABLE 1.2

Mass Attendance Rates of 18- to 29-Year Old American Catholics, the 1970s
(Percent)

ATTENDANCE	GENERAL SOCIAL SURVEY			Catholic Youth
	1972–73 (N = 221)	1974–75 (N = 223)	1976–77 (N = 198)	1979 (N = 721)
Weekly	35	31	24	29
Once a year or less	29	31	40	31

the change in the once-a-year-or-less attenders. While the number of young Catholic adults who took very little interest in church attendance rose over the course of the 1970s, the 1979 figures indicate a drop back to the 1974–75 rates in the proportion of people who fall into this category. This upswing in attendance rates, of course, is tentative and should be followed into the 1980s to determine its staying power.

Table 1.3 offers a fuller view of the 1979 situation—incorporating the Mass attendance, Communion, and Confession rates of both the adolescents (aged 14 to 17) and the adults (aged 18 to 29).

TABLE 1.3

Attendance Rates of American Catholic Adolescents and Young Adults at Mass, Communion and Confession, 1979
(Percent)

Attendance	(N = 1,065)
Mass:	
Weekly	37
Once a year or less	25
Communion:	
Weekly	26
Once a year or less	41
Confession:	
At least several times a year	25
Once a year or less	75

While Mass attendance rates may be improving at present, the respondents display a rather relaxed attitude toward the institutional Church. A full 25 percent of those young people who still think of themselves as Catholic attend Mass once a year or less. Communion fares even worse, with a once-a-year reception rate of 41 percent. And it seems that regular reception of the sacrament of Reconciliation (Penance) has been virtually abandoned by youth, with 75 percent of the population receiving the sacrament once a year or less. (Among young adults that figure jumps to 83 percent—56 percent reporting that they "never" go to confession.)

Of course, there are other means of involvement with the Church besides attendance at Mass, communion and confession. Table 1.4 (page 7) reports the participation rates of young Catholics over a two-year period in a number of alternative activities. Among them, the communications media have touched the greatest proportion of young people. In the last two years, 26 percent of the young population have read a spiritual book and 36 percent have read a Catholic periodical. Fifteen percent have listened to a Catholic radio or television program even though, presumably, such programs are not available to all.

TABLE 1.4

Participation Rates of Young Catholics in Various Religious Activities
(Percent)

Activities	(N = 1,052)
Retreat	16
Days of renewal	11
Read spiritual book	26
Read Catholic periodical	36
Listened to Catholic radio or TV program	15
Talked over religious problem with priest	15
Attended marriage program	13
Charismatic prayer meeting	4
Informal liturgy	8
Religious discussion group	20
Served as lector, reader, or extraordinary minister of communion	9
None of the above	32

Religious discussion groups are also quite popular, with one-fifth of the youthful population having participated in one. Nearly 10 percent of youth have experienced the more public participation in Mass offered to lectors, readers, and extraordinary ministers of communion. Only about a third of the young Catholics have not in the last two years taken part in any of the activities contained in Table 1.4.

Personal Relationship with God

Although young Catholics participate less frequently than previous generations in formal liturgy, they pray often and feel close to God. In fact, while there appears to be an alienated component of young people who have left the Church, many of those who have given up the Catholic religion continue to pray often and to feel close to God. Table 1.5 (page 8) notes how often Catholic and former Catholic young people engage in private prayer. A majority of both groups pray at least once a week. The non-Catholic group is more bipolar—mainly consisting of people who pray very frequently and very infrequently. (Probably those who pray frequently have embraced an alternative religion.) The Catholic group is fairly evenly distributed over the three-prayer categories.

TABLE 1.5

Frequency of Private Prayer, American Catholic and Former Catholic Youth
(Percent)

Frequency	Catholic (N = 1,059)	Former Catholic (N = 179)
Pray every day	32	36
Not daily, but at least once a week	32	16
Less than once a week	36	48

Table 1.6 notes how close Catholic and former Catholic young people feel to God "most of the time." A large majority of both groups feels at least somewhat close to God, with the non-Catholic group again demonstrating a more bipolar pattern of answers. The most common reaction of a young Catholic or former Catholic is to feel at least moderately close to God. However, even among those who still consider themselves Catholic, there remains a group who feels distanced from the deity.

TABLE 1.6

How Close American Catholic and Former Catholic Youth Feel to God
(Percent)

Response	Catholic (N = 1,070)	Former Catholic (N = 177)
Very or moderately close	44	45
Somewhat close	38	20
Slightly close or not close at all	18	35

Besides noting the respondent's sense of closeness to God the Young Catholics Study protocol contained a series of questions on the little-explored subject of prayer. The questions asked the respondents to indicate how often they prayed in certain ways—for example, in their own words, on their knees, using the Bible for reflection. Preliminary analysis shows that young people pray in at least three distinct manners and that the way in which they pray is a fairly good predictor of their sense of relationship to God and their other religious participation rates and attitudes.

The three modes of prayer, which we have labeled "Formal," "Informal," and "Reflective," appear in Table 1.7 along with the behavioral patterns that characterize them. The patterns are obtained by a statistical technique termed factor analysis, which can be used to sift through a large number of items, linking the items which vary in a similar fashion. (See Appendix II for explanations of statistical terms encountered in the report.) For example, in the case of the prayer items, people who often say formal prayers from books or memory are also likely to pray at regular times, to pray to specific religious persons, and to pray on their knees. We have termed this particular way of praying the Formal Mode. Likewise, those who use their own words in prayer—those who pray in the Informal Mode—often pray as if they are talking to a friend, give thanks, pray for a sense of direction or meaning in their lives, and ask for things they need. In contrast, in the Reflective Mode, persons often use the Bible or other spiritual reading for reflection and they also use music to help them talk to God. A few people may combine modes, for example, praying both formally and informally.

TABLE 1.7

Modes of Prayer Among American Catholic and Former Catholic Youth (As Derived From a Factor Analytical Statistical Routine)

MODE		
Formal	Informal	Reflective
Says formal prayers from books or memory	Uses own words	Uses Bible or other spiritual reading reflection
Prays at regular times	Prays like talking to a friend	
	Gives thanks	Uses music when alone to help self talk to God
Prays to specific religious persons such as Jesus, Mary or saints	Prays for a sense of direction or meaning in life	
Prays on knees	Asks for needed things	

Perhaps the most interesting aspect of the prayer modes is their predictive power. Table 1.8 (page 10) notes the relationship between the mode in which young adults pray and their religious participation, their sense of closeness to God and the Catholic Church, and certain demographic characteristics. (Correlation coefficients range from 0 to 1, with the higher numbers indicating a stronger relationship.)

Those who pray formally are much more likely than is the average young adult to attend Mass, to receive communion, and to go to confession on a regular basis. They are also likely to pray frequently and to feel close to God and the Catholic Church. Among young people there is no relationship between a person's educational level and his or her tendency to pray in the Formal Mode. Those who use the Formal Mode of prayer are slightly more likely to be female than would occur by chance.

TABLE 1.8

Correlations Between Prayer Modes and Catholic Participation Rates, American Young Adults (Aged 18-29)

(Coefficient = Pearson's r)

PARTICIPATION	MODE		
	Formal	Informal	Reflective
Frequent Mass attendance	.43*	.11*	.22*
Frequent communion reception	.39*	.20*	.26*
Frequent confession	.32*	.01	.24*
Frequent private prayer	.49*	.50*	.43*
Feel close to God	.40*	.42*	.42*
Feel close to Catholic Church	.39*	.01	.17*
Sex (male)	−.09*	−.18*	−.04
Education level (high)	−.02	.08*	.05

* Significant at .05 level or better.

A tendency to pray in the Informal Mode does not predict a person's religious behavior quite as well as the tendency to pray formally. Those who pray informally are very likely to pray frequently and to feel close to God. They are somewhat more likely than is the average young adult to attend Mass and communion regularly. The relationship, however, between informal prayer and regularly participating in Mass and communion is weaker for informal prayer than for formal. A person's informal prayer patterns offer no help in predicting whether the person feels close to the Catholic Church or goes regularly to confession. However, those who pray informally are somewhat more likely to be female and are also a bit more likely to have achieved a higher educational level.

Probably the most interesting relationships of all occur between Bible reading and the use of music to stimulate private prayer (the Reflective Mode) and religious participation. Among Catholic and former Catholic young adults, those who frequently use the Bible for prayer are also less religiously alienated than those who do not. On the average, they feel close to God and offer private prayers frequently. They are more likely to attend Mass, to receive the sacraments and to feel close to the Church than is the average young adult. They are equally as likely to be male as female, to be well-educated as poorly educated.

Beliefs

In addition to their style of worship and sense of community Catholics have been distinguished from other American religious groups by their beliefs. This section treats the degree to which young Catholics hold the religious tenets and moral beliefs espoused by the Catholic Church. Table 1.9 (page 11) presents a number of religious issues and notes the percentage of young people who offered the orthodox response.

TABLE 1.9

The Proportion of American Youth Who Offer Orthodox Opinions on Certain Doctrinal Issues
Percent

Opinions	(N = 1,060)
There is no definite proof that God exists. (FALSE)	49
God will punish evil people for all eternity. (TRUE)	29
Jesus directly handed over the leadership of his Church to Peter and the popes. (TRUE)	47
The devil really exists. (TRUE)	52
God doesn't really mind how he is worshipped, as long as he is worshipped. (FALSE)	18
It is a sin for a Catholic to miss weekly Mass obligation when he easily could have attended. (TRUE)	44
Under certain conditions the pope is infallible (cannot be wrong) when he speaks on matters of faith and morals. (TRUE)	25
Do you believe there is life after death? (YES)	64

The greatest proportion of young Catholics accept as true the idea of life after death. Interestingly, the next most widely held belief (with 52 percent of the young people agreeing) is that the devil exists. The amount of agreement starts slipping into minority status when it comes to definite proof of the existence of God (49 percent assert proof) and whether Jesus handed Church leadership to Peter and the popes (47 percent agree that Jesus passed on the leadership).

The greatest diversion from the orthodox viewpoint occurs in the areas of papal infallibility (which 25 percent of young Catholics accept) and whether or not God cares how he is worshiped (18 percent assert that God cares). The idea that missing weekly Mass constitutes a sin presents an interesting situation. More young Catholics agree with the sinfulness statement (44 percent) than attend Mass weekly (37 percent).

Besides being asked their opinions on doctrinal matters, the young adult segment of the population fielded questions concerning moral issues. Table 1.10 (page 13) notes the proportion of young Catholic adults who hold the orthodox Catholic viewpoint on moral and sexual issues. When possible, comparisons are made to the attitudes of young Protestants on these issues (as represented in the General Social Survey). The Protestant figures come from the 1978 General Social Survey data; the exception is the homosexuality question, which was last asked in 1977.

A majority of young Catholic adults accept the Church's views on only two issues: the wrongfulness of homosexual relations and of abortion on demand. In contrast, artificial birth control in marriage is viewed as "not doing anything wrong" by 95 percent of young Catholic adults; remarriage after divorce receives the support of 89 percent of the young Catholic population. Even in the area of abortion, 85 percent of young Catholics refuse to take a negative stand when there is the chance of a serious defect in the baby. Similarly, 66 percent of the youthful Catholics reject the Church's teaching against mercy killing.

Except on the issue of homosexuality, young Catholics show an attitude of sexual permissiveness. Eighty-three percent refuse to brand premarital sex as wrong or even "almost always wrong," while 76 percent reject the Church's teaching concerning the wrongfulness of living together out of wedlock.

When the views of young Catholics are compared to those of young Protestants there are few large differences. If anything, young Catholics may, except in the area of homosexuality, be slightly more permissive. Of course, "Protestants" incorporate the diverse religious views of everyone from Southern Baptists to Episcopalians. However, here they are used to illustrate the views of the mainstream of American youth.

The Canadians

The first sections of this chapter have traced the religious devotion of young American Catholics and also their views on doctrinal and moral issues. Two difficulties arise. The first is knowing how unique is the American experience. It could be argued that the condition of the Catholic Church in the United States cannot accurately reflect the condition of the Catholic Church in other parts of the world. A second problem is knowing how to interpret statistics. Thirty-seven percent of young American Catholics attend Mass weekly. Given the imperfection of humankind, is this proportion high or low?

A comparison of American youth to the French-and English-speaking youth in Canada alleviates both of these problems. The French-and English-speaking Canadian youth represent two different cultures to which the American experience might be compared. If French and English Canadians believe and behave in similar fashions as young Americans, this argues that the findings are more generalized phenomena, not peculiar to the American Church. Also, the Canadian data represent a point of comparison which speaks to the problems of interpretation. The Canadian data offer reference points which help define "lows" and "highs."

TABLE 1.10

Proportion of American Protestant and Catholic Young Adults (18-29) Who Espouse Orthodox Catholic Views on Moral Issues
(Percent)

Moral Issues	Catholic (N=883)	Protestant (N=230)
Birth control OK for married couple with as many children as wanted (DISAGREE SOMEWHAT OR DISAGREE STRONGLY)	5	—
Remarriage OK for divorced people in love (DISAGREE SOMEWHAT OR DISAGREE STRONGLY)	11	—
Legal abortion OK if chance of serious defect in baby (NO)	15	15
Legal abortion OK for married woman who does not want more children (NO)	51	56
Euthanasia OK if patient and family request it (DISAGREE SOMEWHAT OR DISAGREE STRONGLY)	34	—
Premarital sexual relations (ALMOST ALWAYS WRONG OR ALWAYS WRONG)	17	23
Unmarried couples living together (ALMOST ALWAYS WRONG OR ALWAYS WRONG)	24	—
Sexual relations between two adults of same sex (ALMOST ALWAYS WRONG OR ALWAYS WRONG)	77	73

The general trend seems to be that American Catholics and English-speaking Canadian Catholics show similar religious behavior and attitudes. French-speaking Catholics are slightly less devout than their English-speaking co-religionists. However, to begin with, French-speaking Catholics are less likely to forsake the religion to which they were born. While 82 percent of young Americans and 87 percent of English-speaking Canadians retain their Catholic religion, the figure is 95 percent for young French-speaking Catholics. French-speaking Catholics, therefore, are perhaps less likely formally to give up their religion even when they philosophically drift away from it.

Table 1.11 adds the Canadian figures to those which appeared in Table 1.3. It can be seen that the differences in the three groups are not startling. While the French Canadians are slightly less likely to attend Mass and communion regularly than the English-speaking groups, their rate of confession is equal to that of the other two groups.

TABLE 1.11

Attendance Rates of American and Canadian Catholic Adolescents and Young Adults at Mass, Communion and Confession, 1979

(Percent)

ATTENDANCE	American (N=1065)	English Canadian (N=228)	French Canadian (N=495)
Mass			
Weekly	37*	36	30
Once a year or less	25*	29	35
Communion			
Weekly	26*	26	21
Once a year or less	41*	42	46
Confession			
At least several times a year	25	29	27
Once a year or less	75*	70	72

* Difference between Americans and French Canadians significant at .05 or better.

Differing rates of participation in other religious activities portray the different styles of the three groups. Again, the habits of the two English-speaking groups are nearly identical; those of the French vary. Here comment will mostly be focused on those activities which show at least a ten percentage point spread between the French Canadians and the Americans (see Table 1.12, page 15). The French, for example, are much less likely to read a spiritual book or Catholic periodical and are much more likely to have listened to a Catholic radio or television program. While 26 percent of Americans have read a spiritual book and 36 percent have read a Catholic periodical in the last two years (the figures are slightly higher for English-speaking Canadians), only 15 percent of French Canadians have read a spiritual book and 21 percent have read a Catholic periodical. Concerning Catholic radio and television programs, however, all Canadians experience a higher rate of participation—the French registering a 36 percent audience, the English Canadians a 30 percent audience, with the Americans showing a 15 percent viewing and listening rate. (Programs, of course, may differ in their availability.)

Religious discussion groups most dramatically divide the different cultures. Roughly one-fifth of American and English-speaking Canadian Catholics participate in religious discussion groups. The comparable figure for French Canadians is two-fifths—double the English-speaking figure. Another activity in which the French Canadians show double the participation of the English-speaking groups is charismatic prayer groups. Eight percent of the French-speaking Canadians have attended such groups; a comparable figure for English-speaking Canadians and Americans is four percent.

TABLE 1.12

Participation Rates of Young American and Canadian Catholics in Various Religious Activities

(Percent)

ACTIVITIES	American (N=1052)	English Canadian (N=250)	French Canadian (N=520)
Retreat	16*	13	7
Day of renewal	11*	9	5
Read spiritual book	26*	31	15
Read Catholic periodical	36*	40	21
Listened to Catholic radio or TV program	15*	30	36
Talked over religious problem with priest	15*	15	12
Attended marriage program	13*	12	11
Charismatic prayer meeting	4*	4	8
Informal liturgy	8*	6	5
Religious discussion group	20*	18	41
Served as lector, reader, or extraordinary minister of communion	9	8	8
None of the above	32*	29	23

* Difference between Americans and French Canadians significant at .05 or better.

Although the French Canadians differ from English Canadians and Americans in their religious activities, they feel just as close to God and pray with the same frequency. There are no statistically significant differences between the three groups either in feelings of closeness to God or in frequency of prayer.

Just as the frequency of prayer finds duplication in the Canadian and American groups, so the modes of prayer differ little in the groups. When the different ways in which Canadian youth pray are entered into a factor analysis, the same three prayer modes emerge—Formal, Informal and Reflective. The factors contain virtually identical variables. The only exception is that some of the weaker variables (with scores under .5) which appear on the Informal factor in the American case like "asking for needed things" appear on the Formal factor in the Canadian case. However, the replication of the three different modes of prayer in two separate countries speaks to their robustness and indicates the need for further research on the prayer phenomenon.

A final way in which the youth of three cultures distinguish themselves is in their beliefs—both doctrinal and moral. As noted in Table 1.13 (page 17), the French Canadians are much less likely to believe in the devil or in the sinfulness of missing Mass. They are somewhat less likely to believe that there is proof that God exists. Along with their English-Canadian counterparts, French Canadians are less likely than American youth to believe that the evil will be punished for all eternity.

However, the youth of the three cultures hold roughly the same views on the infallibility of the pope (a minority believe) and the existence of life after death (a majority believe). Furthermore, the French Canadians take a somewhat more orthodox position than the English-speaking groups on the primacy of the Catholic Church. They are more likely to believe both that Jesus gave his leadership to the popes and that God minds how he is worshiped.

In the area of moral issues, sexual topics most strongly divide the three cultures. As shown in Table 1.14 (page 18), Americans are less likely to approve of premarital sex, cohabitation, or homosexuality than are either the French-or English-speaking Canadians. However, the three groups' views are closer together on birth control, divorce, abortion and euthanasia, even though the differences remain statistically significant. They differ the most in their approach to homosexuality. Homosexuality is considered wrong by more than three-quarters of the Americans, by more than two-thirds of the English-speaking Canadians, but by only half of the French Canadians. Across the board, the French Canadians take the least orthodox positions on the moral issues analyzed here. The Americans and the English-speaking

Canadians are equally likely to assume orthodox positions—with the Americans generally less orthodox on sexual issues.

TABLE 1.13

The Proportion of American and Canadian Youth Who Offer Orthodox Opinions on Certain Doctrinal Issues
(Percent)

OPINIONS	American (N=1060)	English Canadian (N=247)	French Canadian (N=512)
There is no definite proof that God exists. (FALSE)	49*	43	37
God will punish evil people for all eternity. (TRUE)	29*	19	17
Jesus directly handed over the leadership of his Church to Peter and the popes. (TRUE)	47*	46	58
The devil really exists. (TRUE)	52*	50	20
God doesn't really mind how he is worshiped, as long as he is worshiped (FALSE)	18*	22	29
It is a sin for a Catholic to miss weekly Mass obligation when he easily could have attended. (TRUE)	44*	45	24
Under certain conditions the pope is infallible (cannot be wrong) when he speaks on matters of faith and morals. (TRUE)	25*	28	30
Do you believe there is life after death? (YES)	64	68	65

* Difference between mericans and French Canadians significant at .05 or better.

Youthful Catholic Practices: Summary

The purpose of the first portion of this chapter has been to establish where the Church stands in the lives of American and Canadian young people. In view of the quantity of data presented, it seems wise to summarize and discuss the religious state of Catholic youth before proceeding to the analytical portion of the chapter which concerns dimensions of religiosity and closeness to the Church.

The religious status of American Catholic young people in 1979 presents a mixed picture. On the positive side, the great majority of those born Catholic remain Catholic. The Church is speaking to them at some level. A strong minority regularly attends Mass. (Forty-one percent of the Americans who are 18-to 29-years old attend Mass at least two or three times a month; this compares roughly with the Protestant attendance rate of 37 percent for the same age group.) Moreover, the 1979 figures offer some hope that regular Mass attendance may be rising.

TABLE 1.14

Proportion of American and Canadian Catholic Young Adults (18–29) Who Espouse Orthodox Catholic Views on Moral Issues

(Percent)

Moral Issues	American (N=883)	English Canadian (N=176)	French Canadian (N=336)
Birth control OK for married couple with as many children as wanted (DISAGREE SOMEWHAT OR DISAGREE STRONGLY)	5*	8	2
Remarriage OK for divorced people in love (DISAGREE SOMEWHAT OR DISAGREE STRONGLY)	11*	15	7
Legal abortion OK if chance of serious defect in baby (NO)	15*	22	12
Legal abortion OK for married woman who does not want more children (NO)	51*	56	56
Euthanasia OK if patient and family request it (DISAGREE SOMEWHAT OR DISAGREE STRONGLY)	34*	33	27
Premarital sexual relations (ALMOST ALWAYS WRONG OR ALWAYS WRONG)	17*	7	6
Unmarried couples living together (ALMOST ALWAYS WRONG OR ALWAYS WRONG)	24*	18	9
Sex relations between two adults of same sex (ALMOST ALWAYS WRONG OR ALWAYS WRONG)	77*	69	50

* Difference between Americans and French Canadians significant at .05 or better.

The Canadians illustrate that the American case is not an isolated one. Like their American counterparts, most young Canadians who were born Catholic have remained so. This is particularly true of French Canadians who leave the Church in negligible numbers. (Only five percent of French-Canadian youth give up their faith.) A counterpoint to the French-Canadian Catholic Church retaining its members is that it attracts virtually no converts. (Whereas 4 percent of American and English-Canadian Catholics are converts, the figure is .2 percent for the French Canadians.) Presumably, since the great majority of French

Canadians are Catholic, they gain and lose fewer members through intermarriage. A fair minority of young Canadian Catholics also attend Mass regularly, with 37 percent of the English-speaking young adults (18 to 29) and 31 percent of the French young adults attending at least several times a month.

Besides attending Mass and the sacraments, the three cultures express their religious life in different ways. Actually, the division in choice of religious activities falls more neatly between the English-speaking and the French-speaking cultures than among each one of the three. The youth of the English-speaking cultures are much more likely to turn to the printed word—Catholic books and periodicals—for spiritual enrichment. The French, in contrast, engage more often in religious discussion groups and in listening to or viewing Catholic programs on radio and television. (The English-speaking Canadians actually span both groups, following the American trend in reading periodicals and the French trend in consuming Catholic radio and television.)

Catholic youth from both the United States and Canada feel close to God and pray quite often. The mode in which young people pray varies substantially from individual to individual. Some choose traditional methods of prayer—saying formal prayers on their knees and praying to specific persons. Others pray more spontaneously as if they were talking to a friend. Still others feel more comfortable using the Bible or music for contemplation. Although individuals vary in their ways of approaching God, these same patterns of variation appear in two separate countries. In both countries, the way in which a young person relates to the Deity offers an important way of predicting the rest of his or her religious behavior. The reproducibility of three modes of prayer and their importance suggests that more research is needed not only into prayer but also into how people come to an idea of the Deity. Why do young people who share the same faith relate so differently to God?

On the negative side, young Catholics from all three groups seem to have rejected the Church as teacher. The majority accepts only a few doctrinal and social principles—the existence of life after death, the immorality of homosexuality and of abortion on demand. On most doctrinal and moral questions only a minority of young people take the Church's position.

The Church's standing as a moral (as opposed to doctrinal) teacher has been particularly eroded. The Church's position on birth control is rejected by more than 90 percent of the Catholic youth of all three cultures. Likewise the position on divorce is rejected by 85 percent or more of young Catholics from the three cultures. Eighty percent or more of the Catholic young adults reject the wrongfulness of premarital sex.

Two conclusions seem to follow from this rejection of doctrinal and moral teachings. The first is that young people do not feel compelled to leave the Church when they disagree with it. They are perfectly able to function within a Church which takes a stand different from their own. However, the second conclusion is that the moral values of the laity seem to be veering further and further from those advocated by the Church—a rather unhealthy situation. The role of the Church as a moral teacher is one which needs constant attention and discussion. It seems difficult to dismiss the opinions of such huge proportions of the Catholic population as irrelevant, especially as this youthful population grows older and assumes more leadership in the Church.

Having outlined the relationship of American and Canadian Catholic youth to their Church in 1979, we turn in the next portion of the chapter to a related topic—discovering what attracts and keeps these young people within the Church. However, we begin the next section by developing a way to summarize the many dimensions which make up a young person's religiosity. These religious dimensions will be used to predict closeness to the Catholic Church. They will also be used in later chapters to predict a tendency to join fraternal groups and, also, to predict a young person's political views.

PART 2: An Analysis of Religiosity and Closeness to the Catholic Church

This part analyzes the religiosity of young Catholics—the kinds of religion practiced by young adults, the reasons for their particular religious styles, and the impact of religion on other dimensions of their lives. The number of aspects of a person's life which fall under the heading "religious" has been the subject of intense inquiry in the sociological literature. As yet, there is no consensus about the contours of the phenomenon known as religion.

Dimensions of Religiosity

Much recent research is about designating the exact number of religious dimensions present in different populations (e.g. Allport and Ross, 1967; Stark and Glock, 1968; Dejong, Faulkner, and Warland, 1973; King and Hunt, 1975; O'Connell, 1975). Stark and Glock's five dimensions—religious beliefs, practices, knowledge, experience and consequence—are probably most often cited. Yet, other researchers (King and Hunt, 1975) report as many as eleven different religious dimensions in several different test populations.

The important point seems to be that religion is, indeed, multidimensional. People's religiosity encompasses more than the regularity of their church attendance. Exactly how many dimensions compose a person's religiosity depends on the kinds of individual activities that one is willing to enter into the classification scheme. Is personal growth and striving a religious dimension or an aspect of personality? Is financial support for a church important enough to be considered an aspect of one's religiosity? The number of and kinds of variables entered into a factor analysis or other analysis, of course, affect the number of dimensions which emerge from that analysis.

We sidestep the question of the *ideal* number of religious dimensions present among Catholic young people. Instead we hypothesize a number of aspects of contemporary Catholicism which seem discrete from one another and important in the religious life of the young adult. These six selected aspects of the faith—(1) amount of participation in ritual, (2) parish involvement, (3) personal relationship with God, (4) views on doctrinal issues, (5) views on sexual morality, and (6) mystical experience—were subjected to a principal components analysis to test the discreteness of each dimension.

When two to three variables were selected to represent each theoretical dimension and all of the variables were entered into a principal components analysis, the analysis showed that two of the hypothesized dimensions—ritual and parish involvement—really constitute a single dimension, but that the other four hypothesized dimensions are, indeed, discrete. That is, regarding their amount of participation in ritual and their involvement in their parish, young people are likely to show the same behavior patterns. However, each of the other aspects of religiosity represents a separate pattern of attitude or behavior which is not a particularly good predictor of behavior on other dimensions.

Table 1.15 (page 22) illustrates the different attitudes and activities which were included in the principal components analysis. Also listed are the scores on each dimension. It can be seen that the dimensions are quite crisp. When those scores over .3 are listed, as in Table 1.15, only two variables appear on more than one dimension; and each of these two variables is much weaker than the other variables which constitute that dimension.

To summarize: We have discerned five different dimensions which make up young Catholics' religious lives—parish involvement (including attendance at Mass and communion), views on sexual morality, doctrinal views, their personal relationship with God, and their mystical or ecstatic experience. This list may, by no means, be exhaustive. However, it offers a fruitful starting place for studying youthful religiosity.

TABLE 1.15
Scores On Different Dimensions of Religiosity—Principal Components Analysis, Varimax Rotation
(All scores over .3 listed)

Variable	Dimension 1 Ritual/ Parish	Dimension 2 Sexual Morality	Dimension 3 Doctrinal Views	Dimension 4 Relationship With God	Dimension 5 Mystical Experience
Frequency of Mass attendance	.80			.32	
Frequency of communion reception	.78				
Involvement in a parish activity	.67				
Perceived closeness to the parish	.65		.31		
Attitude toward premarital sex		.90			
Attitude toward living together		.89			
Papal infallibility			.78		
Primacy of Peter and Popes			.70		
Sinfulness of missing Mass			.65		
Frequency of prayer				.78	
Perceived closeness to God				.72	
Closeness to powerful spiritual force					.73
Confidence that life has purpose					.70
Direct contact with "the Sacred" or "the Holy"					.68

Religiosity Dimensions and Closeness to the Church: The American Case

If the Catholic Church is to remain a viable institution, it must maintain its membership over succeeding generations. Having defined different dimensions of religiosity, we may use these dimensions to discover which aspect of religiosity best predicts a sense of closeness or distance from the Catholic Church. For example, is it young people's close relationships to God or their orthodox doctrinal views which better predict their closeness to the.

Church? Once the relationships are understood, it becomes possible to offer policy suggestions that will most effectively encourage closeness to the Church.

The amount of affect that young Catholic adults in the United States feel toward the Catholic Church is the subject of Figure 1.1. The respondents in the Young Catholics Study had each looked at a picture of concentric circles with number "1" and the words "very close" appearing in the bull's eye, with the numbers "2," "3," and "4" appearing in ever more distant circles, and with the number "5" and the words "not at all close" appearing in the outermost circle. A question asked the respondents to use these numbers to rate how close or distant they felt in a few relationships. Figure 1.1 shows that, in the case of the Catholic Church, the largest number of young adults who presently consider themselves Catholic choose a median response of "3" when rating their closeness to the Church. However, the trend of response is toward distance from the Church rather than closeness, with a majority of young adults rating themselves at "3" or less close.

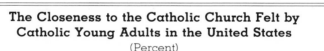

FIGURE 1.1

The Closeness to the Catholic Church Felt by Catholic Young Adults in the United States

(Percent)

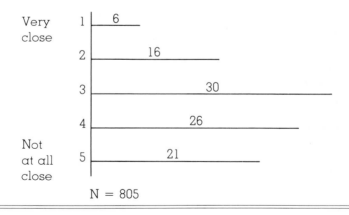

Very close	1	6
	2	16
	3	30
	4	26
Not at all close	5	21

N = 805

Table 1.16 (page 24) notes the strength of the relationship between each of the religiosity dimensions outlined earlier and a feeling of closeness to the Catholic Church. For comparison purposes the table also includes factors which might influence religiosity—religious education and the religiosity of parents and spouse and one's social commitment. The left-hand column shows the simple relationships between each variable and closeness to the Catholic Church. The right-hand column indicates the strength of the relationship when all of the other variables are taken into account. Although each of the five dimensions bears a statistically significant relationship to Church closeness, the ritual/parish dimension shows the strongest relationship. Controlling for the other four dimensions enhances the importance of the ritual/parish dimension.

As an aside here, the theory has been advanced by some that young people distance themselves from the Catholic Church because the Church lacks a strong enough commitment to social action. Table 1.16 shows that those young people who feel a stronger commitment to social action than their compatriots are slightly more likely to feel *closer* to the Church rather than distant. The impact of social action is a relatively small one, however, and is dwarfed by the effect of participation in the sacraments and parish life. The social action variables will receive more attention in Chapter Ten which concerns religion and politics.

TABLE 1.16

The Relationship Between Closeness to the Catholic Church and Aspects of Religiosity Among Young Catholics

	r	B
Ritual/Parish dimension	.62*	.48
Sexual morality dimension	.32*	.10
Doctrinal views dimension	.32*	.10
Personal God relationship dimension	.40*	.15
Mystical experience dimension	.09*	.01
Number years in Catholic school	.03	.09
Number years CCD	.07	.10
Religious parents (Catholic)	.16*	.05
Religious spouse (Catholic)	.30*	.12
Social commitment[a]	.09*	.00

* Significant at .05 level or better.
[a] Social Commitment consists of a scale composed of attitudes toward racial segregation, aid to the poor, and the importance of solving social problems.

The ritual/parish dimension, as noted in Table 1.15, is made up of Mass attendance, communion reception, closeness to the parish and participation in a parish activity. Table 1.17 (page 25) returns to the raw data on each of these variables to form a comparison of the four. Each of the four shows a medium to strong direct relationship with closeness to the Church. However, when all four are entered at once into the closeness-to-the-Church equation, closeness to the parish emerges as by far the most important factor. In other words, among young Catholics, one's experience of the local parish is the *critical* factor in precipitating a feeling of closeness to the Church as a whole. Alone it explains half of the variance which young people show in their identification with the Catholic Church. The comments offered by some respondents confirm this impression. For example, one young adult said:

> I am about to be married and was very disappointed in a certain church that I attended. We had new priests and they were very cold and inconsiderate towards me when I went to talk to them about it. I resigned from this church and didn't have much faith until I joined another church which was better. I now happen to think the Church is the one who decides whether you'll be a good Catholic or not.

TABLE 1.17

The Relationship Between Each of the Components of the Ritual/Parish Dimension and Closeness to the Church

	r	B
Mass attendance	.49*	.12
Communion reception	.46*	.09
Closeness to parish	.72*	.62
Participation in parish activity	.30*	.02

* If a young person is to feel close to the Church, he or she needs a good and vibrant experience of Church at the parish level.

Thus, for young Catholic adults closeness to the Church as a whole begins in the local parish. Persons who feel welcome at the local level seem to translate this acceptance to a larger feeling of affection for the Church as a whole. The next question becomes—what sorts of parishes are most likely to offer young adults spiritual satisfaction?

Table 1.18 (page 26) lists a number of factors that might influence the closeness that young adults feel to their parishes—ranging from the number of available activities for parishioners and the amount of lay influence in the parish to the quality of sermons and the understanding of priests. The table also shows the simple relationship between each variable and closeness to the parish. Most of the variables make statistically significant contributions to predicting a young adult's feeling for the parish, with the exception of the presence or absence of a youth minister.[2] However, when each variable is inspected, controlling for the impact of all of the other variables, those characteristics which emerge as significant are: (1) good sermons, (2) priests who understand a person's problems, and (3) participating in a parish activity.

TABLE 1.18

The Relationships Between Certain Characteristics of Parishes and a Feeling of Closeness to the Parish Among Young Catholics

(Coefficient = Pearson's r)

Number of available parish activities	.16*
Participation in a parish activity	.30*
Lay influence in parish (strong)	.28*
Good sermons	.44*
Priests understand respondent's problems	.43*
Approve of how priests handling job	.33*
Youth minister in parish	.06

*Significant at .05 level or better.

Figure 1.2 illustrates the final model. Good parish sermons, empathetic priests and participation in parish activities all contribute to closeness to the Catholic Church because they cause closeness to the parish. The presence of good sermons in a person's parish is so important that it also makes a direct contribution to the person's closeness to the Church.

FIGURE 1.2

Path Model of Closeness to the Catholic Church Among Young American Catholics

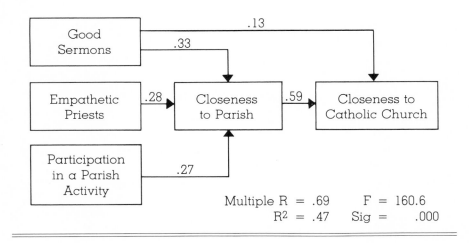

Religiosity Dimensions and Closeness to the Church: The Canadian Case

The patterns among young Canadians are similar to those among young Americans. Figure 1.3 (page 27) notes the degree of closeness to the Church felt by English-speaking and

French-speaking Canadian young adults. The two do not differ statistically either from each other or from their American co-religionists.

FIGURE 1.3

**The Closeness to the Church Felt by
Catholic Young Adults in Canada**
(Percent)

A. English Speaking

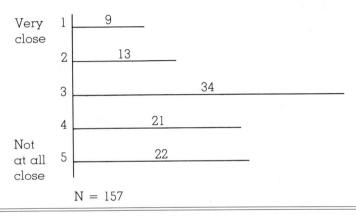

N = 157

B. French Speaking

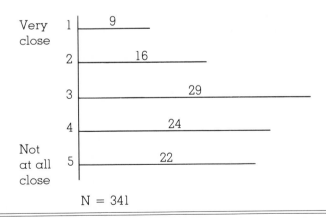

N = 341

Concerning the link between feelings toward the parish and feelings toward the Catholic Church as a whole, similar relationships exist. While we earlier noted a correlation coefficient for Americans of .72 between closeness to the parish and closeness to the Catholic Church, the English-speaking Canadians show a correlation of .79 between the two items, and the French-speaking Canadians register a correlation of .71.

27

However, the final models of Church closeness for Americans and English- and French-speaking Canadians contain slightly different variables. Figures 1.4A and B illustrate the English and French Canadian models respectively. Among the French, being a member of a parish where the laity has a hand in decision-making is a more important predictor of closeness to the parish than it is for the Americans and the English-speaking Canadians. For the French, good sermons exert less of an influence on closeness to the parish and disappear from the model. In contrast, among the English-speaking Canadians, the quality of sermons is by far the most important predictor of a person's closeness to the parish. The ability of priests to understand a person's problems is less important for the English-speaking Canadians than for either the Americans or the French Canadians.

FIGURE 1.4

Path Model of Closeness to the Catholic Church Among Young Canadian Catholics

A. English-Speaking

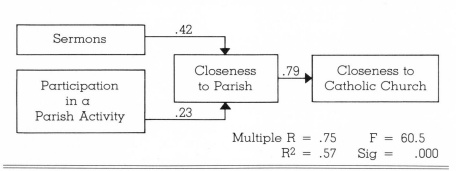

Multiple R = .75   F = 60.5
R^2 = .57   Sig = .000

B. French-Speaking

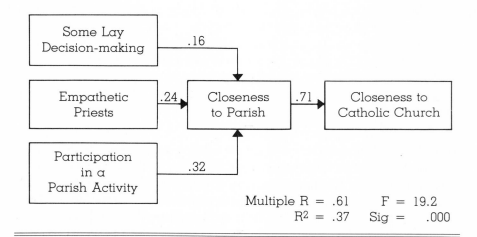

Multiple R = .61   F = 19.2
R^2 = .37   Sig = .000

The French-speaking Canadians, then, feel closer to their parish (1) if they are involved in a parish activity, (2) if the priests are empathetic, and (3) if there is a good deal of lay influence. For the English-speaking Canadians, the critical elements in closeness to the parish are (1) high quality sermons, and (2) participation in a parish activity.

Conclusions

In sum, among three different groups—American, French-speaking Canadians, and English-speaking Canadians—a feeling of closeness to the Catholic Church begins within the parish. Although the most critical parish factors vary slightly from culture to culture, the scenario remains very similar. In order to retain young adults within the Church, one major solution is vibrant parishes. Especially important are quality priests who are able to empathize with young adults and then counsel them. Just as important, however, is the ability of priests to deliver well-planned and articulate sermons. Finally, a parish which makes a special effort to draw young adults into parish activities and decision-making, perhaps by offering activities of special interest to this often neglected age group, will experience smaller rates of attrition.

However, the importance of the priest cannot be overemphasized. A sensitive parish leader who prepares meaningful sermons and relates well to his parishioners strengthens their spirituality. More than anyone else the priest seems to be the person who fosters in young Catholics closeness to the Church as a whole.

Modes of religiosity, then, do not differ drastically in the three separate cultures. For all three groups the quality of the parish attracts and holds the young person within the Church. Likewise, the same modes of prayer manifest themselves in the separate cultures. Youthful Americans, English and French Canadians pray in a Formal Mode, an Informal Mode or a Reflective Mode. For the three groups patterns of prayer predict other aspects of religious behavior. In addition to similarity in modes of religiosity, many details of belief are the same among the youth of the United States and the English- and French-Canadian youth. The three groups, for example, express similar views on life after death, on the infallibility of the pope, on birth control, divorce, and abortion on demand.

However, the details more often separate the behavior and beliefs of at least two of the three groups than bring them together. Overall, the two English-speaking groups, Catholics in the United States and Canada, attend Mass and receive communion a bit more regularly, take a more orthodox position on moral issues and are more likely to read Catholic literature. French Canadians are somewhat more likely to believe in the primacy of the Catholic Church, to participate in religious discussion groups, and to view or listen to Catholic radio or television.

What implications do these findings hold for the Catholic Church? The first is that cultural religious differences continue to exist even within one country—Canada. French young people seem more positive about the primacy of the Catholic Church and yet are less likely to attend that Church regularly; the English are less sure that Christ handed the leadership of his Church to Peter and the popes and that God minds how he is worshiped.

The difference in the French and English groups may well stem, at least partially, from the Catholic Church's minority status in the United States and English-speaking Canada and its majority status in French-speaking Canada. Whatever its source, the existence of cultural differences within the Church emphasizes the need for continuing recognition of the diverse people who make up the Catholic Church. The Church's continuing sensitivity to differences in culture while maintaining its basic beliefs should bring not only the youth, but all Catholics closer to their Church.

In addition, as noted earlier, the fact that the youth of three cultures nearly unanimously reject the Church's teachings on birth control, divorce, and premarital sex, points out the need for continuing consideration of these questions. The division between the official Church position on these issues and the position taken by its people grows wider, not narrower. Ignoring this division imperils the Church's credibility as a moral teacher among Catholic youth. However, young Catholics retain an ability to remain with a Church they no longer look to for moral authority and guidance. This ability relates to parish and also to religious images, a phenomenon which will be explored further in later chapters.

NOTES

[1]Included in the English-speaking group are the 23 Canadian respondents with a mother tongue other than French or English.
[2]The youth minister variable may not be too reliable. The concept of a youth minister is not recognized equally well in different sections of the country. A large minority of respondents, 43 percent, do not know whether or not their parish has a youth minister.

Disidentification with Catholicism

Highlights

1   *Fifteen percent of American Catholics and 22 percent of all Catholics who are married have left the Church entirely and do not consider themselves to be even marginal Catholics.*

2   *The positive impact of worship, family ties, and the value of children are "extremely important" to those who affiliate with the Church.*

3   *One important indicator of possible disaffiliation from the Church comes from the way that parents approach religion. It seems that parents who see religion as a burden might have a more negative influence on children than parents who completely ignore religion.*

4   *The religion of the spouse is the most powerful influence in staying in or in leaving the Church. In religiously mixed marriages, the rate of disaffiliation from the Church is 42 percent; very devout or very lukewarm non-Catholic spouses increase the rate of disaffiliation from the Church.*

5   *"Warm" images of God, Jesus, and Mary are typical of persons within a Church community. "Cold" images characterize the feelings of those persons who are estranged from the Church.*

6   *It seems that the level of disaffiliation of Canadian Catholics is remarkably low compared to their American counterparts.*

7   *Continued affiliation with the Church can be encouraged by featuring the "warm" and positive elements of the Church.*

8   *Special pastoral efforts should be made to help young Catholics who want to be married and those who enter into religiously mixed marriages.*

Chapter 2

Disidentification with Catholicism

About 15 percent of our sample consider themselves to be
ex-Catholics. This chapter deals with the correlates of
disidentification with the Church. Disidentification is not
uncommon among Americans; some studies have found that a
similarly high proportion of all Americans change their religious
identification (Warren, 1970). However, the process of
disidentification is not well understood, because it is typically
measured by asking respondents their *current* religious
identification and his or her identification at an *earlier point in
life*—usually at age 16. The researcher is then left with the problem
of inferring why the respondent changed identifications—and
even a direct question to the respondent may produce unreliable
results. For example, respondents in looking back on their lives
may rationalize an earlier decision to leave one church for another
in terms of their current life experiences. Learning the reason for
disidentification will also be a problem in this chapter. In addition,
this chapter deals only with the process of disidentification among
the young Catholics. Some of those who now report themselves as
Catholics may eventually disidentify and, conversely, some of
those who now consider themselves ex-Catholics may reidentify
with the Church in later life.

This chapter will refer to five groups of Catholics and ex-Catholics.
The *cradle Catholics* are respondents who were reared as
Catholics, who have never left the Church and still consider
themselves to be Catholic. The *converts* were not reared as
Catholics, but are now Catholics. The *marginal Catholics* were
reared as Catholics, but are now ambivalent about their
identification. About 49 percent of the latter reported that they are
now Catholics, although they left the Church for a period. Another
51 percent consider themselves to have left the Church, although
they still report their religious identification to be Catholic. The
switchers were reared as Catholics, but now are members of
another church. The switchers are about evenly divided between
those who are members of mainline Protestant denominations

(Baptist, Methodist, Presbyterian, Lutheran, Episcopalian) and those who report themselves members of "other" religions. Finally, the *unchurched* are those who were reared as Catholics, but now report that they have no religion.

Negative Aspects of Catholicism

One way to approach the issue of disidentification is to examine the negative aspects of Catholicism as reported by the five groups of Catholics and ex-Catholics. Table 2.1 summarizes the percentage of each group who feel that certain negative aspects of the Church are "extremely important." For cradle Catholics the most important single negative aspect is the sex teachings of the Church. Almost one-half of the cradle Catholics report that this is extremely important, although in their cases it has not yet been important enough to lead to disidentification.

TABLE 2.1

Percent Saying Certain Issues Are "Extremely Important" Negative Aspects of Catholicism, by Degree of Catholic Affiliation

(Percent)

Aspect	Cradle Catholics	Marginal Catholics	Converts	Switchers	Unchurched
Sex teachings*	47	62	20	45	66
Doctrine*	29	41	20	58	42
No church attractive*	19	41	40	20	49
Rituals*	36	67	20	47	55
Laity have no say*	21	33	0	43	27
No value system*	29	54	0	60	48

* Significantly associated with degree of Catholic affiliation at .05 or better.

For marginal Catholics the most important negative aspects are a lack of satisfaction associated with rituals, and disagreement with sex teachings, with over 60 percent rating both of those "extremely important." Because of the ambivalence of this group, their response is particularly interesting. As expected, converts find no negative aspect of Catholicism especially important except for a disinclination toward churches in general. One would expect that the convert group would not find teachings or rituals to be important deterrents.

The patterns for switchers and the unchurched are quite different from those for the previous three groups. Over two-fifths of the switchers find the Church's sex teachings, doctrine, rituals, and the role of the laity to be important negative aspects; three-fifths find the lack of a value system important. The unchurched are somewhat more like the marginal Catholics in their disenchantment with the Church's teachings on sexuality and with Catholic rituals; moreover, almost half of them find no church attractive. The fact that the laity have little say in the Catholic Church does not bother the unchurched as much as it bothers the marginal Catholics, perhaps because the unchurched have already "voted with their feet."

The data in Table 2.1 suggest the importance of investigating two areas of Catholicism further—basic beliefs and sexual morality.

Doctrinal Orthodoxy and Disidentification

There are clear patterns of assent to and dissent from Catholic doctrine among the five groups examined in this chapter. As Table 2.2 (page 36) shows, the entire sample remains relatively orthodox in believing in life after death: over 90 percent of the cradle Catholics, converts, and switchers believe in life after death, compared with 82 percent of the marginal Catholics and 76 percent of the unchurched. Beyond that, on the items of belief that Christians share in common (proof that God exists, God punishes evil, existence of the devil), the switchers are overwhelmingly the most orthodox, and the unchurched the least orthodox. Cradle Catholics and converts have similar levels of orthodoxy, with the marginal Catholics about 8 to 10 percent lower in the percentage giving an orthodox response.

On items of belief that are unique to Catholics such as papal primacy and papal infallibility, current Catholics are far more likely to give an orthodox response; the switchers and the unchurched are equally unlikely to give the orthodox response. The level of orthodoxy among cradle Catholics and marginal Catholics is almost twice as high for papal primacy as it is for infallibility, although not even a majority give the orthodox answer on the papal primacy question, "Jesus directly handed over the leadership of his Church to Peter and the popes."

A third pattern appears on questions of ritual. Cradle Catholics are most likely to respond that it is a sin to miss Mass on Sunday when you could have attended easily. Marginal Catholics and converts are less likely to give that response, although they are similar to each other. Switchers and the unchurched are even less likely to answer yes, although they are similar to each other in the level saying yes. This ordering was reversed on the question "God doesn't really mind how he is worshiped, just so long as he is worshiped." The switchers were most likely to say no, the orthodox response, and cradle Catholics least likely to say no. One possible interpretation of these findings is that the cradle Catholics believe attending Mass on Sunday is most important for them, but suspect that God is tolerant about how he is worshiped by others.

TABLE 2.2

Percent Giving Orthodox Answers on Belief Questions, by Degree of Catholic Affiliation
(Percent)

Question	Cradle Cath- olics	Mar- ginal Cath- olics	Con- verts	Switch- ers	Un- churched
Definite proof God exists*	50	40	54	72	24
God punishes evil*	30	19	27	58	9
Devil exists*	53	45	61	75	25
Papal primacy*	48	36	37	16	16
Pope infallible*	26	19	34	12	11
Miss mass a sin*	46	33	32	28	26
God does not care how worshiped*	17	19	22	40	19
Firm disbelief in astrology*	16	23	12	36	18
Life after death*	91	82	90	97	76
N =	1032	70	41	88	114

* Significantly associated with degree of Catholic affiliation at .05 or better.

A final question about belief in astrology was asked as a guide to beliefs that might compete with religious beliefs. Still another pattern appears here, with the switchers and the marginal Catholics most likely to disbelieve in astrology.

Returning to Table 2.1, we saw that dissatisfaction with Church doctrine was strongest among the switchers and the unchurched. Now we can determine that a different process is at work for each group. The switchers tend to be more orthodox on doctrinal issues and the unchurched are the least orthodox. The respondents who are still Catholics are in an intermediate position. People who deviate at both extremes on doctrinal orthodoxy are most likely to disidentify.

Sexual Morality

Table 2.1 suggested the importance of the Church's teachings on sexuality as a negative aspect of Catholicism. The importance of these teachings to disidentification is displayed in Table 2.3. This table shows the percent of each group of Catholics and ex-Catholics who gave orthodox answers to questions of sexual morality. (These questions were asked only of the members of the sample who were age 18 or older, so the sample size is smaller than that in Table 2.2.)

TABLE 2.3

Percent Giving "Orthodox" Answers on Questions of Sexual Morality, by Degree of Catholic Affiliation

(Percent)

	Cradle Catholics	Marginal Catholics	Converts	Switchers	Unchurched
Birth Control Wrong*	6	2	8	5	1
Abortion Should Be Illegal If Baby Defective*	18	16	22	28	6
Abortion Should Be Illegal If Mother Wants No More Children*	63	49	63	59	27
Remarriage After Divorce Wrong*	12	11	17	15	3
Premarital Sex Always Wrong	8	11	18	33	4
Living Together Without Marriage Always Wrong*	10	11	21	34	4
Homosexual Acts Always Wrong*	68	66	66	75	30
N =	633	53	34	74	102

* Significantly associated with degree of Catholicism at .001 or less.

In assessing the responses to these questions, it is important to notice that all groups distinguish between the motives for abortion, and they also distinguish heterosexual activity from homosexual activity. Moreover, it may be significant that the abortion question was phrased in terms of whether it should be possible for a woman to obtain a *legal* abortion under given conditions. Our respondents might have distinguished legality from morality—that is, they might think that abortion is immoral without necessarily thinking that it should also be illegal.

The first fact that emerges from Table 2.3 (page 37) is that there is greater variety in the level of orthodox answers within the same group than there is between groups. The highest percentage of orthodox answers comes on the question of homosexuality; the lowest comes on birth control. But, the range in the percent giving the orthodox answer is about 60 percent in the four groups of church members, and 29 percent among the unchurched. There seems to be far greater consistency among the unchurched than among the churched on these varied aspects of sexual morality, but that consistency is achieved by rejecting orthodox teaching.

Sixty percent of cradle Catholics clearly disapprove of homosexual acts, and abortion (if the mother wants no more children), while only 8 percent disapprove of premarital sex. Marginal Catholics are more permissive in two ways: only half of them believe that abortion should be illegal if the mother wants no more children, and less than 2 percent disapprove of birth control. Converts have a similar pattern of disapproval—most disapprove of homosexuality, and few disapprove of birth control—but, on every other question, the percent who disapprove is higher than among the cradle Catholics. It is particularly interesting that converts are about twice as likely as cradle Catholics to disapprove of living together without marriage.

The switchers are more likely than the cradle Catholics to give the orthodox response, except for birth control and abortion for the mother who wants no more children. Switchers are about four times as likely as cradle Catholics to say that premarital sex is always wrong, and they are three times as likely to say that living together without marriage is wrong. It is interesting that the switchers are somewhat more likely than cradle Catholics to disapprove of abortion when the fetus is defective, but somewhat less likely to disapprove of it because the mother wants no more children.

The least orthodox of the respondents are the unchurched. Their responses on homosexuality are especially striking, because they are only half as likely as cradle Catholics to disapprove of homosexuality. They are by far the most permissive group on abortion, regardless of reason. Furthermore, fewer than five percent of them disapprove of premarital sex, living together without marriage, remarriage after divorce, or birth control.

The switchers and the unchurched once again deviate from the Catholic groups in much the same way as they did on doctrinal questions: the switchers are more orthodox, and the unchurched are less orthodox. In this case, however, the switchers are closer to the Catholic groups, whereas the unchurched give strikingly different responses.

Reasons for Continued Identification

Another way to look at the identification issue is to examine the reasons for continued identification with Catholicism. Table 2.4 shows the percentage of respondents in each group who believe that certain positive aspects of Catholicism are extremely important. The four groups that are still identified with a Church agree that values for children are the most important, with over 40 percent giving this response. Only 18 percent of the unchurched respond in this way.

TABLE 2.4

Percent Saying Certain Issues Are "Extremely Important" Positive Aspects of Catholicism, By Degree of Catholic Affiliation
(Percent)

Aspect	Cradle Catholics	Marginal Catholics	Converts	Swtchers	Unchurched
Source of identity	10	3	9	0	4
Value system	35	18	36	24	18
Worship*	38	33	58	10	5
Family ties*	30	24	36	5	10
Meeting others	6	3	3	14	0
Values for children	49	42	46	48	18
Community Involvement	7	9	9	0	0

* Significantly associated with degree of Catholic affiliation at .05 or better.

It is possible that children are in general more important for those who have Church affiliation—or, perhaps, that their Church affiliation has become more important for them as they have had children. All of the four church-affiliated groups expect to have 2 or more children—2.5 for the cradle Catholics, 2.4 for the switchers, 2.3 for converts, and 2.1 for the marginals. The unchurched expect only 1.8 children.

Worship and family ties are important for those who have remained Catholics, and the value system is important for the cradle Catholics and the converts. Surprisingly, "meeting others" is twice as important for the switchers as for any other group. The unchurched are the least likely to find positive aspects of Catholicism; only 18 percent consider either "values" or "values for children" extremely important.

Except for worship and family ties, the positive aspects of Catholicism do not appear to be associated with Catholic affiliation to the same extent that the negative aspects are. It appears that for all groups, the "push" factors from Catholicism are more important than the "pull" factors to Catholicism. This seems a little puzzling in the case of the continued identification of the cradle Catholics, but it may be that for them an undiffused attraction for Catholicism could not be adequately expressed in the aspects we had prepared in our questionnaire.

Personal Characteristics and Disaffiliation

One would like to be able to predict the background variables that predispose a young Catholic to leave the Church. In this section we attempt to discover the factors that may influence a young Catholic in changing his or her religious identification from "Catholic" to something else. The disaffiliation rate used in this section is the proportion of those who were reared Catholic who no longer consider themselves to be Catholic. Converts are excluded from this section because they were not reared Catholic; the switchers and the unchurched are both considered to be disaffiliated. The overall disaffiliation rate for the sample is 15 percent. In contrast, the data for Canada are dramatically different.

The switchers and the unchurched report that they began having doubts about the Catholic faith about two years earlier, on the average, than those who are still Catholic did. Their doubts began at about age 13; the doubts of those who are still Catholic began at about age 15. (Because not all of the sample has yet reached age 15, it seemed likely that current age is related to disaffiliation.) For children reared as Catholics, it seemed likely that their current religious affiliation would be influenced by their parents' religiosity and by their memories of their childhoods as happy or not. Finally, one's current education might be related to disaffiliation because education is a reasonable proxy variable for exposure to different types of thought and competing ideas, as well as a substitute for social class.

The effect of these variables on disaffiliation is presented in Table 2.5 (page 41). Together these variables account for only 9 percent of the variance, not a very impressive finding. Nevertheless, although the effects are not very important, they are in the expected direction. Column 2 of the table shows the deviation of the disaffiliation rate for a specific group from the grand mean, 15 percent for the whole group. A negative sign means that the group has a lower disaffiliation; a positive sign means more disaffiliation. As expected, the older Catholics are somewhat more likely to be disaffiliated, and the younger ones less likely to be so. The eta-squared of .05 indicates that this variable by itself explains about 5 percent of the variance; the beta-squared indicates that this variable explains only about 1 percent of the variance when the other variables in the table are controlled. Therefore, though there is an effect for age, it is not strong.

TABLE 2.5

Multiple Classification Analysis of the Effects of Personal Background on Probability of Disaffiliation

Independent Variable	Unadjusted Probability	Deviation from Grand Mean	N
Birth Cohort			
1949−52	.234	.089	351
1953−57	.193	.048	388
1958−62	.086	−.059	421
1963−67	.038	−.107	238
$E^2 = .05, B^2 = .01$			
Parents' Relationship			
Lived together	.134	−.011	1174
Child adopted/orphan	.176	.031	17
Divorced	.198	.053	126
One parent dead	.317	.172	41
Other	.138	−.007	29
$E^2 = .01, B^2 = .00$			
Childhood Happiness			
Very happy	.112	−.033	500
Happy	.149	.004	718
Not too happy	.228	.083	149
Unhappy	.294	.149	17
$E^2 = .01, B^2 = .00$			
Father's Religion			
Joyous	.087	−.058	578
Not joyous	.234	.089	184
Not religious	.156	.011	212
$E^2 = .03, B^2 = .00$			
Mother's Religion			
Joyous	.096	−.049	970
Not joyous	.333	.188	132
Not religious	.255	.110	98
$E^2 = .06, B^2 = .03$			
Education Level			
Lt HS	.127	−.018	79
HS	.131	−.014	305
Vocational school	.167	.022	90
Some or jr. college	.211	.066	289
College	.214	.069	131
Some grad/prof	.356	.211	45
Graduate/prof	.325	.180	70
$E^2 = .02, B^2 = .03$			
Grand mean = .145			
$R^2 = .09$			

The parents' relationship variable indicates that the respondent whose parents lived together was less likely to disaffiliate. Children from homes broken by divorce or death, and adopted children, were somewhat more likely to disaffiliate. However, these effects are extremely weak, as the eta and beta statistics show. Remembered childhood happiness is also a weak predictor, even though the very happy are less likely on average to disaffiliate and the unhappy more likely to disaffiliate.

TABLE 2.6

Multiple Classification Analysis of the Effects of Spouse's Characteristics on Probability of Disaffiliation

Independent Variable	Unadjusted Probability	Deviation from Grand Mean	N
Spouse's Religion			
Catholic	.5.423	−.192	240
Not Catholic		.206	215
$E^2 = .24$, $B^2 = .17$			
Religiousness of Spouse			
Very religous	.314	.097	51
Religious	.155	−.062	181
Not too religious	.176	−.041	119
Not religious	.341	.124	91
$E^2 = .04$, $B^2 = .0$			
Marriage Duration			
Newlywed	.500	.283	6
1–5 years	.190	−.027	226
6–10 years	.214	−.003	210
10+ years	.303	.086	33
$E^2 = .04$, $B^2 = .00$			
Marriage by Priest			
Yes	.109	−.108	276
No	.392	.175	171
$E^2 = .11$, $B^2 = .05$			
Education of Spouse			
Lt HS	.194	−.023	31
HS	.141	−.046	142
Vocational school	.333	.116	42
Some college	.255	.038	98
College	.213	−.004	73
Some grad/prof	.308	.091	26
Grad/prof	.241	.024	29
$E^2 = .02$, $B^2 = .00$			
Grand mean = .217			
$R^2 = .28$			

Father's approach to religion and mother's approach to religion were more important predictors of disaffiliation, and mother's approach remained important even when other variables were controlled. If either father or mother were joyous in their approach to religion, the child was less likely to leave the Church. Interestingly, the disaffiliation of the children was higher if the mother were not joyous than if she were not religious at all. This was also true of the father although to a lesser extent. It appears that having parents who view religion as a stern duty or a "chore" is worse than having parents who do not care about religion at all.

The strongest effect in this table comes from current educational level. Respondents who have high school diplomas or less education are less likely to leave the Church; those with more education are more likely to leave. The highest rate of disaffiliation is for those with some graduate or professional training, of whom over one-third have left the Church. The rate for those who have completed graduate or professional training is almost as high. In part, this variable is confounded with the age variable, because the older respondents are also more likely to have more education. The beta-squared indicates that the importance of this variable as a predictor is increased when age and the other variables are taken into account.

Whereas this is a somewhat disturbing finding, it should be remembered that the overall predictive power of the variables in Table 2.5 is rather weak. Even if one knew all of these variables for a group of young Catholics, one could explain less than 10 percent of the variance in their current religious identification.

Other findings in this report suggest the great importance of the family of choice, that is, the family one creates by marriage. It might be that knowing about one's spouse tells more about identification than knowing about one's family of origin. Indeed, this is the case. Table 2.6 (page 42) presents information on several aspects of marriage and disaffiliation rates. The variables in the table account for 28 percent of the variance, a reasonably good job.

By far the most important variable is the religion of the spouse. This alone accounts for 24 percent of the variance, and when the other variables are controlled it accounts for 17 percent of the variance. The overall disaffiliation rate for married Catholics is 22 percent, but for mixed marriages it rises to 42 percent. Religiousness of the spouse is also important, and leads to more disaffiliation either if the spouse is very religious, or if the spouse is not religious at all. This variable accounts for about 4 percent of the variance, but the beta-squared is much smaller, 1 percent. This is because of the interaction effect of religiousness of spouse and mixed marriages. The disaffiliation rates below (shown with case bases in parentheses) show that even a non-religious Catholic spouse cannot draw one away from the Church. But, it is important to note that two-fifths of those married to non-religious, non-Catholic spouses disaffiliated, and three-fifths of those married to non-Catholic, very religious spouses disaffiliated. Thus, in terms of disaffiliation, the devotion of the spouse intensifies the effect of mixed marriage.

Spouse Catholic, very religious	.00	(25)
Spouse Catholic and not religious	.04	(26)
Spouse non-Catholic and very religious	.62	(26)
Spouse non-Catholic and not religious	.47	(64)

A marriage to someone who is not a Catholic also depresses the religious devotion of the Catholic partner, no matter what the denomination (Table 2.7), unless the non-Catholic spouse happens to fall into the residual category of "other." Furthermore, the devotion of a Catholic in a mixed marriage is lower than of a Catholic in a Catholic marriage (Table 2.8, page 45), except when both parents' and spouse's devotion are low.

TABLE 2.7

Religious Devotion of Respondent by Spouse's Denomination
(Percent Respondent High on Religious Devotion Scale)

Spouse	Percent	N
Catholic	34	
		(181)
Baptist	14	
		(21)
Methodist	15	
		(27)
Presbyterian	11	
		(9)
Lutheran	20	
		(20)
Episcopal	25	
		(8)
Other	30	
		(30)
Jewish	0	
		(2)
None	18	
		(332)
All	27	

Respondents in a Catholic marriage are 17 percent higher on the devotion scale when their *parents and their spouse* are also devout. Those in a Catholic marriage are about 27 percent higher on that scale when either their *spouse is devout and their parents were not*, or when their *parents were devout and their spouse is not*. Only in the situation where a respondent's *parents and spouse are not devout* is the person in the Catholic marriage lower on the devotion scale than the respondent in the mixed marriage.

TABLE 2.8

Religious Devotion[1] in Both Catholic and Mixed Marriages by Spouse's Religious Devotion[2] and Parents' Religious Devotion[3]
(Percent Respondent High on Devotion Scale)

| | | PARENTS' DEVOTION | | | |
| | | High | | Low | |
		Catholic Marriage	Mixed Marriage	Catholic Marriage	Mixed Marriage
Spouse's Devotion	High	58	41	35*	8
	Low	42*	14	15	23

* Significantly higher than mixed marriages.
[1] Scale composed of prayer, Mass attendance and reception of communion. To be high on the scale the respondent has to do two of the three following things: pray at least several times a week, go to Mass every week, receive communion several times a month.
[2] Spouse's prayer and church attendance. To be high spouse has to go to church every week and pray several times a week.
[3] Parents' reception of communion. Parents must both be Catholic and both have received communion at least several times a month.

As long as a mixed marriage is of a Catholic from a devout family to a devout spouse, the marriage seems to have only a minor effect on the respondent's devotion, as distinguished from affiliation. In other cases, even when the family of origin is devout, the mixed marriage seems to correlate with a devastating decline in personal devotion for young Catholics.

Finally, a spouse's devotion is more important than the parents' (Table 2.9), and both are more important than a mixed marriage. A sixth of mixed marriages occur in circumstances where both the background and the devotion of the spouse are sufficiently high to minimize the effect.

TABLE 2.9

Standardized Coefficients (Beta) With Religious Devotion of Respondent

Mixed Marriage	.12
Parents' Devotion	.19
Spouse's Devotion	.24

Returning to Table 2.6, we see that disaffiliation is related to marriage duration; the most recently married and those married the longest have the highest disaffiliation rates. At first blush, this seems contradictory to the findings which we will describe in Chapter Five of a "mini life cycle" of religious practice during the first decade of marriage.[1] However, two points should be noted. First, this table refers to complete disaffiliation, not to religious practice. Second, the variable of marriage duration is inevitably confounded with age, which, as we saw in Table 2.5, had an independent effect on disaffiliation. The issue of age and marital duration considered jointly will be taken up below.

Next to mixed marriages, the second most important variable is having been married by a priest. The disaffiliation rate dropped by half for couples married by a priest, and it rose by 18 percent for those not married by a priest.

Finally, education of the spouse explains about 2 percent of the variance by itself and none at all when the other variables are controlled. There is no clear relationship between the spouse's education and disaffiliation as there was with one's own education. The low disaffiliation rates for those with a high school diploma or less might be due to younger age.

Table 2.10 presents the disaffiliation rates by both current age and duration of marriage. The first column of the table indicates that the younger one was when married, the higher the disaffiliation rate is likely to be. The second column shows the same thing except for those most recently married. And a similar finding emerges from the third column—the earlier one is married, the more likely one is now disaffiliated from Catholicism. The rows indicate the same thing for marriage cohorts. For persons married 3-5 years, the disaffiliation is highest for the youngest and decreases for the older couples. The same pattern is seen for those married 6-8 years. The two incomplete rows seem to present a discrepant pattern, but the last row is also the group that married the earliest and has the highest overall disaffiliation rates.

TABLE 2.10

Disaffiliation Rates of Married Persons by Age and Duration of Marriage

| Marriage Duration | Age Now | | |
	20–24	25–29	30
0–2 Years	.151	.276	—
3–5 Years	.213	.196	.167
6–8 Years	.267	.234	.188
9+ Years	—	.209	.237

One concludes from this analysis that the characteristics of the spouse are enormously important for one's continued identification as a Catholic, and that marriage at a somewhat later rather than an earlier date is conducive to continued affiliation. In part, these findings might be artifacts of Church policies in some areas of the country. For example, some priests refuse to conduct weddings for very young couples or to perform ceremonies where the non-Catholic spouse refuses catechesis, as might be the case with a very devout non-Catholic. Another important ambiguity, and one that could not be tested in the data, lies in the possibility that it is the less committed Catholics who are attracted to non-Catholic spouses. In other words, the process of disaffiliation may have begun well before the wedding. The weak but consistent effects of the background variables suggest that one's family of origin plays some role in disaffiliation.

Religious Images and Disaffiliation

Some of the discussion in other parts of this report centers on the "warm" or "cold" religious images of our respondents. Table 2.11 shows that the disaffiliated are less likely to have warm images of God. The cradle Catholics, the switchers, and the converts are most likely to have warm images. It is the marginal Catholics who are most likely to have cold images, and the cradle Catholics and the switchers who are least likely to have them. The rank-order correlation coefficent of −.38 indicates that a group that is high in one ranking is low in the other—in other words, the group that is ranked high in warm images is likely to rank low in cold images.

TABLE 2.11

Religious Images and Degrees of Affiliation		
	Warm Images	Cold Images
High	Cradle Catholics	Marginal Catholics
	Switchers	Converts
	Converts	Unchurched
	Marginal Catholics	Cradle Catholics
Low	Unchurched	Switchers
Spearman's rank-order correlation coefficient = −.38.		

The information on religious images suggests one more aspect of the motivation to remain attached to a church. Whether it is Catholicism or another church, membership seems to be related to one's images of God, Jesus, and Mary as warm and welcoming. Those who are estranged from the Church, on the other hand, have a more forbidding mental image of God.

As Table 2.12 shows, the level of disaffiliation in Canada is remarkably low. (All but one of the converts, 33 percent of the marginal Catholics, and 60 percent of the unchurched are non-French speakers.) French speakers, even though they may not attend Mass, continue to think of themselves as Catholics. This is strikingly different from the case of the American Catholics, where 15 percent may be considered out of the Church. It is interesting to compare French-Canadian descendants in the U.S., of whom only 7 percent are disaffiliated, and French descendants in the U.S., of whom 37 percent are disaffiliated. (Non-French-Canadian descendants in the U.S. have a 25 percent rate of disaffiliation.)

TABLE 2.12

Identification With Catholic Church: Canada

(Percent)

Affiliation Group

Total	100.0
Cradle Catholics	93.3
Converts	1.1
Marginal Catholics	4.3
Unchurched	1.4

N = 730

Percent Giving Orthodox Response

	Cradle Catholics	Marginal
No proof God exists	39.6	16.1
God will punish evil	17.9	3.2
Papal primacy	55.8	43.3
Devil exists	29.9	22.6
God does not care how he is worshipped	27.2	29.0
Papal infallibility	31.0	9.7
Life after death	90.5	89.5

This indicates that there may be something distinctive about French-Canadian Catholics that endures even in another culture, and which is not shared either by French Americans or Canadian Americans who do not speak French. But there also appears to be a distinct Canadian effect when even non-French-speaking Catholics in Canada are compared with their descendants in the U.S. and with U.S. Catholics as a whole. (In the United States, the ethnic groups least likely to disaffiliate from Catholicism are the Eastern Europeans—Poles, Czechs, and Hungarians—and the Hispanics, except for Puerto Ricans.)

Despite these rates of affiliation, however, the Canadian Catholics are not strikingly more orthodox, except, perhaps, on the issue of papal primacy. There are distinct differences between the cradle Catholics and the marginal Catholics in Canada, however, especially on the belief that God will punish evil for all eternity and on papal infallibility. Interestingly, the marginal Catholics are somewhat more likely than the cradle Catholics to disagree that God does not care how he is worshiped as long as he is worshiped. However, these differences should only be taken as rough indicators because so few of the Canadians may be considered marginal Catholics.

Conclusions

About 15 percent of American Catholics and 22 percent of married American Catholics who were reared as Catholic no longer report themselves as Catholics. The most important background determinant of one's continued affiliation with Catholicism is how joyous one's mother's approach to religion was. It also helps to have come from an intact family and to have remembered one's childhood as happy. Continued affiliation with Catholicism does not necessarily mean doctrinal orthodoxy nor agreement with the Church's teachings on sexuality, but it is associated with warm images of God. Catholics who remain in the Church are more likely than others to associate Catholicism with positive family values for themselves and their children. The greatest disaffiliation occurs in mixed marriages, and especially mixed marriages in which the spouse is devout. However, at least statistically, being married by a priest can "cancel" the effect of a spouse's religiousness on disaffiliation. And although being young is usually associated with continued affiliation, being *married* at an early age is not.

That this pattern of disaffiliation is not inevitable but can be affected by outside interventions seems obvious from the fact that the pattern in Canada is so different. Indeed, even within the United States there are ethnic patterns of disaffiliation.

Some Pastoral Considerations

Is there anything the pastor can do to encourage continued affiliation with the Church? Several considerations seem to be important. The first is encouraging Catholics to view themselves in terms of a warm relationship with God, Jesus, and Mary, and not just in terms of formal assent to doctrines or to teachings. Almost all of the sample had encountered some doubts about Catholicism. Whether those doubts later turn into reasons for leaving the Church appears to depend on one's religious environment. This includes parents with warm and joyful attitudes toward religion, a secure and intact family, and one's own religious images. The

Catholics who remain affiliated to the Church are especially likely to see the Church's encouragement offered to families as a positive aspect of Catholicism.

Unfortunately, some pastoral practices that are currently popular may drive young people in the opposite direction. One of these is the insistence on doctrinal and ritual conformity before young people are married in the Church. Being married in the Church is an important predictor of later affiliation with the Church. Being kept away from a sacramental marriage, whether because one still has religious doubts or because one's devout non-Catholic spouse refuses a long period of catechesis, may have little deterrent effect on the wedding's eventually being performed and may needlessly drive young people from the Church.

A more difficult issue is young marriages. Marriage at a young age tends to be associated with disaffiliation, and it is also associated with a number of other negative consequences, including marital instability. But the pastor who tries to discourage a young couple from marrying must do so very cautiously, lest he further alienate the young people. It is possible that young marriages attract couples who are in some ways rebellious and wish to escape from the influence of their own families. It is an easy extension from this to rebellion against the Church as well.

When the Church is considered as a sort of club in which everyone must agree to the bylaws and must subscribe to the same beliefs, then the disaffiliation rate is astronomical. Doctrinal orthodoxy of young Catholics, by these standards, is very low; many of our most "orthodox" young people have joined other churches. The majority of young people continue to belong to the Church, however, and to believe what they can believe. Accepting them where they are—and convincing them that God accepts them where they are—is an important step toward maintaining their loyalty. And as our life cycle perspective in Chapter Five will indicate, there is reason to believe that people "grow into" their faith over time.

NOTES

[1]The "mini life cycle" of religious practice refers to the amount of religiosity experienced at different stages of life—in this case those years between 14 and 29. Chapter Five reveals decreased religiosity in the early and middle twenties with a rebound in the late twenties.

Religious Images, Prayer, and Marital Fulfillment

Highlights

1   Persons' openness to "grace" experiences and their sense of hopefulness about life find vivid expression in their religious imagery and stories.

2   Warm childhood experiences and relationships generate warm religious imagery. This warmth has a "ripple" effect because it affects a person's marital intimacy in a positive way.

3   The way that one pictures Jesus, God, Mary, and the afterlife affects the married couple's satisfaction and sexual filfullment.

4   As they overcome and resolve relational problems in the middle years of the first decade of marriage, Catholic spouses have a resurgence of warm religious imagery within their family circle.

5   Prayer and sexuality are intimately connected. Expressions of human love relate strongly and positively to expressions of love for God.

6   Spouses whose religious imagination are nurtured by daily prayer and warm religious images have the greatest possibility of sexual fulfillment within their marriage.

7   The majority of the couples who reported their sexual fulfillment as excellent pray together every day and share warm religious images.

Chapter 3

Religious Images, Prayer, and Marital Fulfillment*

It is appropriate to begin this chapter with a brief summary of the theory of the sociology of religion which has directed the present analysis. (A more detailed elaboration of the theory can be found in William McCready and Andrew Greeley, *Ultimate Values of the American Population*, and Andrew Greeley, forthcoming, *Religion: A Secular Theory*.) Religion, it is assumed by this theory, is rooted in the human capacity to hope; a capacity which Lionel Tiger (1979) has recently suggested may be genetic, but is, in any case, uneradicable. Reinforcing this propensity to hope, and probably a consequent of it, is the human capacity to experience moments of "grace"; such moments (David Tracy in *Blessed Rage for Order* calls them "limit experiences") may be relatively minor, such as a beautiful summer day, a cold silent sheet of ice on the lake in winter time, a touch of a friendly hand, a smile of a two-year old. Or they may be the major ecstatic experiences of the sort described by William James, or any kind of intense moments of "revelation" or "gratuity" that would appear on a continuum between these extremes (for greater detail and discussion of these experiences, see David Tracy's *Blessed Rage for Order*, John Shea's *Stories of God*, and Andrew Greeley's *The Mary Myth*). These moments of gratuity or "grace"—are "sacraments" (with a small "s"), or "revelations" (with a small "r") which seem to reveal a secret design or purpose or goodness or order at work in this cosmos. In these experiences of "grace," one may find the origin both of religious heritages which developed through history and of the religious perspectives which developed through the biography of an individual person.

These experiences are resonated and recounted to a person as "symbols" or "images" or "pictures" which spontaneously arise in his or her own imaginative process to help him or her articulate what has been experienced. Such "symbols" are drawn both from religious tradition and from the general repertoire of powerful imagery which is at the disposal of humankind (sun, moon, light, water, fire, food, sex, etc.). Often the core of religious heritage can be found by examining what use it makes of the human symbol repertoire.

Such religious symbols, resonating, representing, and articulating—still at the imaginative level and in the imaginative dimension of the personality—are in fact "stories" which purport to provide meaning both to the life of the individual person and the existence of the cosmos. These religious stories implicitly and imaginatively link the experiences of an individual's life with that Higher Order which one experienced in moments of "gratuity" or "grace." One might add that in this approach to religion, Sacraments (with a capital S) and Revelations (with a capital R) are those experiences and symbols—the death and resurrection of Jesus, for example—in which a given religious tradition emphatically reaffirms, confirms, validates, and revalidates the fundamental moments of hopefulness that all humans encounter in their lives.

A religious symbol, then, is an articulation of an experience of hope. Such symbols are implicitly "stories" which link the stories of a life of an individual person with what the person perceives to be the Larger Story of the cosmos. Such symbols not only represent for the person and give meaning for what has happened so far in his or her own story, but they also shape the development of that story since they describe the "scenery" and the "setting" within which the rest of the story will unfold.

All of this activity occurs initially and primordially in the creative or the imaginative dimension of the personality—that which is called by Lawrence Kubie (1961) "the preconscious and the creative imagination," by Jacques Maritain (1955) "the creative faculty" and "agent intellect" (here Maritain would be following Aquinas and Aristotle), and by St. Paul "our spirit" (to which the Spirit speaks). Since humans are more than imaginative and poetic creatures, they very quickly reflect intellectually on, philosophize about, and then theologize about their moments of grace. Finally, they express a digested version of these theologies in creedal statements and catechetical propositions. Such statements and propositions, of course, are "religious," but they are not primordially religious in the sense that the experiences of grace and the stories which produce these experiences can be said to be primordially and fundamentally religious. If one wishes, then, to know the religious orientation of a human personality, one must look not only to his or her catechetical propositions and creedal statements but also, and more importantly, to his or her religious imagery and the stories implicit in such imagery. For the purpose of the present research we assume two things about experiences of childhood relationships. First, they are "sacramental," revealing to a child something about the nature of the cosmos and the possibility of his or her own existence. Second, they affect an adult's religious imagery and that religious imagery in turn affects his or her approach to human intimacy and human love. Succinctly, the warmer the childhood experiences have been, the warmer a person's religious imagery will be; the warmer will be his or her own marital intimacy. No argument is made that *all* the religious imagery is shaped by childhood experience or that the entire quality of the marital warmth is shaped by the partner's warmth in religious imagery. Such an expectation would be absurd because both religious imagery and marital satisfaction are complex phenomena likely to be shaped by many different aspects of a person's biological, psychological, cultural, and biographic background. We do not, in other words, expect particularly high correlations among the variables with which we will be working, but we do expect there to be real and statistically significant correlations.

Religious Imagination and Marital Success

Four items were selected as measures of "warm" religious imagery—God as a lover, Jesus as warm, Mary as warm, and the afterlife as a "paradise of pleasure and delight." (Each of these images, incidentally, is a story because it implies an ongoing relationship.) Seventy-four percent of young Catholic married people think of Mary as warm. Sixty-eight percent of young Catholic married people think of Jesus as warm. Forty-one percent think of God as a lover. Only 13 percent think of the afterlife as a paradise of pleasure and delight (see Table 3.1.)[1]

TABLE 3.1

Religious Imagery Among Young Catholics	
(Percent)	
God as "lover"	41
Jesus as "warm"	68
Mary as "warm"	74
Afterlife a "paradise of pleasure and delight"	13

A substantially smaller proportion of Catholic marriages are characterized by common religious imagery between husband and wife. In half of all of the marriages, husband and wife both describe Jesus as warm and Mary as warm, but only 12 percent of them share an image of God as a lover and only 5 percent an image of the afterlife as a paradise of pleasure and delight. (See Table 3.2, page 56).

On the other hand, if a married person thinks of God as a lover or of heaven as a paradise, there is more likely to be a similar image in the mind of his or her spouse than there is likely to be a correlation between husbands' and wives' images of Jesus as warm and Mary as warm. In other words, if you think of Jesus as warm, there is not much reason to believe that your spouse has the same thought; but if you think of God as a lover or of heaven as a paradise of pleasure, there is a much higher probability (though still the correlations in Table 3.3 are rather low) that your spouse will have the same religious imagery. (See Table 3.3).

TABLE 3.2

Joint Religious Imagery — Husband and Wife Both

(Percent)

God as "lover"	12
Jesus as "warm"	51
Mary as "warm"	53
Afterlife a "paradise of pleasure and delight"	5

TABLE 3.3

Correlations Between Spouses' Religious Imagery

(Coefficient = Pearson's r)

God as "lover"	.24*
Jesus as "warm"	.10*
Mary as "warm"	.08*
Afterlife a "paradise of pleasure and delight"	.24*

*Correlation is significant at the .05 level or better.

After analyses were made on both the respondent's religious image patterns and the spouse's religious image patterns, these two factors were combined to produce a "joint religious image scale." This scale correlates positively and significantly with sexual fulfillment in marriage. (See Table 3.4, page 57).

If there is an atmosphere in the marriage in which husband and wife tend to share warm religious imagery, then their marriage satisfaction, their sexual fulfillment, and their value consensus is likely to be higher than if they do not share such religious imagery. How their imagination perceives Jesus, God, Mary, and the afterlife does indeed affect their marital satisfaction and their sexual fulfillment. Religious images do indeed have an impact on what goes on in the bedroom (though, of course, people need not be aware of this impact).

Furthermore, religious warmth declines in the middle years of the first decade of marriage. Within this time frame, spouses are experiencing an increase in problems in their marital life, and individual respondents are experiencing problems in their religious belief systems. However, in the last two years of this first decade of marriage, the warmth scale seems to rebound to where it was at the beginning of the marriage. Religious images are not only a story, they are also involved in the story of decline and growth-one might even say of death and rebirth (see Tables 3.5 and 3.6).

TABLE 3.4

Joint Marital Adjustment by Joint Image Scale
(Percent)

Marital Adjustment	Image Scale	
	High ("Warm")	Low ("Cool")
Percent both "excellent" sexual adjustment*	36	22

* Difference is significant at the .05 level or better.

TABLE 3.5

Image Scale by Duration Of Marriage
(Z Scores)

0–2 Years	.25
3–8 Years	−.13
9–10 Years	.23*

*Rebound is significant at .01 level.

TABLE 3.6

Sexual Fulfillment by Duration of Marriage
(Both Spouses Say It Is "Excellent")
(Percent)

0–2 Years	33
3–8 Years	20
9–10 Years	42

We have noted that the path of decline and rebirth of marital happiness is paralleled by a decline and rebirth in religious attitudes, images and behaviors. We now ask whether one decline can account for the other.

This question can be answered by using a technique of multiple regression analysis called "residual" anaylsis. Briefly, it is sufficient to say that one endeavors to diminish percentage point differences by taking into account the influence of variables which are hypothesized as being accountable for the differences. Thus, for example, one finds a 50 percentage points difference between Irish Catholics and Jews in the amount of alcohol consumed at a given sitting, and one hypothesizes this difference as a result of mother's and father's drinking behavior. One first mathematically eliminates the impact of the father and then the impact of the mother (or vice versa) and sees how much the difference between the two ethnic groups' drinking has been diminished. If, when the mother's drinking behavior is put into the regression equation, the residual percentage diminishes from 50 to 30, then one can say that two-fifths of the difference between Irish and Jews in drinking is accounted for by the fact that Irish mothers drink more than Jewish mothers. If another 10 percentage points decrease occurs when the father's influence is included in the regression equation, then one can say that the joint influence of mother and father diminishes the difference by 30 percentage points, and thus "explains" three-fifths of the difference between the Irish and the Jewish in drinking and leaves two-fifths difference unexplained by a model which takes into account only maternal and paternal drinking.

In Table 3.7 a similar technique is used to account for the decline in 13 percentage points on the joint agreement by spouses that their sexual fulfillment is "excellent" between the first two years of marriage and the middle years of marriage. The difference declines by 3 percentage points when one takes into account religious images.

TABLE 3.7

Model to Explain Decline of Sexual Fulfillment (Both Spouses "Excellent") Between the First Two Years of Marriage and Third to Eighth Years of Marriage

	Difference	Proportion of Decline Explained
Simple difference	−13%	
Taking into account "warm" religious imagery	−10%	.24

Precisely the same pattern may be observed in explaining the increase in sexual fulfillment between the middle years and the ninth and tenth years of the marriage. In this critical turning point, the level of sexual satisfaction goes up 21 percentage points and more than three-fifths of that increase can be accounted for by family experience and warm religious imagery (the latter of which is indeed the funnel for childhood experiences). (See Table 3.8.)

TABLE 3.8

Model to Explain Increase in Sexual Fulfillment (Both Spouses "Excellent") Between the Third and Eighth Years of Marriage and the Ninth and Tenth Years

	Difference	Proportion of Increase Explained
Simple difference	+21%	
Taking into account "warm" religious imagery	+ 8%	.62

In the process of working out the sexual problems in the middle years of the first decade of marriage, Catholic spouses—in all likelihood and quite unself-consciously—are powerfully influenced by a dramatic resurgence in the climate of warm religious imagery in their family. As we have said before, doubtless the causality is reciprocal. The increase in sexual fulfillment is sacramental and revelatory, and this gives the couple greater confidence in the loving warmth of God. On the other hand, the loving warmth of God seems also to give them greater confidence, enabling them to strive for stronger, better sexual intimacy.

Research priority ought to be given to the study of the crisis which occurs between the middle and the end of the first decade of a Catholic marriage in order to sort out the intricate relationship between religious imagery and sexual fulfillment. Presently we must be content to say that it seems more likely that the changing image of God influences changing marital satisfaction than vice versa. Even so, both still influence one another.

Human Intimacy and Divine Intimacy: An Empirical Test

Christian religious theory has always maintained that there is a link between human love and divine love. Marriage is, according to Paul, a "great sacrament"—that is to say, a "revelation" of Christ's love for his people. As husband and wife love one another, so do Christ and the Church. Similarly, husband and wife ought in their relationship to try to imitate the love of Christ for the Church. The imagery is a two-way street: marriage revealing the passion of Christ's love for his people, and the generosity of Christ's love providing an ideal for the married life. Paul himself frequently gets his syntax confused as he tries to go in opposite directions on the symbolic street.

In traditional Christian marriage catechesis much has been made of the relationship between "the two loves." If human spouses love God strongly, it is argued, they will also love one another strongly. Their faith in God will strengthen their faith in one another, and their love for one another will motivate them to grow in love of God.

It is often difficult to tell how seriously this catechesis is taken. Does the overarching "story" of God's love affect the emerging "story" of "our love," and does "our love" for one another rebound back to intensify our involvement in God's story? Does divine intimacy really affect human intimacy and vice versa? How closely are the two love stories related? Is the relationship merely a matter of conventional piety without any measurable impact on people's lives?

If one takes prayer as a fair measure of intimacy with God and sexual fulfillment as a fair measure of intimacy with one's spouse, it is possible to fashion a rough empirical test of the nature of the relationship between the two loves. What effect does the prayer life of a young Catholic married couple have on their sex life? Prayer is nice, one might be told, and sex is nice, but most people think the two really do not mix.

In approximately a quarter of the Catholic marriages we have studied, both members of the couple pray every day. In forty-two percent of those families both husband and wife described their sexual fulfillment as "excellent." On the other hand, where one or both of the spouses does not pray every day, only twenty-four percent described their sexual fulfillment as "excellent" (Table 3.9, page 61). The difference is statistically significant, and the coefficient of association (gamma) is quite high—.50. Prayer and sex do indeed mix, and the two loves do indeed relate strongly to one another.

Moreover, the association between husbands' and wives' prayer (Table 3.10, page 61) increases with the duration of marriage. The gamma in the early years of marriage is .31. It diminishes to .21 between the third and the eighth year of marriage but then rises to .42 during the last two years of the first decade of marriage.

As "your" story and "my" story, "both of us" are more likely to get involved with God (though not necessarily together, since the question merely revealed whether the respondent and the spouse pray every day, and not whether they pray together).

TABLE 3.9

Sexual Fulfillment By Family Prayer
(Percent both spouses report sexual fulfillment as "excellent")

Both Pray Every Day	One or the Other Does Not Pray Every Day
42*	24
Gamma = .50	

*Significant at the .05 level or better.

TABLE 3.10

Association Between Husband's and Wife's Prayer by Duration of Marriage
(gamma)

0–2 Years	.31
3–8 Years	.21
9–10 Years	.42

We know that there is a correlation between warm images and sexual fulfillment, and we are not surprised (Table 3.11, page 62) to see that those who have warm images of the cosmic personages are also more likely to communicate with them. Hence, prayer, sexual fulfillment, and warm religious images intercorrelate with one another. The more a husband and wife pray, the more likely they are to have sexually fulfilling marriages; and the warmer the religious imagery, the more likely they are to have sexually fulfilling marriages. Furthermore, both of these variables, while they are related to each other, also make an independent contribution to sexual fulfillment (Figure 3.1). They are not substitutes for one another. The greatest probability of sexual fulfillment comes in marriages in which there is both daily prayer by the two spouses and warm images in the religious imagination of the two spouses. Indeed, it is precisely among such marriages that the difference in sexual fulfillment occurs. (See Table 3.12, page 62.)

More than half of them report excellent sexual fulfillment (by both husband and wife), twice as many as in the other three categories. In the technical parlance of social science, daily prayer *specifies* the difference in sexual fulfillment between those families that share warm imagery and those that do not. It is precisely the combination of the two that accounts for the difference in sexual fulfillment in a young Catholic family.

The proportion of Catholic families in which both husband and wife pray every day increases as the marriage ages (Table 3.13, page 63). It is not merely, then, that "your" story and "my" story become more closely related, and that "your" story of "your" relationship with God and that "my" story of "my" relationship with God tend to converge, as we saw in Table 3.10. It is also true that "our" joint relationship with God improves through the years of the marriage, just as "our" relationship with one another is improving. As "our" story gets better, so "our" involvement in God's story becomes more active.

TABLE 3.11

Correlations Among Daily Prayer, Sexual Fulfillment and Warm Images

(All measures are family scores—both husband and wife)
(Coefficient = Pearson's r)

	Prayer	Sexual fulfillment
Sexual fulfillment	.20*	
Warm images	.19*	.26*

* Significant at the .05 level or better.

FIGURE 3.1

Standardized Correlations
(Beta)

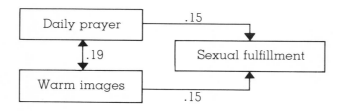

TABLE 3.12

Sexual Fulfillment By Daily Prayer By Warm Images (Family Measures)

(Percent both excellent "sexual fulfillment")

	Both pray daily*	
	Yes	No
Warm images	53	27
	22	22

* Significantly different both in row and column at the .05 level or better.

TABLE 3.13

Daily Prayer by Duration of Marriage
(Both husband and wife)
(Percent)

0–2 Years	22
3–8 Years	20
9–10 Years	30

It is impossible, of course, with our present data to sort out the influence flow between the two loves. Paul's difficult syntax as he shifts back and forth manifests the same problem that the researcher faces: the two loves are so closely connected that it is hard to chart the ebb and flow one upon the other.

However, if one pursues the model suggested in Table 3.14 (page 64) and assumes at least some influence of prayer and warm images on the changing level of the sexual fulfillment in young Catholic families, one can say that prayer makes an additional contribution to the explanation of the rebound between the middle and late years of marriage and sexual fulfillment. The difference between the third and the eighth year, on the one hand, and the ninth and the tenth year, on the other, is twenty-two percentage points. When the warm imagery is taken into account, the difference diminishes to nine percentage points. In other words, three-quarters of the increase in sexual fulfillment can be accounted for by changes in the religious imagery of the spouses between the middle and the end of the first decade of their marriage. When one adds to that the daily prayer of spouses, the difference diminishes even more to six percentage points; and one has accounted for three-quarters of the change in sexual fulfillment. Whether religion influences sexuality or sexuality influences religion is hard to determine. That they both have an extraordinary impact on one another is now beyond any doubt.

A final comment is in order about whether the influences reported are perceived by the husbands and wives involved. Do men and women know that they are being influenced religiously by their mate? One of the questions in the survey asked the respondent to rate a number of potential religious influences on a four point scale (mother, father, friends, priests, etc.). If correlations exist between the conscious rating of the spouse's influence and the family religious styles analyzed in this report, then it would follow that not all the husband-wife, wife-husband influence is preconscious or subconscious (about 18% say that their spouse has a "great deal" of religious influence).

TABLE 3.14

**Prayer and Warm Images as Explanation for Increase in
Sexual Fulfillment (Both Spouses) Between Middle and End of
First Decade of Marriage**

	Percent Difference	Proportion explained
Difference between 3−8 years and 9−10 years in percent of couples in which both spouses say sexual fulfillment is excellent	+22	
Taking into account warm images of both spouses	+9	.59
Taking into account whether both spouses pray every day	+6	.73

In fact (Table 3.15), there are statistically significant correlations between the perception of spouse's influence and the joint imagery, joint prayer, and joint sexual fulfillment measures. We cannot say with certainty that there is a consciousness that the spouse is leading the respondent to pray more or to have warmer religious imagery, but there is a consciousness that the spouse is exercising influence.

TABLE 3.15

Correlations With Acknowledged Religious Influence of Spouse
(Coefficient = Pearson's r)

Both warm images	.23*
Both pray daily	.23*
Both sexual fulfillment	.16*

*Significant at the .05 level or better.

Furthermore (Table 3.16, page 65), this influence seems to wane, then wax during the first ten years of marriage, as do so many other aspects of the relationship. In the final years of the decade, the spouse's religious influence is more likely to be perceived as stronger than during the earlier years. Also, the correlations between imagery and prayer on the one hand and perceived influence of the spouse on the other seem to go through the same "U curve." The relationship between the perception of the spouse's influence and the joint imagery and joint behavior is strongest during the final years of the first decade of marriage (Table 3.17, page 65).

TABLE 3.16

Spouse Religion Influence
by Duration of Marriage
(Z score)

1–2 Years	+.04
3–8 Years	−.02
9–10 Years	+.10

TABLE 3.17

Relationship Between Spouse Having "Very Much" Religious
Influence on Respondent and Warm Images
and Daily Prayer by Length of Marriage

	Warm Images and Spouse Influence
1–2 Years	.57*
3–8 Years	.45*
9–10 Years	.65*

	Prayer and Spouse Influence
1–2 Years	.67*
3–8 Years	.24
9–10 Years	.58*

*Significant at the .05 level or better.

Not only do joint prayer and joint imagery increase in the "rebound" period, so does the perception of the spouse's influence and the relationship between such a perception and prayer and imagery. Not only are "your" story and "my" story becoming "our" story, but "we" are becoming self-conscious about the fact that it is "our" story.

Figure 3.2 demonstrates one possible influence flow. Husband and wife have warm religious images. This sharing of "stories of God" makes it more likely that the two of them will pray frequently. A combination of the "stories" and the mutual (if not common) prayer leads them to perceive that they are having more religious influence on one another. All three factors improve their sexual fulfillment.

If one adds self-consciousness about religious influence to the explanatory model developed to explain the "rebound" in sexual fulfillment, the three-quarters of the 22 percent increase between the 3rd and 8th and the 9th and 10th years can be accounted for.

Earlier in the chapter it was noted that 52 percent of those couples, both of whom pray every day and both of whom have warm religious images, report that their sexual fulfillment is excellent. If one adds self-consciousness about spouse's influence, the figure rises to 57 percent, 10 percentage points higher than those with images and prayer but without the self-consciousness and 35 percentage points higher than the rest of the sample (Table 3.18).

FIGURE 3.2

Images, Prayer, Spouse Influence and Sexual Fulfillment

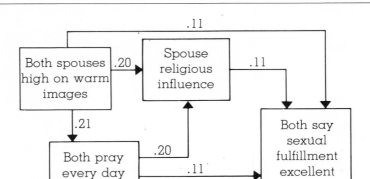

TABLE 3.18

Prayer, Spouse Influence and Sexual Fulfillment

(Both Spouses High on Warm Images)

(Percent both say sexual fulfillment excellent)

	Both Pray Daily	One or Both Do Not Pray Daily
"Very much" influence by spouse	57 (14)	43 (14)
Not "very much" influence	47 (17)	21 (52)
Total	52 (31)	26 (52)

(One Or Both Low on Warm Images)

"Very much" influence by spouse	36 (11)	*
Not "very much" influence	21 (88)	29 (14)
Total	22 (99)	22 (18)

* Fewer than 5 cases.

Thus, not only is there some self-consciousness about religious influence of the spouse, but this self-consciousness heightens the impact of the influence.

Conclusions

The religious imagination, which is grounded in the human capacity for, and experience of, hope is empirically linked with the decline and rebirth of marital satisfaction and sexual fulfillment in the first decade of marriage for young Catholics. The hope that is embodied in the stories of their faith also now appears in their up-and-down roller coaster first ten years of marriage, and the linkage between religious imagery and marital success seems to be a strong and productive one for the young family.

The present research has identified the fact of the sexual and religious rebound during the first decade of marriage, and it has also demonstrated the strength of the relationship between marital success and the religious imagination. We need to know more, however, about the process by which this occurs and the true directions of the influences. Undoubtedly sexual fulfillment and religious imagery influence each other. Greater fulfillment can reveal and build confidence in the hopefulness that is at the foundation of faith, while renewed imagery of a warm and loving God can contribute to the trust and vulnerability necessary for satisfying intimacy. However, we know too little about the ways in which this happens within marriages. Such information would aid the Church in formulating plans and visions which would recognize and assist this rebound at the end of the first marital decade.

It may well be that if we were able to take apart the religious imagery/sexual fulfillment puzzle more thoroughly, the information gained would provide insights on how the Church could more successfully overcome the liabilities it has incurred in the past because of the lukewarm reception to its teaching positions on sexuality. These data give the Church something positive to contribute to the "sexuality dialogue" in a way it has not had for a long time. Good sex and good religion go together. We do not know why in all the details, but the relationship certainly is clear. This empirically-based insight could be very helpful to many people whose marital lives are confused and tumultuous. It should also be helpful to the planners and visionaries responsible for charting the course of the Church into the future.

NOTES

*The material in this chapter is excerpted from the book, *The Young Catholic Family* by Andrew Greeley (Thomas More Press, Chicago, 1980), written from the materials available in the Knights of Columbus project.

¹In each of these cases we are dealing with those who say they are "extremely likely" to have such imaginations.

The Madonna in North America: A Specific Example
of the Impact of Religious Imagery

Highlights

1   *The overwhelming majority of young Catholics think of Mary as gentle, warm, and comforting.*

2   *The childhood experience of a warm, consoling, life-giving maternal figure carries over into married life. The image of Mary in the Church links the experience of childhood with the experience of married life.*

3   *Among all the ethnic groups under study, it is the Irish Catholics who have the most positive attitudes about Mary.*

4   *The "stories" of God that we have, do not have their origin in declarations of dogma, but rather come from the imagination and are often clothed in warm Madonna imagery.*

5   *Contrary to the views of those who believe that Mary is a symbol of conservatism in the Church, Mary is at the vanguard of liberalism and liberation for young Catholics, especially men.*

6   *Husbands and wives who share warm Madonna images have excellent sexual fulfillment within their marriage.*

7   *As young Catholics who have been estranged from the Church recall the warm memories and the symbolic attraction of the devotion to Mary, they tend to reidentify with the Church.*

8   *The more that the Church is seen as "mother"—warm, welcoming, comforting, affectionally strong—the more those who have left the Church will want to return.*

Chapter 4

The Madonna in North America: A Specific Example of the Impact of Religious Imagery*

The broken Mary Myth cannot compete,
A loser in the symbolic marketplace,
Like the mighty dollar now debased,
Turned tinsel tattered in a slushy street
Rejected, madonna, as obsolete,
Discarded in ecumenical distaste
A worn out image buried with all due haste
And quickly forgotten by a smug elite.

Yet sounds of happiness in the winter cold:
A young mother's joy shouted at the skies,
A young woman's laugh chasing dreary pain
Capricious, our universe will not stay closed,
Like the magic star Mary glows surprise,
And her hint that God is tender love remains.

This chapter focuses on the unique finding that even though current Catholic religious education and parochial practice often ignore Marian mythology, the image of the Virgin is still powerful and effective, even among Catholics under thirty.

We propose four tasks for ourselves in this chapter:

■ To report on the phenomenon of the survival of strong Marian imagery among young Catholics in North America

■ To fit such a survival within a social science theory of religion which might lead us to expect it

■ To make some predictions about the antecedents and the consequences of Marian imagery in the life of a young person, and to test these hypotheses against empirical evidence

■ To examine the way in which Marian imagery aids the process of reidentification with the Church

First of all, the survival of the Madonna: our respondents were asked to rate Jesus, Mary, and God on a number of descriptive nouns and adjectives. It seemed reasonable to think that the portrait of the Madonna as gentle, warm, patient, and comforting is a fairly accurate description of the tradition. Eighty-one percent of the respondents in the United States said that they were extremely likely to think of Mary as gentle; seventy-five percent as warm; seventy percent as patient; and seventy-five percent as comforting. These show a substantially higher proportion than her Son or the Father in heaven were able to earn (St. Bernard of Clairvaux's famous dictum, "If you fear the Father, go to the Son; if you fear the Son, go to the Mother," still seems to hold; see Table 4.1). English-Canadian young people were virtually identical in their strong, positive image of the Madonna, although French-Canadian young people were somewhat less positive than their English-speaking counterparts—nonetheless, they were still very positive.

TABLE 4.1

The Madonna Image Among Catholics Under 30
(Percent "Extremely Likely To Think Of Her As")

	U.S.A.	English Canada	French Canada
Gentle	81	85	85
Warm	75	79	69*
Patient	70	74	71
Comforting	75	78	69*

*Significant at .05 level or better.

Almost two-thirds of the respondents in the United States said they were extremely likely to think of Mary in all four terms; thus (Table 4.2) fifty-seven percent of the men and seventy-three percent of the women endorsed as "extremely likely" all four components of the Madonna image. (In subsequent tables we will analyze only the respondents in the United States, turning to Canada at the end to see if the analytic models developed for the American population can be replicated across cultural lines.)

TABLE 4.2

The Madonna Scale By Sex
(Percent High — "Extremely Likely" On All Four Images)

Men	Women
57 (631)	73* (699)

*Significant at the .05 level or better.

Secondly, religion finds its origins in the human propensity to hope, as we have said previously. We hope; we hope against hope; we hope in spite of ourselves; and we hope when the situation is hopeless. Sudden death and resuscitation research both show that there is a tendency for us to depart life in an ecstacy of hope. Freud says that the unconscious believes in its own immortality. Other psychoanalysts find hope manifested irresistibly in our dreams. Our previous research has discovered hopeful or optimistic responses to life tragedy situations from almost ninety percent of the American population (McCready & Greeley, 1974). The religious question, perhaps the only religious question that really matters, is whether we ought to trust this propensity to hope. Or is it a self-deception, the ultimately cruel trick of a cruel and deceiving universe? Such theological and existential issues are beyond the scope of this chapter. We assume, however, that religion would not exist if we did not hope, if we did not suspect (sometimes with greater confidence than at other times) that, as G.K. Chesterton remarked at the conclusion of a sudden-death experience of his (long before the research), "life is too important ever to be anything other than life."

We also assume that our hope periodically is reinforced during the course of life by experiences of renewal, of rebirth, and of recreation. These experiences may be spectacular. They are frequently more ordinary events: experiences of love, of beauty, of goodness, which can happen in everyday existence and which confirm our suspicion that life is too important ever to be anything but life. Reconciliation after a quarrel, the touch of a friendly hand, a desert sunrise, a solution to a complex problem, a smile on a little kid toddling across the floor—all of these are limit experiences, horizon experiences, experiences of gratuity, or in Peter Berger's phrase, "rumors of angels," or in a phrase we prefer, "experiences of grace."

Thirdly, these experiences of grace are especially likely to be occasioned by the most powerful forces at work in our lives: sun, moon, water, fire, sexual differentiation, food, drink, community leadership, the passing of the seasons, childbirth, marriage, death futility—these are the gracegenerating experiences *par excellence*. (As Nathan Scott and Karl Rahner have said, for some things to be Sacramental with a capital "S," all things must be potentially sacramental with a small "s." Grace, in other words, is everywhere.)

Fourthly, images of the reality that occasion grace experiences remain in our creative imagination (preconceptual intellect, poetic imagination, preconsciousness, agent intellect—call it whatever we want) after the experience is over. These images serve to recall the experience both for ourselves and for sharing with others. Such images with the potential to recall and share experiences are called "symbols."

Fifthly, symbols—at least religious symbols—tend implicitly to be narrative, to describe relationships, to be accounts or stories of our own experiences which we can share with others, and by which we can replicate the experience. These stories give shape and meaning to the story of our lives precisely because they link our story with the other people's stories and some overarching story which has been handed down to us by a religious tradition. We experience grace; we tell stories about the experience so that we may tell the story of our own life and share it with others. The way we tell the story is in part shaped by the symbolic repertory which we have inherited from our religious tradition—probably very early in life.

Finally, we conclude, therefore, that religion is primarily and primordially an exercise for the imagination, the preconceptual intellect, the poetic faculty, or whatever else we might want to call it. Our experiences of grace occur in this dimension of our personality; and the images, powerful and primal, which are the residue of these experiences, persist there. Paul describes a sociologically accurate truth when he says that the "Spirit" speaks to "our spirit," meaning that religious reality hinges primarily on the creative expansive "fine point" of the personality. Indeed, we may and must reflect on the meaning of our experience. We may and must impose propositional, catechetical, creedal, philosophical, and theological order on our stories. The propositions, catechisms, creeds, and philosophical systems are derivative. However necessary and however good, they will soon lose their power if they do not periodically revisit their origins in the preconceptual imagination.

On the other hand, if the conceptual intellect turns away for a time from a powerful symbol and an important story, the story and the symbol are likely to continue with the life of their own, if only because they are rooted in powerful human experiences which transcend philosophical and catechetical systems.

The notion that the divine is somehow androgynous (having both male and female qualities) is very common in human religion. Folk Judaism in the second-temple era retained the memory of the shekinah of Yahweh—his spirit and his presence, indeed (as a matter of fact, the shekinah became the "Holy Spirit" of Christianity) also had a feminine counterpart, a residue of Yahweh's spouse from the preprophetic time. The feminine component of the deity can be conveniently subsumed under four experiences: the madonna, the virgo, the sponsa and the pieta. These are four dimensions of womanliness that men experience in their relationship to women, and that women also experience in their relationship to men.

The experience of woman as warm, consoling, life-giving, mother, of Mary as Madonna, reflects the experience of grace in and through maternity, loving a mother, being a mother, sharing with a mother, being aware of one's potentiality of being a mother, or of producing children together with someone who has that potentiality. These are raw, primal experiences in the human condition which, on some occasions, can be gracious in the sense of hope-confirming. They suggest that whatever reality is responsible for the cosmos is, in part, rather like a mother; and they suggest that the story of our life and the story of the cosmos is, in part, a story of a relationship with a mother.

Out of this theoretical perspective, we hypothesized that warm images of the Madonna would correlate with warm and powerful experiences with one's mother in the family of origin, with a sense of the sacramentality of the lifegiving forces of nature and, consequently, with warm experiences with one's spouse in the family of procreation. A man or a woman who has had a warm experience of maternity growing up will have a warm experience in sharing maternity with his or her spouse in the family which one has founded, *and* Madonna imagery will serve as a link between the two experiences.

We would have expected before the research began that our Hispanic respondents would score highest on the "Madonna" scale. To be high on the Madonna scale a respondent had to believe that he or she was "extremely likely" to think of Mary as gentle, warm, patient and comforting. The power of the Guadalupe history in Mexican-American religion would seem to have virtually guaranteed such a finding. However, in fact, among our Catholics under thirty (Table 4.3, page 76) it is the Irish who are most likely to score high on the Madonna scale. Indeed, the difference between the Irish and non-Irish respondent is statistically significant. In other NORC research we have discovered that the Irish and the Jews, of the American ethnic groups, are the most pro-feminist. (A recent Common Market study has indicated that Ireland and Denmark are first and second among the nine nations in a wide variety of measures indicating powerful positions for women in the social structure.) We lack the evidence in the present research to investigate the possibility that the high score of the Irish on the Madonna scale (high for both men and women) is a function of their feminist proclivities. But it is, at least, a possibility to be investigated further.

A high score on the Madonna scale as hypothesized correlates at statistically significant levels with the respondent's perception of his or her mother as having exercised "very much" religious influence, a characterization of the mother's approach to religion as very joyous, the involvement of the mother in the family decision making, either making the decisions herself, or making them jointly with the father, and the mother's frequent reception of communion (Table 4.4, page 77). Those who come from families in which the mother was personally devout, was involved in decision making, was joyous in her approach to religion, and was perceived by the respondent as having a powerful influence on the respondent's religious life are precisely those who are most likely to score high on the Mary scale. Satisfying experience of maternity in the family or origin, in other words, produces both for young men and young women high scores on the Madonna scale.

TABLE 4.3

Ethnic Background and Madonna Scale
(Percent High on the Madonna Scale)

Ethnic Group			
Irish			72
German			61
Italian			66
Polish			65
French			65
Hispanic			59
Other			67
	Men	Women	Total
Irish	62	82	72*
Not Irish	55	71	64

* Significant at the .05 level or better.

The prediction that there would be a relationship between the Madonna scale and nature as a source of religious reflection was also sustained. Both "mother" and nature are sources of life, and both correlate with the Madonna as a symbol of benign life experiences, although the childhood maternity experiences apparently do not correlate with the experience of nature as a religious source (Table 4.5, page 77).

The Madonna, then, serves as a recollection of benign experiences of the mother and of nature as a religious source. Is the persistence of this image in contemporary America, however, merely a curious phenomenon or does it have any impact on people's lives? First of all, those young Catholics who are high on the Madonna scale are more likely to pray every day, to attend Mass every week, to be active in their parish, and to believe in life after death (Table 4.6, page 77).

TABLE 4.4

Mother Influence and Madonna Scale
(Percent High on Madonna Scale)

Mother's Religious Effect	Men	Women	Total
"Very much"	64*	77*	78*
Other	44	60	58
Mother's Approach to Religion Very Joyous			
Yes	70*	80*	77*
No	52	70	62
Mother Involved in Family Decision Making			
Yes	58*	74*	67*
No	47	63	54
Mother Frequent Recipient of Communion			
Yes	61*	77*	70*
No	50	66	60

* Significant at the .05 level or better.

TABLE 4.5

Nature as a Religious Source and Madonna Scale
(Percent)

	Men	Women	Total
Learn a "great deal" about religion from nature	64*	79*	72*
Other	52	69*	61

* Significant at the .05 level or better.

TABLE 4.6

Madonna Scale and Religious Devotion
(Percent)

	High on Scale	Low on Scale
Daily Prayer	62*	42
Weekly Mass	49*	34
Active in Parish	14*	7
Belief in Life After Death	68*	53*

* Significant at the .05 level or better.

Furthermore, the Madonna scale correlates much more strongly with frequent prayer than does a doctrinal orthodoxy scale made up of propositions concerning papal primacy, papal infallibility, the existence of the devil, the existence of hell, and other similar propositions (Table 4.7, page 78). It is the "story of God" that one carries around in one's preconceptual imagination embodied in the Madonna imagery that makes one more likely to pray, and *not* one's propositional orthodoxy.

TABLE 4.7

Madonna Scale Frequent Prayer and Doctrinal Orthodoxy Scale
(Coefficient = Pearson's r)

	Orthodoxy	Madonna
Madonna	.02	
Prayer	.07	.23

A number of recent writers on the role of Mary in the Catholic tradition (most notably Marina Warner in *Alone of All Her Sex*) have argued that the Madonna image has been a means of imposing on women a conservative, traditionalist, Catholic, familial and sexual ethic in which women are condemned to early marriage, large families, and household drudgery. Whatever might be said of the past there is no evidence in Table 4.8 (page 79) that the Madonna image today supports such a role definition for women. There is no difference between those who are low on the image scale and those who are high on it in their definition of what is an ideal number of children, what is a large family, what is a small family, or how many years a woman ought to wait before having her first child. There is only a three-tenths of a year difference in their judgment as to what is the best age for a woman to marry (an age which in both cases, by the way, is substantially above the expectation and the practice of non-Catholic Americans).

For married respondents there are also no differences between the two groups in age of marriage, number of children, or number of expected children. (Since most of our sample is not yet married there is a lower actual age at marriage for those who are married than there is an ideal age for the whole sample.)

Parallel findings can be reported for Canada and for the English-and French-Canadian samples: in none of the three cultures is the Mary image tied to a fertility cult.

TABLE 4.8

Madonna Scale and Marriage Age, Family Size by Sex

	Madonna Scale	Men	Women	Total
Best age for women to marry	High	24.0	24.5	24.3
	Low	23.7	24.3	24.3
How many years before first baby?	High	3.4	3.7	3.6
	Low	4.2	3.0	3.7
Ideal number of children	High	2.6	2.7	2.6
	Low	2.5	2.7	2.6
"Large" family	High	5.2	5.4	5.3
	Low	5.2	5.3	5.2
"Small" family	High	1.5	1.6	1.5
	Low	1.4	1.6	1.5
(For Married Respondents)				
Total number of children ever had	High	0.8	1.0	0.9
	Low	0.9	1.0	0.9
Number of children expect to have	High	2.5	2.3	2.4
	Low	2.2	2.4	2.3
Age at marriage	High	21.7	20.6	21.0
	Low	21.8	20.3	21.0

Those high on the Madonna image scale are somewhat less likely to think that premarital sex is not wrong and somewhat more likely to think that abortion is wrong when the reason for it is the woman does not want any more children (Table 4.9, page 80). However, there is no difference between those who are high and low on the scale in their approval of legal abortion when a child is expected to be defective, and their approval of birth control and their approval of divorce. In other words, some sexual matters are differentiated by the Madonna scale, but many others are not. Furthermore, there is no evidence in either Table 4.8 or Table 4.9 for the allegedly conservative, familialist exploitation of Mary by the Catholic Church.

Further (Table 4.10, page 80), there is no difference between those high and low on the scale in their rejection of the notion that the working mother harms children. Those high on the Madonna scale are more likely to think that the Church should update its sexual teaching, and that working on social problems ought to be an important life goal. Moreover, for men the Madonna scale correlates statistically with a sense of obligation to work towards ending racial segregation and also with support for the ordination of women. Note well, it is precisely men who have warm images of Mary who are more likely to support the ordination of women. For them, the Madonna image does not interfere with the feminist position on the ordination of women, but reinforces it.

TABLE 4.9

Madonna Scale and Sexual Attitudes
(Percent)

	High	Low
Premarital sex not wrong	50*	56
Birth control not wrong	94	96
Divorce not wrong	89	87
Legal abortion of defective child not wrong	82	84
Legal abortion wanting no more children not wrong	62*	60

* Significant at the .05 level or better.

TABLE 4.10

Madonna Scale and Social Attitudes
(Percent)

	High	Low
Working on social problems important life goal	29*	22
Should work to end racial segregation (men)	36*	29
Church should update its sexual teachings	55*	47
Support ordination of women—Men	45	38
Women	48	44

* Significant at the .05 level or better.

The Madonna image, then, is not just a curiosity. It correlates with sexual liberalism, with social commitment, and for men, with a position against racial segregation and support for the ordination of women. Far from being a messenger of conservatism and oppression, Mary is rather a herald of liberalism and liberation for young Catholic adults, and especially for young Catholic men—and *at statistically significant levels*. We also hypothesized a relationship between the Mary myth and warmth in the relationship with one's spouse. This was not to be merely a relationship between the Mary image and general happiness in the marriage relationship, but also between the Mary image and sexual fulfillment in marriage. This hypothetical connection, was to say the least, atypical in social science circles. And yet, there is a .16 correlation between the Madonna scale and sexual fulfillment in marriage. It is only in this aspect of the marriage relationship where there is a significant correlation.

Table 4.11 shows that sixty-six percent of those who were high on the Madonna scale say that their sexual fulfillment is excellent, as opposed to fifty percent who were low on the scale. Thus, we know that the Madonna scale correlates with one's spouse in adulthood.

TABLE 4.11

Sexual Fulfillment in Marriage by Madonna Scale and Maternity Scale
(Percent Sexual Fulfillment High)

Madonna Scale	High	66*
	Low	50
Maternity Scale	High	56*
	Low	40

* Significant at the .05 level or better.

It also turns out that there is a significant association between one's relationship with one's mother and with one's spouse. A "maternity" scale was constructed out of the variables considered in Table 4.4—powerful religious effect of the mother acknowledged, a mother who participated in decision making, a mother whose approach to religion was very joyous, and a mother who frequently received communion. Fifty-six percent of those who were high on the scale (i.e., they scored three or four) also reported excellent sexual fulfillment as opposed to forty percent who were low on the scale.

The question then arises as to whether the Madonna image intervenes between recollection of childhood relationship with one's mother and current sexual fulfillment with one's spouse. In Figure 4.1 (page 82), we see that it does. For both the men respondents and the women respondents the Madonna image is the "channel" which links childhood maternal relationship with adult familial relationship. For men there is also a direct path which does not flow through the Madonna image. However, this direct path is over and above the influence channeled through the Madonna image and not a substitute for it. The hypothesis proposed in the beginning of this chapter, then, is sustained. The Madonna symbolism weds the story of one's childhood experiences to the story of one's marital experiences. One's image of the Madonna is in part fashioned by one's experience with one's mother, and in its turn shapes in part one's experience with one's wife or with one's husband.

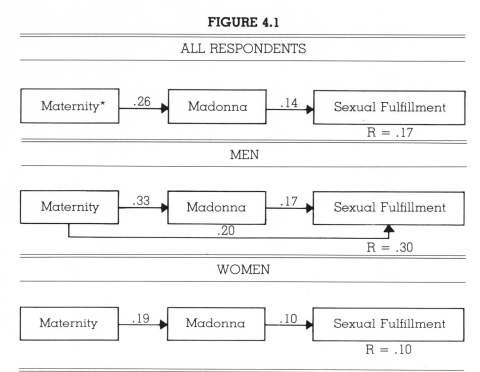

FIGURE 4.1

ALL RESPONDENTS

MEN

WOMEN

*Scale composed of mother involved in decision, mother joyous, mother had religious effect, mother frequent communicant.

Since Canadian young adults were interviewed as well as young adults in the United States, it is possible to ascertain whether the Madonna image plays the same role in two other cultures—English-Canadian and French-Canadian. We observe in Figure 4.2 (page 83) that the flow of influence in English Canada is the same as in the United States; indeed, the relationship between the Madonna image and sexual fulfillment in marriage is virtually the same. Among French Canadians, however, the matter is somewhat different. The Madonna image is, indeed, affected by recollections of childhood relationships, and those recollections also affect sexual fulfillment in marriage. However, there is no relationship among French Canadians between the Madonna image and sexual fulfillment, perhaps because the Madonna imagery is somewhat less powerful in French Canada than it is in English Canada or in the United States.

Questionnaires were also administered to the spouses of respondents in the United States. It became possible, therefore, to obtain a measure of the family environment as well as of individual attitudes and behaviors. In twenty-five percent of the couples in our survey, both husband and wife said that their sexual fulfillment was excellent. For those in which both were high on the Madonna scale the proportion went to thirty-three. For those in which one or both were not high on the Madonna scale the proportion fell to twenty-two percent. In other words, in those families in which husband and wife share strong Madonna images, the chances are half again as likely that both will report that the sexual fulfillment of their marriage is "excellent." Figure 4.3 demonstrates that the maternity/Madonna/fulfillment model can also be applied to couples as well as individuals (though the maternity scale represents the opinions of the respondent and not of the respondent's spouse).

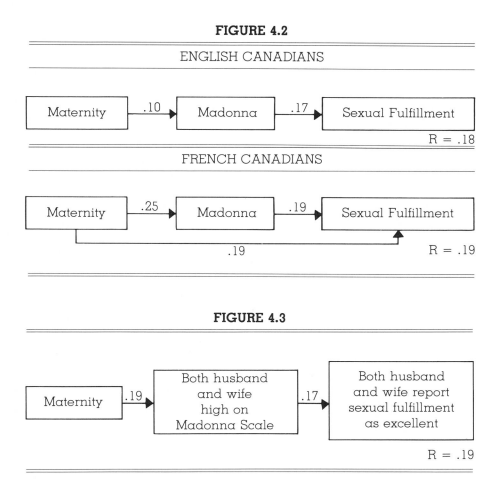

FIGURE 4.2

ENGLISH CANADIANS

Maternity — .10 → Madonna — .17 → Sexual Fulfillment

R = .18

FRENCH CANADIANS

Maternity — .25 → Madonna — .19 → Sexual Fulfillment

.19

R = .19

FIGURE 4.3

Maternity — .19 → Both husband and wife high on Madonna Scale — .17 → Both husband and wife report sexual fulfillment as excellent

R = .19

The correlation between a respondent's sexual fulfillment as "excellent" and his or her spouse's sexual fulfillment is .51 if both are high on the Madonna scale and .29 if one or the other is low on the scale. If husband and wife share, in other words, the same "story" of the womanliness of the Ultimate, they are also more likely to share the same story of their life together.

A final way in which the Marian symbol influences young Catholics has to do with the way in which some of them, having once moved away from the Church, reidentify, in part, because of the symbolic power of the Madonna.

In Chapter Two we were able to link the return to religious devotion of young people approaching their thirties with a reintegration into society associated with marriage. We explained those turning thirty *as a group* were more devout because as a group they were more likely to be married. However, we have no information either on their previous levels of devotion or on their self-consciousness about the apparent change in levels of religious devotion. We lack this information not because there was no means to obtain it through retrospective questions, but rather because we did not anticipate such a sharp "mini life cycle" phenomenon.

However, we do have retrospective information on the closeness of the respondents' identification with the Church five years previously. It is thus possible to select a group of young people who were only marginally identified with the Church five years ago and who now have moved closer to it. Having identified such a group, it is then feasible to search for an explanation of their return. What is it, in other words, which has led the reidentifiers back into the Church?

Four hundred seventy-one respondents said that five years ago they were either "slightly close" or "not at all close" to the Church. Of these, 74 say that they are now either "very close" or "moderately close" to the Church—a jump of at least two rings in our five concentric rings (question 26) representing degree of identification with the Church. There are no important differences between the returners and the nonreturners in age, sex, and marital status.

There are two explanations which might be advanced for the "return" or "reidentification." It may well be that the returners and the nonreturners are differentiated by sexual and authority issues which loom so largely in the mass media accounts of the "troubles" in the Church. Those who stay on the margins may be more "liberal" on matters of sexuality and more restive on questions of authority.

Or the differentiation may be more religious in the strict sense of the word. The returners may be attracted back by worship, by fond memories of childhood warmth in the Church, and by the ministry of the clergy. Obviously, it is possible that all these forces may be at work. The "religious" dimensions may attract young people back into the Church, and the moral/authority dimensions may force them towards the margins.

The media issues do not seem to differentiate the returners sharply from the nonreturners. The relationships between doctrinal orthodoxy and return, and the ordination of women and the return are both trivial and not statistically significant. The relationship of return with "permissiveness" (living together and premarital sex) and approval of papal job performance (.10 and .14 respectively) are significant but weak, and they disappear in the multiple regression equation combining all the variables (Table 4.12). Only a sex mores index (birth control and abortion) seems to have a moderate differentiating effect between the returners and the nonreturners (.24).

TABLE 4.12

Correlates of Stronger Identification
With the Church
(Coefficient = Pearson's r)

Morality and Authority	
#Mores	.24*
##Permissiveness	.10*
Orthodoxy	.01
Papal approval	.14*
Ordination of women	.03
Religion	
Maternal scale	.23*
Madonna scale	.21*
Quality of sermons	.35*
Church a way of worshiping God	.34*

#Abortion and Birth Control.
##Premarital Sex and Living Together.
*Significant at the .05 level or better.

On the other hand, four "religious" variables are all statistically significant—the maternal scale, the Madonna scale, the quality of sermons, and the attraction to Catholicism as a satisfying way to worship God (.23, .21, .35, and .34 respectively). When all nine variables are put into a multiple regression equation (Table 4.13, page 86), they produce an R of .53 and thus account for 28 percent of the variance between returners and nonreturners. (If the sexual/authority items are removed from the equation, 22 percent of the variance is still accounted for.)

Thus, reidentification with the Church seems to be almost entirely a matter of religious motivation. There is little difference between the returners and the nonreturners in their attitudes towards birth control or the ordination of women. Ninety-six percent of the nonreturners reject the teaching, but so do 87 percent of the returners. Forty-seven percent of the nonreturners think that the ordination of women is an important issue as opposed to 43 percent of the returners. But two-thirds of the returners say that the Church is "extremely important" to them as a "satisfying way to worship God" as opposed to a fifth of the nonreturners. Seven percent of the nonreturners report hearing "excellent" sermons as opposed to 37 percent of the returners. That a priest may be crucial in the return is further confirmed by the fact that while 12 percent of all our respondents say they have had a serious talk about religion with a priest in the past year, and nine percent of the nonreturners have had such a talk, 26 percent of the returners report a conversation with a priest.

TABLE 4.13

Correlates of Stronger Identification
for Married People

	r	beta
Mores	.12	.00
Maternal scale	.23	.15
Sermons	.38	.33
Madonna	.30	.24
Spouse church attendance	.22	.13
R = .53	Variance explained = 28 percent	

It is interesting that the return to the Church correlates with the maternal and Madonna scales. As we saw previously, the former represents a recollection of a strong, religious, affectionate mother, and the latter is a religious symbolization (or "story") of the experience of God as mother. It may well be that to the extent that "Mother Church" is able to join itself to this memory of loving maternity and appear as a strong, religious, and affectionate mother, it (she) becomes attractive as a mother to whom to return.

The path diagram in Figure 4.4 (page 87) illustrates this possibility. Both the maternal scale and the Madonna scale exercise their influence on the returners through their conviction that the Church is extremely important as a way to worship God. A rewarding childhood experience with one's mother leads to a strong Mary image; and both in turn seem to induce a greater need to worship God and, hence, a propensity to reidentify with the Church, even if one does not agree with its sexual ethic. This story of a warm and loving God represented by a warm and loving Church may be especially attractive when it is presented by an "excellent" preacher.

FIGURE 4.4

A Model to Explain Stronger Identification
with the Church

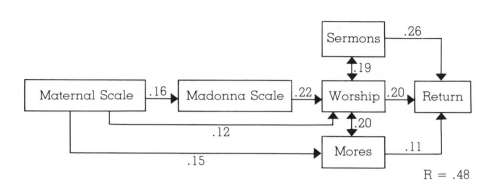

We can find no evidence that sexual or doctrinal problems are inhibiting a reidentification of young people with the Church. Those who do return seem to have a strong need to worship, powerful images of Mary, and happy recollections of their relationship with their mother. They also need to hear better sermons.

By way of summary, the Madonna symbol still seems to be for North American young people a "story" which reflects the memory of a strong, joyous, and devout mother, and for the English Canadians and Americans it also is a symbol which relates (for both men and women) positively with a passionate relationship with one's spouse. The experience of maternity in childhood channeled through the Madonna image seems to deepen and enrich the experience of potential maternity or a relationship with a potential mother in adulthood. It also facilitates the process of reidentification with the Church for some proportion of young Catholics who have drifted away. The Madonna is alive and well and living in North America, and the reason, it would seem, is that there is still a role for her to play.

We end as we begin, turning from numbers to images, images which now, however, have been empirically substantiated.

> *Wild rainbow wit, lady dear, made the world*
> *(Though we in loss of nerve oft turn in gray)*
> *Flowers red, foam white, lake green, sunset gold*
> *Thunderbolts of color on your harvest day*

And Matthew red, Mollie blond, Norae brown
Toothless grins, rotten dids, fun and funny
faces
Mad, comic God and a few Irish still around
Multicolored mischief, wild and merry chases
Too much for us, lady, you know the thought
He made them; from then on 'twas Mary's show
Like us, always watching kids, you've been
caught
So praising you, God as Mother, we all know
That you look down with laughter from above
And God sees each of us with a mother's love.

Notes
*Presented at the symposium "In Her Image," University of California, Santa Barbara, April 23, 1980.
Sponsored by The National Endowment for the Arts.

The Religious Life Cycle

Highlights

1   *Catholics who are now approaching their thirties seem to be coming out of the faith crisis which marked their early and middle twenties.*

2   *One of the most effective means for the Church to deal with the problem of sexual permissiveness is to preach constantly the warmth and love of God. A Church that speaks harshly will not receive an attentive hearing from young Catholics.*

3   *Young people in their twenties undergo a period of alienation from the established order, including the Church. When they marry, this alienation tends to disappear and a religious reintegration takes place.*

4   *On a scale of religious devotion, the highest proportion of devout Catholics can be seen among those who have devout spouses and who share warm religious imagery with one another.*

5   *The way that the Church can help young adults in their religious reintegration counteract the sense of alienation and promote healthy sexual attitudes is to share with the people the stories and images of Jesus, Mary, and God as warm and loving, and the afterlife as a place of delight.*

Chapter 5

The Religious Life Cycle

Other NORC research has indicated a return by Catholics in their 30s to religious practice, particularly by those who attended college and those of Irish ethnic background. Therefore, it seemed reasonable to ask whether there was any sign of either decline or rise of religious practice among the respondents in the Young Catholics Study. Table 5.1 indicates that on all measures there is a sharp decline in religious practice after a person becomes 22 years old. However, at the end of the 20s there is an upturn, and the members of the last three-year age group, for example, are as likely as the youngest respondents to say they pray several times a week. Whereas their Mass attendance, communion reception, and a sense of closeness to the Church and to the parish have not returned to the levels of their late teens and early 20s, nonetheless, the level of their religious practice increased over the three-year age cohort just beneath them. Furthermore (the bottom half of Table 5.1, page 92), our respondents seem to be aware of this change in themselves. The people in their late 20s think of themselves as being closer to God than they were five years previously, and the same for those between 28 and 30.

There are two possible explanations for the "U curve" in religious behavior which seems to occur to young Catholics during their 20s. It may be an actual "life cycle" phenomenon, with some young people manifesting a decline and then a rise in religious practice. Or, it may be a "generational" phenomenon. Those Catholics in their late 20s today may have always been more devout than those in their middle 20s, and those in their middle 20s may also be less devout than those in their early 20s. There is not, then, a change of behavior, but a change of personnel in age categories.

The fact that those in their late 20s now seem to be conscious that they feel closer to their parish than they were seems to indicate an authentic life cycle change. Furthermore, the annual NORC General Social Survey, taken every year, enables us to ask how the age cohort now turning thirty behaved religiously at earlier points in the last decade. In the first column of Table 5.2 we see that there was, in fact, a lower level of religious practice of this cohort in the early and middle years of the 1970s and a sharp increase in the last two years. It would appear that Catholics turning thirty at the present time seem to have experienced a religious crisis or, at least, a crisis of religious behavior in their early and middle 20s and are now in the process of "rebounding" out of that crisis—an authentic life cycle phenomenon and not a generational change.

TABLE 5.1

Age and Religious Behavior
(Percent)

Religious Behavior	18 –21	22 –24	25 –27	28 –30
Mass (nearly weekly)	46	35	24	32
Communion (monthly)	41	27	21	25
Prayer (several times a week)	58	53	52	57
Living together wrong	25	15	25	29
Close to		(Z Score)		
God	.04	−.07	.02	.06
Church	.24	−.01	−.15	−.07
Parish	.22	−.04	−.14	.00

Conclusion: There seems to be a religious trough in years from 22 to 27 with increase in religiousness in years after 28.

Change in closeness to God and parish over past five years as perceived by respondents (according to age)+ = closer.

God		.02	.21	.43	.53
Parish		−.55	−.48	−.15	.11

TABLE 5.2

Church Attendance by Catholic Age Cohorts
(NORC General Social Survey)
(Percent)

Cohort	1949–51	1946–48	1943–45	1939–41
Age:				
22–23	33			
24–25	35	54		
26–27	29	46	54	
28–30	55	43	36	56
31–33		43	43	35
34–36			44	58
37–39				65

One cannot find, however, evidence of a similar life cycle crisis for Catholics who were born before 1949. Indeed, Catholics who were born between 1939 and 1945 seem to have experienced a sharp dip (of more than 20 percentage points) in church attendance in their early 30s, and then, also, to have rebounded as this decade of their life went on.

It may be, then, that there are two major "dips" or "U curves" in religious behavior for Catholics, one in the middle 20s and the other in the early 30s. We will only be able to confirm this possibility when we can follow the cohort presently turning thirty into the next five years of its life.

An alternate possibility (and one which seems more reasonable to us) is that young Catholics in the present situation in the Church go through a period of disillusionment from which many of them recover after a certain period of time. An earlier generation experienced this disillusionment at a somewhat older age in life. But now the disillusionment has "filtered down" into the middle 20s and has ended by the time young people turn thirty.

The phenomenon of the "U curve" does not seem to be limited to Catholics in America. A Gallup release at the time this report was being finished (Table 5.3) shows a parallel decline in church attendance for the whole American population during the middle 20s, then a rebound—and a very sharp one—of 18 percentage points in the early 30s.

TABLE 5.3

American Church Attendance By Age In 1979*	
Age	Percent Attending Church in a Typical Week
18	34
19	34
20	35
21–24	26
25–29	20
30–34	38

*Gallup Poll, 1979.

This age cycle of religious devotion seems to parallel so closely the cycle of marital satisfaction described in Chapter Three that it seems safe to assume as a working hypothesis that the two phenomena are related, if not identical. In our attempt to explain the religious life cycle, then, we propose the following hypotheses:
1. Decline of religious devotion of American Catholics is a form of institutional "alienation": a partial withdrawal of affiliation from

the institutional Church which parallels a withdrawal from other institutions in society.

2. Given the enormous disagreement between the attitudes on sexual matters of young Catholics and the teachings of the institutional Church, their views on premarital sex and living together before marriage make a strong contribution to the devotional decline of young Catholics.

3. Given what we have seen previously about the relationship between marriage and religion, a substantial part of the rebound phenomenon will be explainable in terms of marriage reintegrating young people into social institutions, and in particular into the Church. A marriage between two Catholics, and especially a marriage to a devout spouse, will facilitate this reintegration.

4. "Warm" religious imagery will in part cancel the effect of attitudes of sexual permissiveness and the increase of shared warm religious imagery in a marriage will reduce even more the effect of attitudes of sexual permissiveness.

The last point is worth dwelling on because it is a theoretical proposition derived from the perspective on religion described in Chapter Three: warm images of the Cosmic Powers combined with, reinforced by, and enhancing a warm marital relationship will tend to reduce the effect of attitudes supportive of sexual promiscuity and sexual intimacy without public commitment.

Note well that the expectation described in the previous paragraph runs strongly against the conventional wisdom. First of all, it would seem unlikely that a young person's images of God, of Mary, and of the afterlife would have much, if any, effect on his or her approach to premarital sex, not in a "pagan," "hedonistic," and secularist society like our own. Secondly, if one were to expect any influence at all, one might well think it reasonable that someone who believes that God is a lover and that heaven is a paradise of pleasure and delight would also think that there is nothing wrong with the delightful pleasures of love in this life being enjoyed whenever and wherever possible. That warm religious imagery, in other words, which in Chapter Three was demonstrated to promote sexual fulfillment in marriage, would also reasonably be expected to promote sexual freedom before marriage.

Nonetheless, we hypothesize the opposite phenomena. "Stories" implicit in the "warm" religious images are stories of fidelity, commitment, promises made, honored, and kept permanently. We, therefore, predict a negative correlation between warm images and attitudes of sexual permissiveness. At least, unlike other statements about youthful sex, this one can be tested immediately.

And if it is proven correct, the best way the Church can deal with permissive sexual attitudes among young people is not railing against the attitudes, nor denouncing the behavior as sinful, but by preaching ever more vigorously the warmth and love of God.

There is a sharp decline from the middle teen years to the middle 20s in religious devotion (as measured by a scale composed of prayer, Mass attendance, and the reception of communion). Sixty-four percent of those between 14 and 18 are high on this scale, while those in their later 20s (between 26 and 28) only place 22 percent high on that scale. (See Table 5.4.)

TABLE 5.4

Religious Practice by Cohort

(Percent High On Devotion Scale)[1]

18–21 Years Old	48
22–25 Years Old	33
26–28 Years Old	22*
29–30 Years Old	29**

[1]Scale composed of prayer, Mass attendance and reception of communion. To be high on the scale the respondent has to do two of the following three: pray every day or at least several times a week, go to Mass every week, receive communion several times a month.

*The decline in devotion is statistically significant at .05 or better.

**The rise at the end of the 20's is statistically significant at .05 or better.

There is a modest rebound of religious activity in the late 20s, from 22 to 29 percent. It is possible to say that the religious revival which seems to occur at the end of the decade of the 20s (bringing young people back to approximately the level of religious devotion in their early 20s) represents a significant upward change of young Catholic religious behavior.

The cycle seems to be at work in both men and women. Women are more devout than men, and their cycle is approximately 10 percentage points higher than that of the men, starting out at 69 percent, declining at 27 percent and rebounding to 34 percent. Men, on the other hand, begin at 60, decline to 17 and bounce back to 22 percent.

Figure 5.1 (page 96) is a graphic presentation of the first three hypotheses stated at the beginning of this chapter. Sexual permissiveness is measured by a scale composed of attitudes toward living together before marriage and premarital sex. Alienation from the Church is measured by questions asking the respondents to place themselves on a five-point scale indicating how close or how far they feel from the Church.

Organizational alienation is based on a factor created from the items in question 102. (The item on confidence in organized religion is omitted from the scale.) A spouse is considered Catholic if the spouse's present religious affiliation is Catholic, and the distinction is between married and "non-married" so that the latter includes widowed, divorced, separated, and those living together who are not married.

FIGURE 5.1

**Alienation Model to Explain
Religious Life Cycle in the Twenties**

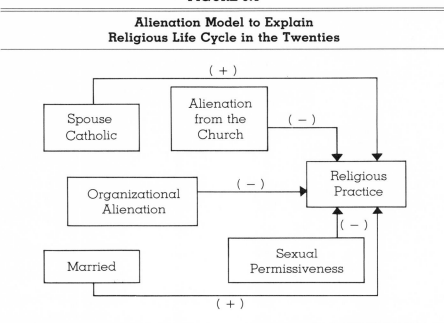

In Figure 5.2 (page 97) this model is applied to religious practice in the United States. The R is about .5, meaning that approximately one-quarter of the devotion and religious practice can be explained by the model. Religious practice is influenced directly by the religion of one's spouse, by alienation from the Church, and by sexual permissiveness. Alienation from the Church, in its turn, is directly influenced by spouse's religion, sexual permissiveness, and organizational alienation. Sexual permissiveness and organizational alienation are both influenced by whether one is married or not. Marriage, then, seems to produce a higher level of opposition to sexual permissiveness and a greater degree of confidence in the organizational and institutional structures of the society. Young people go through a dramatic period of alienation in their 20s, turning off all social institutions including the Church. However, when they "settle down" and begin a family of their own, they become both more hostile to permissiveness and more confident of the organizational structures of the society. Marriage, apparently, reintegrates them into the society and also into the Church—especially in the latter case if the spouse is Catholic.

FIGURE 5.2

Alienation Model to Explain Religious Life Cycle in the Twenties

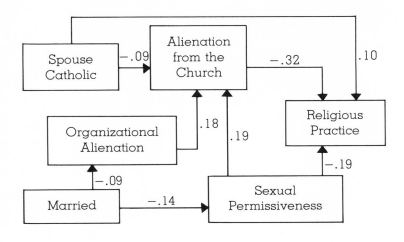

We now propose to use the same technique of "residual analysis" used in Chapter Three to see if the variables in our model can account for much of the religious life cycle—both the decline from the early to the middle 20s and then the rise at the end of the late 20s. Data in Tables 5.5 and 5.6 (page 98) confirm this expectation. By merely taking into account marriage and the religiousness of spouse one can account for almost nine-tenths of the 26 percentage points difference in the religious devotion scale between those in their early 20s and those between 26 and 28 in the United States. In other words, those in their early and middle 20s who are married do not experience the sharp decline in religious practice that singles experience, particularly if they are married to Catholics. Marriage, and especially a marriage to a Catholic, reintegrates them into the social structure of the country and into the organizational structure of the Church.

Similarly, almost nine-tenths of the rebound which occurs between 26-28 and 29-30 years of age can be accounted for by factors related to marriage (Table 5.6). The apparent religious life cycle is in fact part of a larger life cycle. Those who are married are more likely to be religious than those who are not, presumably because marriage, particularly to one of the same faith, puts higher value on social and institutional integration.

TABLE 5.5

Model to Explain Decline in Religious Devotion Among Young People Between 18-21 Years and 26-28 Years

	Percent Difference	Proportion Explained
Decline	−26	
Taking into account marriage and religiousness of spouse	−3	.88

TABLE 5.6

Model to Explain Rise in Religious Devotion Between 26-28 Years and 29-30 Years

	Percent Difference	Proportion Explained
Increase	+7	
Taking into account marriage and religiousness of spouse	+1	.86

Marriage, in other words, cancels the alienation that goes on among the "non-married." Three-fifths of the decline among the "non-marrieds" in the United States can be accounted for by the same model (Table 5.7). The decade of the 20s is a time of alienation from social institutions and from the Church, an alienation reinforced and strengthened by the conflict between young people's sexual attitudes and the sexual attitudes of the Church. Marriage seems to cancel out much of this alienation and to account entirely for the rebound.

TABLE 5.7

Model to Explain Decline in Religious Devotion Among Non-Marrieds

	Percent Difference	Proportion Explained
Decline	−30	
Organization alienation	−23	.23
Sexual permissiveness	−18	.40
Alienation from the Church	−12	.60

The dynamics of the religious life cycle are now clear. Religious behavior goes up in people's late 20s because more people are married in their late 20s. Sixty-nine percent of Catholics between 22 and 25 are not married, and 44 percent of those between 26 and 28 are not married; while the proportion of Catholic marriages increases from 17 percent of those between 22 and 25 to 46 percent of those between 29 and 30. Could it be that those Catholics who wait longer to get married are more likely to marry other Catholics? There is no change in the proportion of the population that are in mixed marriages after the age of 26. It may also be, however, that young Catholics feel freer to enter religiously mixed marriages or that there are a higher number of converts among the spouses of Catholics in their late 20s.

Similarly, there is also an increase in the devotion of married people as they get somewhat older and, perhaps, begin to work out a joint family approach to religion. Not only are people in their late 20s more likely to be married, but those married people in their late 20s are also more likely to be devout. Note especially in Table 5.8 that entering a religiously mixed marriage does not seem to make all that much difference in the devotion of a Catholic. Among those between 29 and 30, 18 percent of the "non-married" are high on the religious devotion scale, whereas 26 percent of the Catholics in mixed marriages, and 46 percent of Catholics in Catholic marriages are also at the top end of this scale.

TABLE 5.8

Religious Devotion By Marital Status
(Percent High on Religious Devotion Scale)

			CATHOLIC MARRIAGE	
Cohort	Not Married	Mixed Marriage	Spouse Low On Religious Devotion Scale	Spouse High On Religious Devotion Scale
22 – Years Old	30	14	27	81*
26 – 28 Years Old	19	28	12	67*
29 – 30 Years Old	18	26	13	72*

* Significantly different at .05 or better from spouse-with-low-devotion respondents.

We have answered the question of why married people are more likely to be devout than single people: they are less alienated, though if they are in a religiously mixed marriage they are not much less alienated from the Church. Two remaining questions must be answered: What goes on in a Catholic marriage that leads to a resurgence of religious devotion, and why do some Catholics choose to marry other Catholics and some choose to marry non-Catholics?

Figure 5.3 introduces religious images into our discussion of the first question. It hypothesizes that warm religious images will have an effect on both permissive attitudes and the feeling of alienation from the Church and, hence, affect the levels of religious devotion in Catholic marriages. If a couple shares warm "stories of God," they will be more opposed to permissiveness, less alienated from the Church, and hence, more devout. This, the most controversial hypothesis stated at the beginning of the present chapter, is demonstrated in Figure 5.4. Religious imagery does, indeed, diminish both permissiveness and alienation. Those who have warm stories of God in their creative imagination are more opposed to premarital sex and living together than those who do not and are also likely to feel less alienated from the Church. In families where couples share these warm religious images, there will be less support for permissiveness, less feeling of alienation, and greater religious devotion.

FIGURE 5.3

**Model to Explain
Why Marriage Improves Level of Religious Devotion**

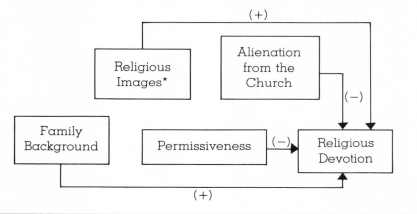

*Both spouses high on "warm" image scale.

We must now determine why these warm religious images work in Catholic marriages to "de-alienate" Catholic young people. First of all (Table 5.8), high levels of religious practice in Catholic marriages are only to be found when both the respondent and the spouse are high on the religious devotion scale. There is virtually no difference between those in religiously mixed marriages and those who do not have a devout spouse in their own religious devotion. Indeed, of the 29 and 30 year level, those in mixed marriages seem more devout than those in Catholic marriages without a devout spouse. In those marriages where the spouse is devout, the respondent's level of religious devotion declines from 81 to 67 percent between the early and middle 20s, but then bounces back to 72 percent in the late 20s. Can the model presented in Figure 5.5 explain some of the differences in religious devotion between those Catholics who have devout spouses and those who do not?

FIGURE 5.4

Model to Explain Religious Devotion in All Marriages in Which Both Partners Are Catholic

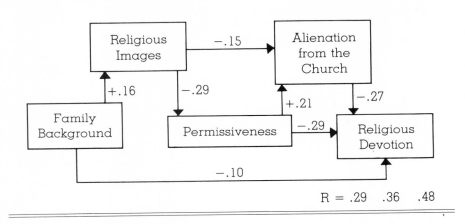

R = .29   .36   .48

FIGURE 5.5

Mixed Marriages

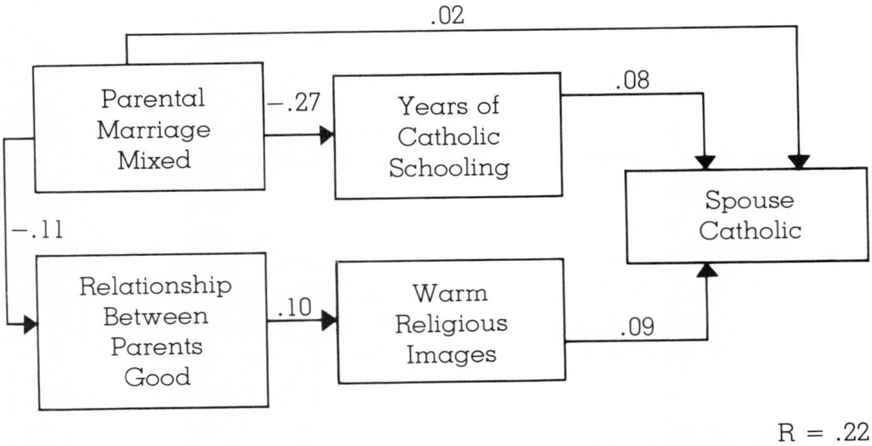

R = .22

Table 5.9 shows that approximately one-half of the 55 percentage points difference in religious devotion between the two kinds of Catholic marriages can be accounted for by the model, and more than half of that half by the fact that in devout Catholic marriages the husband and wife share warm religious images. It is precisely the "stories of God" which husband and wife have worked out together that play a major role in explaining why they are devout and their counterparts who do not have these stories are not devout.

TABLE 5.9

Model to Explain Difference in Religious Devotion in Catholic Marriages Between Those Who Have Devout Spouses and Those Who Do Not

	Percent Difference	Proportion Explained
Increase	+55	
Family background taken into account	+55	.00
Warm religious images	+40	.27
Alienation from Church and sexual permissiveness	+28	.45

Furthermore (Table 5.10), warm religious images also account for half of the differences in alienation from the Church between those who are high on the permissiveness scale and those who are low. Permissive young Catholics are 16 percentage points more likely to be alienated from the Church than non-permissive, and this can be attributed to the fact that the non-permissive share warmer "stories of God."

TABLE 5.10

Permissiveness and Alienation from Church by Warm Family Religious Images

	Percent Difference	Proportion Explained
Percentage point difference in alienation from Church between those who are above the mean on permissiveness and those who are below the mean	+16	
Taking into account the effect of warm religious images	+ 8	.50

The impact of images of God on devotion (Table 5.11), permissiveness (Table 5.12), and alienation (Table 5.13) can also be presented in percentage form. Forty-five percent of those who have warm images are high on the religious devotion scale as opposed to 27 percent of those who do not have such images, and the highest proportion of devout Catholics can be found among those who have both devout spouses and joint warm imagery. Seventy-eight percent of those with devout spouses and warm imagery are themselves high on the religious devotion scale as opposed to 58 percent of those who have devout spouses, but who lack warm "stories of God" (Table 5.14, page 104). It is a help, of course, if your spouse is devout, but the help is much greater (and "significantly" greater) if you also share common "warm religious imagery."

TABLE 5.11

Religious Imagery and Religious Devotion in Marriages Where Both Spouses are Catholic
(Percent of Respondents High On Religious Devotion)

Images Warm	Images Not Warm
45*	27

*Significantly different from not warm at .05 level.

TABLE 5.12

Permissiveness and Religious Imagery
(Percent High On Permissiveness)

Images Warm	Images Not Warm
57*	84

*Significantly different from not warm at .05 level.

TABLE 5.13

Alienation From the Church and Family Religious Imagery
(Percent Not Alienated)

Images Warm	Images Not Warm
32*	19

*Significantly different from not warm at .05 level.

A third of those with warm images describe themselves as close to the Church, significantly different from one-fifth of those who do not have warm images (Table 5.13). Furthermore, there is not a statistically significant difference in alienation between those who are more permissive and those who are less permissive if they have warm images (Table 5.15). It is only among those who lack such images that the more permissive are statistically more likely to be alienated. Indeed, those who have high permissive attitudes and warm images are as likely to be close to the Church as those who have low permissive attitudes, but lack the warm images. Imagery, in other words, seems to cancel out the relationship between permissive sexual attitudes and alienation from the Church. Warm religious images not only lead to a decrease in sexual permissiveness, but they also seem to eliminate the relationship between permissiveness and alienation.

TABLE 5.14

Religious Imagery, Religious Devotion and Spouses' Religious Devotion in Marriages Where Both Spouses are Catholic

(Percent of Respondents High On Religious Devotion Scale)

	Images Warm	Images Not Warm
Spouse low devotion	19	14
Spouse high in devotion	78*	58

* Significantly different at .05 level from those whose images are not warm.

TABLE 5.15

Alienation From the Church Religious Imagery and Sexual Permissiveness

(Percent not alienated)

	PERMISSIVENESS	
	High	Low
Warm images	26	44
Not warm images	4	27*

* Significantly different at .05 level from low permissiveness.

Warm stories of God do not eliminate, by any means, the propensity of young people to be tolerant of sexual permissiveness, but they do diminish it substantially. Eighty-four percent of the people in marriages where the spouses do not have a common warm story of God are high on the permissive scale as opposed to 57 percent of those whose family have developed a mutual warm religious imagery (Table 5.12). Forty-three percent of those with warm images think that living together before marriage is wrong as opposed to 17 percent who lack such images (Table 5.16, page 105). However, there is virtually no difference between the two groups in their attitudes on birth control.

TABLE 5.16

Attitudes Towards Sexual Issues by Religious Imagery
(Percent)

	Images Warm	Images Not Warm
Percent living together almost always or always wrong	43*	17
Percent birth control wrong	6	2

* Significantly different at .05 level from not warm.

The stories of God that a husband and wife share, then, play an important part in the decline in the modest religious revival which occurs at the end of the late 20s, especially because these images have a notable impact on that group from which the religious "revivalists" are most likely to come, marriages in which both partners are Catholic. If the Church is interested in facilitating this religious revival and diminishing the levels of alienation from the Church and in contending against sexual permissiveness, the most effective way of doing so on the basis of the data presently available to them would be to reinforce as strongly as it can the stories of Jesus and Mary as warm, of God as lover, and of heaven as a paradise of pleasure and delight.

If we could account for other effective processes by which Catholic marriages produce greater levels of religious devotion, we are much less successful in explaining the mixed marriage phenomenon (earlier attempts at explaining religiously mixed marriages were also unsatisfactory; see Greeley, *Crisis in the Church*, 1979). Only four variables relate at statistically significant levels to mixed marriages (Table 5.17, page 106): poor relationship between parents when a respondent was growing up; being a child of a religiously mixed marriage; Catholic education; and warm religious images (of the respondent, not of the family). However, the multiple R of the model presented in Figure 5.5 is only 22, meaning that less than 5 percent of the variance in marital choice can be accounted for. It would appear that only longitudinal research in which young people are followed through the life cycle as they make their marriage choices would offer an explanation why one young Catholic chooses a Catholic spouse and another does not.[1]

Marriage adjustment, then, and religious life cycle are both powerfully and importantly affected by a person's religious images, and in particular by the joint religious images that a husband and wife share. These images do not explain the whole of marital satisfaction nor the whole of the religious revival which seems to occur in the late 20s. No one could reasonably expect that they would. For human behavior, particularly behavior as complex as religious devotion and marital relationships, is affected by a variety of biological, cultural, educational, biographical, and psychological factors—as well as, of course, by free human choice. Our point, rather, is that religious imagery (particularly the common religious imagery that a husband and wife share) plays a role, an important role, and, indeed, in the religious revival at the end of the 20s, a very important role. These images present an aspect of the Church's doctrine which can be reinforced and emphasized with relative ease, and which promise a very substantial payoff both in binding married people more tightly together into satisfying relationships and in leading the alienated and disaffiliated back into the Church.

TABLE 5.17

Correlations for Mixed Marriages **	
(Coefficient = Pearson's r)	
	(r)
Parents in mixed marriages	.15*
Years of Catholic schooling	.12*
Warm religious images	.10*
Parent relationship to each other close	.10*

*Significant at .05 level or better.
**Spouse not Catholic.

It should be clear on the basis of the past two chapters that there is an intricate process by which husbands and wives in the first decade of their marriage work out, perhaps implicitly, a common religious posture. The posture is affected by their past experiences and affects many of their present attitudes and behaviors, and will, doubtless, shape their future. It is the formation of a family religious "stance" that is intimately affected by and intimately affects the general satisfaction of their relationship, even though they themselves do not seem to perceive this because the process is so subtle and complex. In this report we have been able to describe some of the dynamics which seem to be at work, dynamics which may seem to many readers to be very complex. In fact, these models are much too simple, and the reality of husband/wife interaction as they resolve their problems and fashion a religious story which is no longer "yours and mine," but "ours," is infinitely more complex than that indicated by the models which have been presented in the last two chapters. We would emphasize here that the present report is merely the beginning of a study of how "your story" and "my story" converge into "our story" and then profoundly influence every aspect of "our" lives. Further research into this complex familial process ought to be high on the agenda of the Church as it moves into the years ahead.

NOTES
[1]It is worth noting, by the way, that there is absolutely no relationship between attendance at Catholic schools and warm images of Cosmic Powers. No matter how many years one has attended Catholic schools, he or she is no more likely to think of God as a lover, heaven as a paradise of delight, or Jesus and Mary as warm than if he or she did not attend Catholic schools at all—a somewhat dismaying and disturbing finding for the partisans of Catholic education, who otherwise will find much to console themselves in the present NORC research.

Catholic Education and Life Cycle

Highlights

1   *It is important for the Church to improve the quality of its religious instruction. This will have a much stronger effect than forcing persons to attend programs of religious education.*

2   *Catholic schools are found to have a significant impact on what young people read, believe, practice, and value in their lives.*

3   *Even more than the influence of family and spouse, it is participation in a Catholic school that makes persons feel a sense of closeness to the Church. When young Catholics are overcoming their sense of alienation, their return to the Church is helped along by their Catholic school experience and the length of time spent in the Catholic school environment.*

4   *Participation in Catholic schools helps to integrate young adults into the life of the Church when they go through their life cycle crisis in their twenties.*

5   *Catholic schools are important to the Church in terms of their religious influence upon young adults—as well as providing the skills and creativity for marital stability.*

Chapter 6

Catholic Education and Life Cycle

Previous NORC reports documented both the influence of Catholic schools in adult life for those who attended such schools and the increase of their impact during the transitional years after the Second Vatican Council. The correlations between Catholic school attendance and adult religious behavior *increased* between 1963 and 1974, which indicates that Catholic schools were more important to the Church after Vatican Council II than before the council. These correlations were especially strong *(Catholic Schools in a Declining Church*, 1976) for Catholics under thirty. In this chapter of our report we continue our investigation of the impact of Catholic schools, and compare the impact of Catholic education in the United States with the impact of Catholic education in Canada. Finally, we ask what the impact of Catholic education is on the religious "mini life cycle."

Catholic Religious Education

It is said frequently by religious education authorities that more than six million Catholics receive no religious education. The methodology by which this statistic is derived is, to say the least, problematic. More importantly, little distinction is made by those who cite the statistic between those who are not receiving any religious education now and those who have received at least some religious education in the course of their childhood and adolescence.

Seven-eighths of the respondents between 18 and 30 report in the Young Catholics Study that they have received at least some kind of Catholic instruction (Table 6.1, page 113). Two-thirds of those who received some sort of instruction attended Catholic schools for a time. Thus, only a minority had all their education in Catholic schools, whereas two-thirds of those who received some religious instruction obtained some of it in parochial grammar schools.

Two-fifths of those Catholics who received religious education had eight years of that education in Catholic grammar school, and more than half of those who did not spend eight years in Catholic grade schools received at least four years of religious instruction. Thus, one comes to the conclusion that, contrary to the implication of the "six million" statistic, the Catholic Church did a commendable job in providing some kind of religious instruction at the elementary school level for those Catholics who are now between 18 and 30 years old. Whether the 13 percent of Catholic young people in this age group who did not receive any religious instruction is small or large depends on one's point of view. In the order of human beings with free choice, 13 percent does not seem to be very high; in the ideal order, Catholics would undoubtably like to see that proportion diminished.

However, the Church's performance at the secondary level of religious education seems much less impressive. Half of the Catholics in our sample between 18 and 30 received no religious education in high school. Twenty-five percent attended Catholic high schools (of whom 17 percent had four years of secondary schooling in Catholic high schools), and the other 25 percent attended CCD classes (of whom 8 percent had four years of such instruction). Only one-quarter of the Catholic young people between 18 and 30, therefore, reported four years of religious instruction. About two-thirds of that group received their religious instruction in Catholic high schools, the other one third in CCD.

Furthermore, almost three-quarters of those who attended public schools at least some of the time said that for some of the years they did not receive religious instruction. Most of those years, presumably, would have been at the secondary level.

However, the reasons given for not receiving religious instruction would seem to suggest that the Church would be hard put to overcome the obstacles to expanding the amount of religious instruction its teenagers receive. Twenty percent of the respondents mentioned poor teaching and thirteen percent said there were no classes available in their parish. The Church could improve the quality of the teaching and could insist that classes be available for all Catholic adolescents; but it would find it much harder to overcome the lack of interest in religion (49 percent), the fact that the young person's friends were not going (11 percent), that their parents did not care (14 percent), and that the young person felt he or she already knew enough religion (11 percent).

The Church has provided at least some religious education to approximately nine out of ten of its members. More than half of these young people received some of their religious education in Catholic primary schools. Yet, it has been able to provide religious instruction to half of its adolescent members, and only half of that half received that instruction in Catholic secondary schools. The reasons for not seeking religious instruction seem to have more to do with peer pressure and religious indifference on the part of parents and children than they do with failures in Church's efforts to organize religious instruction.

TABLE 6.1

Catholic Educational Facts

88% of the respondents between 18 and 30 have had some kind of Catholic instruction.

64% of those receiving some kind of instruction have attended Catholic grade schools for a time.

36% attended Catholic grade schools for all their elementary education. More than one-third of those who did not spend all their years in Catholic grade schools spent at least four years in religious instruction.

BUT

50% received no religious instruction in high school.

25% attended Catholic high schools.

25% attended CCD.

> 17% had four years of Catholic high schools
> 8% had four years of CCD

AND

73% of those who attended public schools at least some of the time said there were years when they did not receive religious instruction.

Reason: [a]

Poor teaching	26%
No interest in religion	49%
Friends weren't going	11%
No classes	13%
Parents didn't care	14%
Already knew enough religion	11%

SO

Church gets some instruction to most of its members, a lot to elementary school children, much less to high school students.

BUT

Poor teaching and unavailability of religious education classes accounts for only about one-third of non-attendance.

[a] Totals to more than 100% because of multiple responses.

In this chapter we will examine the following questions:

■ The impact of Catholic education in the United States and Canada.

■ The possibility that Catholic educational impact may, in fact, be the result of religiousness of family background and not of Catholic school attendance.

■ The possibility that the decisive explanation for the impact of Catholic education is that Catholic schools solidify the commitment to the institutional Church.

■ The impact of Catholic schools in the religious revival that seems to occur among young Catholics in their late 20s (and documented in the companion volume to this report, *The Young Catholic Family)*.

■ The subtle impact that Catholic education may have on choosing not only a Catholic spouse, but a more devout spouse.

Catholic Education in Three Cultures

Attendance at Catholic schools continues in the late 1970s to have the same moderate and statistically significant impact on the behavior of young Catholic adults, as has been found in our earlier studies. More than eight years of Catholic schooling does not produce a statistically significant impact on attitudes towards birth control, living together, and frequency of prayer. Neither did Catholic education produce such an impact in the analysis reported on the education of Catholic Americans based on 1974 data (Table 6.2, page 115). Nor is there a significant difference between those who had more than eight years of Catholic schooling. However, on all the other tested variables—Mass attendance, communion reception, belief in life after death, activity in parish organizations, thought of religious vocation, Catholic periodical reading and TV watching, participation in home liturgy and study groups, and opposition to abortion—Catholic schools do have a statistically significant effect.

How impressive is the magnitude of that effect? The question is no more easy to answer now than it was in either our 1965 or 1975 reports. Those who attended Catholic schools are twice as likely to receive communion almost every week, to belong to parish organizations, to think of religious vocations, and to attend home liturgies. Indeed, only 12 percent of them have considered a vocation, but that is twice as many as the 6 percent who have not had more than eight years of Catholic schooling; and only 10 percent have attended a home liturgy, but that is still twice as high as the 5 percent of those who have not had more than eight years of Catholic schooling. Are these differences large or small? Almost

70 percent of those who have had more than eight years of Catholic school do not go to communion almost every week. In that respect, clearly, Catholic schools have failed. Furthermore, a little more than a quarter of those who have attended Catholic schools are uncertain about life after death (less than 10 percent say they do not believe in life after death, the others report they do not know for certain). If the goal is 100 percent commitment to human survival, then Catholic schools have failed. If the goal is notably and significantly to improve the likelihood of believing in life after death, then Catholic schools have succeeded.

TABLE 6.2

The Results of Catholic Schooling
(Percent)

	More Than Eight Years	Eight Years or Less
Mass attendance (almost weekly)	43*	32
Communion (almost weekly)	32*	17
Pray (at least several times a week)	57	53
Believe in life after death	72*	60
Member of parish organization	13*	5
Thought of vocation	12*	6
Read a Catholic periodical	37*	25
Watch Catholic TV	21	8
Attended home liturgy	10*	5*
Participated in study group	17*	11
Opposed abortion (if no more children wanted)	64*	54
Living together sinful	23	20
Birth control sinful	4	6

* Significant at .05 level or better.

In the propaganda for Catholic schools many years ago, it often seemed to be said that Catholic schools would turn out almost without exception exemplary Catholics. The critics of Catholic schools, taking that "argument" as a norm, have never ceased to point out enthusiastically the schools simply do not achieve such a goal. The defenders of Catholic schools who accept such a statement of the question have been embarrassed and defensive.

Any serious reading of the educational impact literature would reveal that schools should not reasonably be expected to undo the work of home, family, peer group, neighborhood, social class, and ethnic culture. Though schools can make a difference under some circumstances, the boundless American faith in the power of formal education has never been sustained either by empirical evidence or by everyday impression.

Where does this leave us on the subject of the effectiveness of Catholic schools? They do not produce graduates who are universally exemplary Catholics. They do have some effect. How much effect? Far more effect in terms of statistical size than is used to justify racial integration. Is the effect worth the cost? One would think, given the difficulty of affecting human religious behavior at all, that the effect is worth the cost until an alternate system, technique, or method can be devised that does as well.

This interpretation is basically the same one that was originally presented in the *Education of Catholic Americans* and appeared in *Catholic Schools in a Declining Church*. Catholic schools do have a limited effect, a not unimpressive effect as educational impact effects go. It does not seem reasonable to give up on them unless one has an alternative system which will produce the same effect at less cost.

There are striking similarities and some interesting differences in the effectiveness of Catholic schools in the United States and in French and English Canada (Table 6.3, page 117). Indeed, the correlation coefficient for the United States and for English Canada between number of years of Catholic education and adult religious attitudes and behaviors, for instance, is frequently identical. In English Canada, Catholic schools produce a stronger impact on belief in life after death; in the United States a greater likelihood of thinking seriously of a religious vocation, of being active in a parish organization, of being opposed to mercy killing and abortion, of describing self as one who is close to the Church, and of marrying a Catholic spouse. On the whole, as measured by the summary "Catholicity" scale (measuring communion reception, belief in life after death, consideration of religious vocation, membership in a parish organization), Catholic schools have a somewhat higher impact in the United States than they do in English Canada.

In French Canada, however, the picture is rather different. Catholic schools do have a significant impact on the reception of communion and belief in life after death, and, also, a stronger impact than in the United States on the sense of closeness to the Church, and a stronger impact than in English Canada on a pro-life position. But, generally, the correlation coefficients are lower in French Canada than they are in English Canada or in the United States—suggesting that, perhaps, in a mostly Catholic culture (in the same sense that other religious denominations are a very small minority) such as French Canada, cultural forces may be far more important in affecting things like religious vocations, parish activity, and Sunday church attendance than the number of years of Catholic school the person has attended. It also may be that in a situation where virtually all primary education and much secondary education is carried on under Catholic auspices, the schools will have somewhat less effect than in a pluralistic society where there is more freedom of choice. However, the authors of the present report do not propose to be specialists on this phenomenon in Canada and must leave further examination of these data and more sophisticated and subtle interpretations to Canadian scholars.

TABLE 6.3

Correlations with Number of Years of Catholic Education in the United States and Canada

(Coefficient=Pearson's r)

	USA	English Canada	French Canada
Mass	.10*	.10	.03
Communion	.16*	.17*	.10*
Prayer	.05	.05	.03
Life after death	.12*	.18*	.11*
Vocation	.16*	.08	.06
Parish activity	.15*	.05	.03
Close to church	.09*	.06	.14*
Pro life	.13*	.02	.10*
Permissiveness	.06	.08	.04
Catholic marriage	.13*	.00	.04
"Catholicity" scale	.25*	.19*	.02

* Significant at .05 or better.

The Effect of Catholic Schools: Real or Imagined?

In the previous NORC report, the possibility that it might well be Catholic families, either of origin or procreation, which produce the apparent effectiveness of Catholic schools, was considered. Perhaps those who come from religious families are more likely to go to Catholic schools and hence, will appear more Catholic in adult life—but will the real reason be their family and not their school? Perhaps, also, those from devoutly Catholic families will marry devout spouses and the spouse will contribute to the level of Catholicity. Could it be that what appears to be the Catholic school effect is, in fact, an effect of the family in which one is reared and the family which one is formed?

Figure 6.1 (page 118) presents two alternative models to test this possibility. The first one, while conceding that the family affects the choice of the spouse as well as religious behavior, and also has an effect on whether one goes to Catholic schools, does not account entirely for the impact of Catholic schools. The second model, with a dotted line between school and religious behavior, says that when the effect of the family of origin and the spouse are taken into account there will be no Catholic school impact, at least not one that is statistically significant or worth noticing substantively.

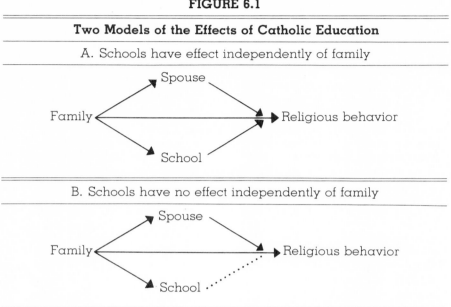

FIGURE 6.1

Two Models of the Effects of Catholic Education

A. Schools have effect independently of family

B. Schools have no effect independently of family

The appropriate regression equations were written to enable us to choose between the two models for both the United States and Canada. The religiousness of the family of origin (measured by whether the family was religiously mixed and dogmatically Catholic and by how often the parents went to Mass and received communion) and the religiousness of spouse (measured by the respondent's description of his or her spouse's religiousness) and the religious "joyfulness" of the respondent's parents (the religious "image" scale described in Chapter Three) were included in the equation. (A high score on the image scale indicates that the respondent is likely to think of Jesus and Mary as "warm" and of God as a "lover" and of heaven as "paradise of pleasure and delight." This scale correlates powerfully with religious devotion, marital satisfaction, sexual fulfillment in marriage, rejection of sexual permissiveness, and social commitment.) All of these factors do, indeed, make their own independent contribution to a person's position on the Catholicity scale (Table 6.4, page 119). However, the impact of Catholic schools is not diminished greatly by taking these other factors into account, and for unmarried respondents is second only to the religious "images" in its effectiveness in producing "Catholicity." There is no connection between the number of years of Catholic schooling and warm religious images, suggesting a major opportunity for improvement in the Catholic educational enterprise. For married respondents, the religiousness of the spouse has somewhat more impact than does Catholic education, but it is still a strong correlate of religious behavior. For the third time, then, NORC research has demonstrated that the effectiveness of Catholic schools is *not* a function of the religiousness of the family in which a person comes or of the family which the person has formed. Catholic schools have their own statistically significant independent effect, which as educational impact effects go is important enough.

TABLE 6.4

Standardized Correlations with "Catholicity" Scale Testing Models in Figure 1

(beta)

	Unmarried respondents	Married respondents
Family religiousness	.11	.14
Religiousness of spouse		.21
Family spirit "joyful"	.13	.13
Catholic education	.19	.17
(Religious images)	.26	.19
English Canada		
Family	.38	
Schools	.16	
French Canada		
(Communion reception the dependent variable)		
Family	.14	
Schools	.21	

Furthermore, the same phenomenon can also be reported in Canada. Indeed, in French Canada, once the religiousness of the family is taken into account, the correlation between the years of attendance at Catholic school and the increased reception of communion suggests that the presence in French-Canadian Catholic education of a considerable number of young people from less devout families depresses the measured impact of Catholic school attendance. This raises the interesting possibility that the rather lower correlations for French Canada noted in Table 6.3 (page 117) are the result of the fact that in French Canada there is not nearly so much self-selection on the basis of family religiousness and the enrollment of young people in Catholic schools.

Catholic Schools and Identification with the Church

What is the secret of the "modest" or "moderate" or "important" effect of Catholic education on the behavior of young Catholic adults? Readers may choose their own words depending on their criteria for educational success—though we would remind them that in most educational research, betas of .15 and .20 are taken very seriously indeed. How can the effectiveness of Catholic schools be explained? Is it the result of specific religious instruction, of different techniques used, or the various courses taught? Is it the integration of religion with other parts of the curriculum, or, perhaps, the integration of the educational experience with the liturgical life of the parish or school?

Our assumption at the beginning of the present project was that, however important any of these factors might be, the primary effectiveness of Catholic schooling was based on cultural and social structural factors. Those who attended Catholic schools, we suspected, would have a closer sense of affiliation to the Church simply because they had spent more time on Church property and would more likely have more experience with religious personnel, over and above the influences of their families, either of origin or procreation. We argued it is precisely this sense of "closeness" to the Church which would be the primary intervening variable between Catholic schooling and religious behavior in adult life. Figure 6.2 (page 121) presents a schematic model describing this expectation.

It will be recalled that there was a modest statistically significant correlation between Catholic education and self-description as being "close to the Church" (on a five point scale describing a number of concentric circles from the center to the periphery of the Church). Even though the size of this correlation was small, it still seemed to us that it would be a decisive factor.

To test our expectation we used residual analysis to reduce the difference between two groups by taking into account various intervening factors. In Table 6.5 (page 121) we apply the model presented in Figure 6.2 to the twenty-two percentage points difference in those high on the Catholicity scale between respondents who had more than eight years of Catholic education and those who had less than eight years, or no Catholic education. One by one prior variables are introduced into the residual model—in this case, the religious background of one's family of origin and the religious identity of one's spouse. About a third of the difference between those who have had more Catholic education and those who have had less can be accounted for by familial factors, but *all* of the rest of the difference is accounted for by the fact that those who have gone to Catholic schools feel that they are closer to the Church. It must be remembered that this feeling of "closeness" is over and above whatever closeness to the Church might be accounted for by either spouse or family of origin. It is "pure" Catholic school effect.

FIGURE 6.2

Model to Test Explanation of Effect of Catholic School Being Attributable to a Greater Sense of Closeness to (or non-alienation from) the Church

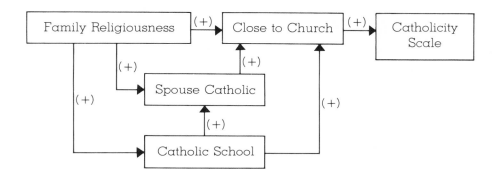

TABLE 6.5

Table Test of Model in Figure 2

	Eight Years	Less	
Difference in "Catholicity" between those who have more than eight years of Catholic education and those with less.	57%	35% = 22%	
			Proportion Explained
Family background	5 points		.23
Spouse Catholic	7 points		.32
Closeness to Church	10 points		1.00

The secret of the schools, if it may be called that, is that they integrate young people more closely into the Catholic institutional community. However, not all those who go to Catholic schools are close to the Church. But, it is the greater "closeness" of some of those who go to Catholic schools which "explains" virtually all of the religious effectiveness of Catholic education. The point for Catholic policy makers is clear: If you can find another institution that can have the same effectiveness in integrating young people into the Catholic community and Catholic institutions, you do not need Catholic schools. Unless and until we find such a technique, then the continuing decline of the proportion of Catholic population in Catholic schools will inevitably lead to a *diminished* level of Catholic commitment in years ahead.

Catholic Schools and Life Cycle

In Chapter Five we identified, described, and explained a "mini life cycle" which affects many young Catholics in their 20s. Religious practice declines sharply in the early and middle 20s and then rebounds, though not quite so sharply, at the end of the 20s. Does attendance at Catholic schools facilitate that rebound, impede it, or have any effect at all?

First of all (Table 6.6), the relationship between the number of years at Catholic schools and the Catholicity scale is higher the more mature a person is. The correlation is .37 for the age cohort 29 and 30 years old. The greatest impact of the Catholic schools, in other words, is precisely at that time in life when young people are beginning to return to regular religious practice. A quite powerful payoff for Catholic schooling seems to take place at that time.

TABLE 6.6

Impact of Catholic Schools and CCD
(Coefficient = Pearson's r)

	Catholic Schools	CCD
Mass	.10*	.08*
Communion	.16*	.06
Prayer	.05	.01
Life after death	.12*	.01
Parish organizations	.15*	.00
Vocation	.16*	.04
Pro life	.13*	.01
Permissiveness	−.06	+.07
"Catholicity" scale	.25*	.02
Closeness to Church	.09*	−.03

* Significant at .05 or better.

The age cohort effect of Catholic schools can be demonstrated also by percentage differences. In Table 6.7 (page 123), for example, the rise in the proportion high on the Catholicity scale is confined almost entirely to those who have had more than eight years of Catholic schooling. For this group, between the middle and late

20s there is an increase in 15 percentage points in the proportion high on the Catholicity scale, whereas for those who had eight years or less of Catholic schools, the increase is only 3 percentage points. In the regular (nearly every week) reception of communion, those who have had eight or more years of Catholic school declined from 49 to 20 percent between the early and middle 20s, and then rebounded to 32 percent, whereas those who do not attend Catholic schools more than eight years declined from 29 percent to 11 percent, and then only increased 2 percentage points in the final years of their 20s. Finally, the Mass attendance of those who have gone to Catholic schools goes up 17 percentage points, while those who had less Catholic education only increases 3 percentage points. The religious revival of the late 20s is almost exclusively concentrated in that proportion of the young Catholic population which has had substantial amount of time in Catholic schools.

TABLE 6.7

Evaluation of CCD and Catholic Education

	CATHOLIC SCHOOLS	CCD
Teaching quality excellent or very good (percentages)		
Grammar	42	28
High school	45	21
Classes somewhat or very "informal" (percentages)		
High school	31	58
Involved in "some or more" activities outside the classroom (percentages)		
High school	32	18
Simple correlations between quality and methods of teaching and "Catholicity scale"		
Informality	.27	.02
Activities	.30	.04
Years	.25	.02

For ecclesiastical policy makers this is an extremely important point to reflect upon: If you are going to get young people back at the end of their 20s, then you better have provided them with an opportunity for more than eight years of Catholic education.

The explanatory model for the effectiveness of Catholic schools presented in Figure 6.2 (page 121) also operates when it is limited to the oldest age cohort in the sample—those at the end of the decade of their 20s. Those who have attended Catholic schools are more likely to return to the Church because they have more religious spouses and because their feelings of closeness to the Church are increasing (Table 6.8). Maturity and marriage seem to intensify that identification with the Catholic community and with Catholic institutions, which Catholic schools have inculcated.

TABLE 6.8

Catholic Behavior by Catholic Schools and CCD
(Percent)

Behavior	Average	10 or More Years in Catholic Schools	10 or More Years in CCD
Mass (2 or 3 times a month or more)	24	49	45
Communion (2 or 3 times a month or more)	21	34	21
Pray (several times a week)	53	65	55
Pope infallible	24	34	20
Seriously considered vocation	6	13	2
Birth control wrong	5	5	3

Conclusion: So duration of CCD attendance does not improve relative impact compared to Catholic schools.

Finally, does Catholic school attendance incline a young person to choose not merely a spouse who is a Catholic, but also one who is more likely to be a devout Catholic and therefore more likely to activate and reactivate a respondent to religious devotion? The question is hard to answer because it is difficult to separate spouses' influence on respondents from respondents' influence on spouses. Yet, if one considers the three variable model presented in Figure 6.3 (page 125), one can see that it is possible to make a tentative test. We know that Catholic education affects the communion reception of our respondents. We also know there is a relationship between Catholic education, between the respondent's own communion reception, and the spouse's communion reception. Logically, there ought not to be a direct correlation (the line at the top of the triangle) between the number of years a respondent went to Catholic schools and the communion of her or his spouse. How, after all, could a husband's Catholic education affect a wife's communion reception, except, say, through the example of the husband's communion reception?

FIGURE 6.3

**Spouse's Communion Reception and Own Catholic Education,
Holding Constant Respondent's Communion Reception**

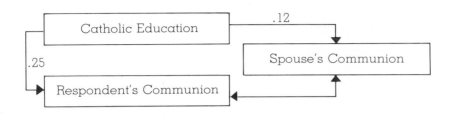

If there is a statistically significant standardized correlation (beta) on the direct path between Catholic education and spouse's communion reception, then there is at least some evidence the spouse was more devout to begin with and was in part chosen precisely because of his or her devotion. Indeed, the beta coefficient on the top line of the triangle is statistically significant at .12. Thus, it would appear that those who attended Catholic schools do choose somewhat more devout spouses than those who did not attend Catholic schools. Succinctly, the more Catholic schooling one has, the more likely that person will choose a devout spouse.

This phenomenon, however, seems to be limited to women. If the model in Figure 6.3 is run separately for both sexes, the coefficient on the top line deteriorates to zero for men, and for women rises to .17. The longer a young woman has attended a Catholic school, the more likely she is to seek and find a husband whose religious devotion will reinforce her own.

Summary

In our 1974 report we argued that the Catholic schools seemed even more important to the Church in times of transition than they did in times of stability. (In 1963 a study had been undertaken before most of the effects of the Second Vatican Council were experienced by the Church.) The present study, limited to Catholics who have matured since the Second Vatican Council, confirms and reinforces this conclusion, both for the United States and for Canada. The answer to Mrs. Ryan's famous question, "Are Catholic Schools the Answer?" as the research evidence shows, seems to be that they may not be the absolute answer, but they are the best answer that exists and they are getting to be a more important answer with the passage of time. Catholic schools seem to be especially important at the decisive religious (and as we have demonstrated in *The Young Catholic Family)* and marital turning point that takes place at the end of the decade of the 20s. The tables that are presented in this chapter should make somber reading for those ecclesiastical administrators who have been reluctant to build Catholic schools and who have stood by taking little action as the proportion of Catholics attending such schools has declined. It is possible, of course, that those who had less Catholic education may return to religious practice at a later stage in their lives. They certainly do not do so, however, by the end of their 20s.

The first NORC report *(The Education of Catholic Americans,* 1966) demonstrated that Catholic schools had an effect independent of the families' religious background. The second report demonstrated that this effect was more important in the post-conciliar Church than previously thought, and was especially strong for young people. In this report we have added two critical new bits of information:

1. The Catholic schools are especially important for young people at the religious turning point at the end of the third decade of their lives.

2. The schools exercise their effectiveness primarily through an integrating effect: tying people into the Catholic community and Catholic institutions.

Other research carried on in such disparate countries as Australia and Peru, and our own preliminary investigation of Canada, parallels the NORC findings (1966) on the "Education of Catholic Americans." The problem posed by Peter H. Rossi (to whom this report is dedicated in the year of his presidency of the American Sociological Association) twenty years ago has basically been solved: How much impact on adult Catholics do Catholic schools have and by what dynamics are such influences produced?

The fact that Catholic school enrollment continues to decline, almost entirely because of the failure of Church leaders to build new schools (Greeley, McCready, McCourt, 1976), in the light of these continued research findings must be considered a telling example of the failure to use research as an important component in the process of ecclesiastical decision-making.

Attitudes Toward the Vocations to the Priestly and
Religious Life

Highlights

1   *The encouragement of mothers and religious professionals is
    absolutely essential in the development of religious vocations
    among the young.*

2   *Those persons who have considered following a vocation in the
    priesthood or religious life are influenced by their family's regular
    attendance at Mass, prayer life, being an altar boy, and hearing
    about a fraternal group such as the Knights of Columbus.*

3   *Participation in a Catholic school has an influence upon whether or
    not a person ever considered a vocation to the priestly and religious
    life.*

4   *Persons from the most religious backgrounds and who are
    themselves deeply religious have the least negative attitudes
    towards vocations. This is especially true if one of their children
    wanted to become a priest or religious.*

5   *Personal encouragement, Catholic education, familial devotion,
    and warm religious imagery surfaced in responses as crucial factors
    in determining whether or not a person gave serious thought to a
    priestly or religious vocation.*

6   *For those persons who have thought about a priestly or religious
    vocation, celibacy is a problem, but not the most important problem
    in developing this vocation.*

7   *If the Church wants young people to think about and to follow
    priestly and religious vocations, then priests, religious, and
    immediate families must increase their encouragement of the
    young people in this regard.*

Chapter 7

Attitudes Toward the Vocations to the Priestly and Religious Life

Between 1950 and 1978 the Catholic population in this country increased by 45 percent and that portion of the population between the ages of 14 and 24 years of age increased by 84 percent. During the same period the number of young men in seminary training *decreased* by 41 percent. Previous research (Greeley, McCready, and McCourt, 1976) has described the way in which parental support, as well as the support of the clergy, for vocations had eroded over the years, partially as the result of the general malaise in the Church, and partially as the result of the movement of Church activity away from young people.

In this chapter we will examine the vocational aspirations of the respondents and their attitudes which related to these aspirations. The chapter consists of three sections. The first explores the demographic and the social background characteristics of respondents with different attitudes and experiences regarding vocations to the priestly and religious life. The second section is organized around a series of models constructed to show the dynamic interrelationships between the factors and influences which either support or hinder such vocations. The final section consists of a discussion of the types of changes which might produce more vocations and includes some general guidelines useful for formulating policy discussions.

In order to provide an initial orientation, the first data to be presented are the responses to the two key vocational questions, one for the adults and one for the adolescents. Both were asked about their vocational status and aspirations, but the format of the questions was changed slightly to account for the greater potential experience of the adult respondent.

The adolescents were asked:

Which of the following best expresses your attitudes toward a religious vocation?	n	percent
I am seriously thinking about a religious vocation and am now in the minor seminary or have begun training.	0	0
I am seriously thinking about a religious vocation, but have not begun training.	6	2
The idea of becoming a priest, brother or nun has entered my mind, but I am not now thinking seriously about it.	111	31
I have never thought about a religious vocation.	247	68

The adults were asked:

Which of the following best expresses your attitudes toward a religious vocation?	n	percent
I am presently a priest, brother or nun.	3	.3
I am presently training for the religious life.	6	.7
I am seriously considering a religious vocation, but have not begun training.	5	.6
I have trained for a religious vocation or have actually taken vows, but later decided that the religious life is not for me.	8	.9
I have seriously considered a religious vocation, but decided against it before entering a seminary or convent.	39	4.4
The thought of becoming a priest, brother or nun has entered my mind, but I have never really seriously considered it.	237	27
I have never considered a religious vocation.	581	66

Given that these distributions are highly skewed toward the "never considered" end of the scale, the data were collapsed into a more easily analyzed form.

We can see in Table 7.1 (page 131) that approximately 94 percent of the respondents fall either into the marginal vocation or the non-vocation type. Only 6 percent are in either vocation or ex-vocation. The preliminary demographic analysis will use the full typology, but, due to the small number of cases in two categories, the latter phase of the analysis will focus on differences between the marginal vocation and the non-vocation types.

TABLE 7.1

Vocational Typology for the Respondents

	Percent	N
Vocation		
(Respondents who are either in the religious life, training for it, or seriously considering it)	2	(20)
Ex-Vocation		
(Respondents who were either in training or thinking seriously about a vocation and stopped)	4	(47)
Marginal Vocation		
(Respondents who once considered a vocation, but not very seriously)	28	(348)
Non-Vocation		
(Respondents who never considered a vocation at all)	66	(828)
	100	(1243)

Background Characteristics

Females, both adolescents and adults, are more likely to have considered religious vocation than males are, although the differences are quite modest. Also, approximately 10 percent of the adult males have at least given serious thought to the religious life or actually trained for it at one time or another. In general the adolescents and the adults are rather similar in their vocational typology with the majority, usually over two-thirds, falling in the non-vocation category (Table 7.2A).

TABLE 7.2A

Vocational Typology By Sex By Age
(Percent)

	ADOLESCENTS		ADULTS	
	Male	Female	Male	Female
Vocation	1	2	3	1
Ex-Vocation	—	—	7	4
Marginal Vocation	28	33	23	30
Non-Vocation	71	65	67	66
	100	100	100	101
N	(184)	(180)	(407)	(472)

Female adolescents are more likely than female adults to say that they would consider becoming priests, if such an option were available, and the adult women are quite a bit more likely to say that they would definitely not entertain such an ambition (Table 7.2B). This is not due to the difference in marital status between the adult and the adolescent women.

TABLE 7.2B

Females Who Would Consider Becoming Priests
(Percent)

	Definitely or Probably or Maybe	Probably Not	Definitely Not	
Adolescents	14	41	45	(181)
Adults	7	26	67	(479)

The adolescent females are also the group most likely to express interest in becoming deacons. In Table 7.3 (page 132) we can see that there is generally very little interest in the diaconate with three-quarters or more of most of the groups not interested. However, adolescent women are about twice as likely as adult women and three times as likely as adolescent men to say that they are interested in this vocational form. It may be that adolescent girls are simply more religious, or are more inclined to think of serving others in some way. While the inferences about these data must be speculative for now, it is possible that these young women represent a new source of recruitment should the Church entertain the idea of women deacons.

TABLE 7.3

**Amount of Interest Expressed
in Becoming a Deacon by Age and Sex**
(Percent)

	ADOLESCENTS		ADULTS	
	Male	Female	Male	Female
Very interested or interested	4	12	5	6
Neutral	22	23	19	16
Not very or not at all interested	74	65	76	79

Among those who have offered encouragement toward a vocation have been brothers, sisters, priests, or the mothers of the respondents. However, among those who are committed to a vocation (or thinking very seriously about one), mothers and religious (brothers or sisters) tie for the first place, with friends close behind. It is possible that the influence of friends stems from those one meets during the training period. This is actually the influence of the peer group after the decision to follow a vocation has been made. In general, the dominant influences seem to come from those already in the religious life and from one's mother (Table 7.4A).

TABLE 7.4A

Proportion of Respondents Reporting that the Following People Have Encouraged Them Toward a Vocation
(Percent)

	Other*	Vocation
Mother	9	32
Father	4	11
Sibling	2	5
Grandparent	4	16
Relative	3	11
Priest	10	11
Religious	12	32
Friend	3	26

* Other includes ex-vocation, marginal vocation and non-vocation.

Encouragement of some kind certainly appears to have an impact on whether or not the respondent ever thought about a vocation to the religious life. In Table 7.4B we can see that there is a large difference in having "ever been encouraged" between those who have at least considered a vocation and those who never thought about one. Over four-fifths of the non-vocation type report that no one has ever encouraged them toward a vocation, while only about half of the marginal vocation type report the same situation.

TABLE 7.4B

Proportion of Respondents Reporting That They Have Never Been Encouraged By Anyone Toward a Vocation By Typology
(Percent)

Marginal vocation	53
Non-vocation	86

There are other kinds of vocational encouragement which stem from the example of people around one rather than from explicit statements of encouragement. In the next table (Table 7.5), we examine the differences between those in the marginal vocation group and those in the non-vocation group with regard to devotional factors, their previous experience as altar boys, and whether or not the Knights of Columbus was a "presence" in their families. (We have concerned ourselves with these two groups only because the size of the other groups makes generalizations very speculative.) Those who considered a vocation were much more likely to have parents who were weekly Mass attenders. They are also more likely to attend Mass every week themselves than the non-vocation group. The level of daily prayer is greater for the marginals than for the non-vocation group. Those who at one time at least thought about a vocation were also more likely to have been altar boys. And finally, they were more likely to have at least heard about the Knights of Columbus from someone in their family.

TABLE 7.5

Devotional Characteristics in the Lives of the
"Considered" and the "Secular"

(Percent)

	Marginal Vocation	Non-Vocation
Fathers attended Mass weekly	72*	60
Mothers attended Mass weekly	79*	66
Respondent attends Mass weekly	33*	22
Respondent prays daily	41*	28
Respondent was an altar boy (Asked of males only)	59*	36
Father or someone in family belonged to or told the respondent about the Knights of Columbus	38*	30
	(348)	(828)

* Significant at the .05 level.

Just as we saw in Table 7.4B that the previous data supported an impression that the marginal group came from backgrounds in which vocation was at least discussed, so these data point to a familial milieu for the marginal type in which religious expressions are commonplace and available for the young to experience. The major difference between the marginal and the non-vocation type seems to have been their general level of exposure to religious experiences and devotional examples.

Another factor to be considered in accounting for the background of a religious vocation is the extent to which the respondents were exposed to Catholic education when they were growing up. In Table 7.6 we can see that those who considered a vocation are likely to have experienced their education in Catholic institutions to a greater degree than those who never considered a vocation at all. For example, there is a 10 percent difference between the types at the elementary school level regarding the proportion attending Catholic school for eight years. Although this is the only difference that is statistically significant, the directions of the differences for high school and college are the same.

TABLE 7.6

Proportion of Time Spent in Catholic Schools by Vocational Typology
(Percent)

	ELEMENTARY SCHOOL		
	All Catholic	Some Catholic	None Catholic
Marginal vocation	45	30	24
Non-vocation	35	27	38
	HIGH SCHOOL		
Margin vocation	38	13	48
Non-vocation	33	15	52
	COLLEGE OR UNIVERSITY		
Marginal vocation	10	9	81
Non-vocation	8	4	87

The different vocational types also have different levels of Catholic activities as can be seen by examining Table 7.7 (page 136), ranging from reading religious books to attending charismatic prayer groups. It is clear from these data that those who have at least considered a vocation are more likely to have engaged in some religious activities than those who have not. The adolescents who have not considered a vocation are just about on the mean while the adult non-vocation types are about a quarter standard deviation below the mean. One interesting comparison is between the adolescent and the adult marginals. For the young people there is a high level of activity, while for the older group the activity level is just about at the mean. This may reflect a greater level of adolescent activity in all types, or some change in the relationship between activity and considering a vocation.

TABLE 7.7

Levels of Catholic Activities for Vocation Types By Age
(Z scores)

	Vocation	Ex-Vocation	Marginal Vocation	Non-Vocation
Adolescents	.93	—	.76	.08
Adults	.47	.57	.04	−.26

In addition to the demographic and behavioral background characteristics we will also consider some of the attitudinal characteristics which are related to the vocational typology. One purpose of this will be to see if the different types are also different in the ways in which they think about religious issues and vocation-related topics.

As can be seen in Table 7.8 (page 137), there are different attitudes expressed by the types on different religious issues. For example, the vocation type is less likely to approve of the way priests are doing their jobs than are the other types, and they are also less likely to say that the Church ought to update teachings about sexual morality. The percent who say that they pay attention to the words or actions of the new pope is relatively small among all types, except the ex-vocation type. Furthermore, there is only moderate support for the attitudes that allowing priests to marry and allowing women to be ordained are extremely important issues. There are virtually no differences between the marginal and the non-vocation type on any of these issues, indicating that while they may have different backgrounds, their present attitudes about religious issues are very much the same.

In the next table, Table 7.9 (page 138), we can see that there are more differences between the types with regard to vocation-related topics than the previous issues. For example, those with a vocation and the non-vocation type are more likely than the others to agree that priests ought not discuss social issues from the pulpit. The marginal are slightly less likely than the others not to expect the laity to be leaders. The marginal and those with no vocation are more likely to say that priests can get involved in national politics. This is an interesting difference since the types less likely to agree with this position are those with a "closer" perspective on vocation, i.e., they are either actively pursuing or were actively pursuing the religious life.

The non-vocation type is more likely to say that they would be unhappy if a daughter wanted to become a nun, and both the marginal and the non-vocation type are more likely than the others to say that priests are not as pious as they used to be. There is little support for the idea that priests have lost interest in people's problems, and those closest to the situation feel that seminaries are not doing a good job in training priests today.

TABLE 7.8

Specific Religious Issue Attitudes
For Vocation Types
(Percent)

	Vocation	Ex-Vocation	Marginal Vocation	Non-Vocation
Priestly job performance (approve)	67	78	84	81
Pay attention to pope (great or some)	16	26	11	6
Church should update teachings on sex (extremely important)	26	57	55	50
Allow priests to marry (extremely important)	26	36*	22	22
Allow female priests (extremely important)	16	26*	22	20

* The ex-Vocation also had the highest proportion "not at all important" responses.

Among the more interesting generalizations from these data are the following: over half the respondents feel that priests expect the laity to be followers; well over half of the two largest groups feel that priests are not as pious as they used to be; and there is no general feeling that priests have lost interest in people's problems.

In addition the people who are *most* religious and who come from the *most* religious backgrounds are also those who are *least* likely to have any negative vocation-related attitudes. As can be seen from Table 7.10 (page 139), all the correlations listed are negative and this means that people with frequent Mass attendance are likely to *disagree* with the statement. For example, people who go to Mass often disagree that having a daughter become a nun would make them unhappy. In the same way the .36 relationship between "Attitude toward the Church" and being unhappy if a daughter became a nun means that those with positive attitudes toward the Church would be less likely to be unhappy.

The evidence in this table indicates that there is some attitudinal consistency between general religious characteristics and specific vocational attitudes. Those respondents who are most religious are also most supportive of vocations. They would be happy if a daughter had a vocation to the religious life; they do not feel that priests have lost piety; they do not feel that priests have become more self-centered; and they think seminaries are doing a good job training priests.

TABLE 7.9

Responses to Vocation-Related Attitudes by Vocation Type
(Percent agree)

	Vocation	Ex-Vocation	Marginal Vocation	Non-Vocation
Priests should not use the pulpit to discuss social issues.	50	39	38	47
Most priests don't expect the laity to be leaders, just followers.	60	61	51	59
It's all right for a priest to get involved in national politics if he wants to.	50	50	64	61
It would make me somewhat unhappy if a daughter of mine became a nun.	25	13	25	34
Priests are not as pious as they used to be.	33	49	57	63
Priests have lost interest in the problems of the people and are concerned only about themselves.	18	14	15	19
Catholic seminaries are not training priests well.	58	37	27	25

The respondents were given a series of possible reasons why they did not choose a vocation ranging from institutional reasons about rules and regulations, celibacy, and poor pay to more personal reasons such as disappointing a parent, weakness of their own faith, or the lack of a challenging career. They rated each of these reasons as to how important they were for them in not choosing to follow the religious life. In Table 7.11 (page 140) we compare the marginal and the non-vocation type of these attitudes. (The ex-vocation are presented because the reasons given may have to do with why they left the vocation, but the size of the group is too small to do any but the most speculative analysis.)

TABLE 7.10

Correlations Between Selected Religious Characteristics of the Respondent and Selected Vocation-Related Attitudes

(Coefficient = Pearson's r)

	RELIGIOUS CHARACTERISTICS			
	Mass Atten-dance	Attitude Toward Church	Mother's Religious Perspective	Father's Religious Perspective
It would make me somewhat unhappy if a daughter of mine became a nun.	−.25*	−.36*	−.16*	−.09
Priests are not as pious as they used to be.	−.08	−.10	−.13*	−.11*
Priests have lost interest in the problems of the people and are only concerned about themselves.	−.20*	−.31*	−.15*	−.10
Catholic seminaries are not training priests well.	−.26*	−.43*	−.16	−.17*

* Significant at .05 level or better.

The reasons mentioned by the majority of both those who considered a vocation and those who never thought about it was the fact that priests and religious are not allowed to marry. The second most often mentioned reason was that the respondent's own faith was not deep enough. The third reason was the lifelong nature of the commitment. There were no significant differences between the marginal and the non-vocation types with regard to these three reasons; however, there were interesting differences on some of the other issues. For example, poor pay in the religious life was more of an issue for those who had never considered a vocation than for those who had. The feeling that the work was uninteresting had the same characteristics, as did the feeling that there were too many rules and regulations, poor professional standards, and that it presented an unchallenging career. For all these topics there were significant differences between those who had never considered the religious life and those who had. The opposition of those respondents in the non-vocation type was more widespread, as befits people who have not shown an interest in a vocation. This indicates that the typology is an accurate reflection of their vocational profile. The fact that the marginal, those who had at least thought about a career in the religious life, were only concerned about three reasons also indicates that there might be some specific policy targets which the institution could focus on in order to nurture some of that interest into vocational decisions.

TABLE 7.11

Reasons Why Respondents Were Against Vocation for Themselves by Typology

(Percent very important)

	Marginal	Non-Vocation	Ex-Vocation
Not allowed to marry	51	55	41
Poor pay	5	14*	4
Lifelong commitment	33	41	17
Lack of privacy	20	28	17
Uninteresting work	5	19*	9
Too many rules and regulations	27	37*	20
Poor professional standards	5	12*	6
Undemocratic church structure	19	23	17
Parents would be disappointed	2	4	2
My faith is not deep enough	47	52	30
My friends would be disappointed	2	4	0
Met unattractive priests or religious	6	6	8
Priests are lonely	14	14	17
I don't know enough about the life to be interested in it	18	30*	8
Not a challenging career	7	21*	2
	(348)	(828)	(47)

* Significant at .05 level or better.

The respondents were also requested to respond to a series of items which asked about those characteristics of a religious career which they found personally attractive, even if they did not choose to follow the religious life. Those who had considered a vocation differed from those who had never thought about one on only three of the ten items. The former were more likely to say that serving God and man, helping people find meaning, and doing God's will were very important aspects of the religious life. Both the marginal and the non-vocation tended to reject the notions that leading a disciplined life, support from a religious community, working with other religious, and leaving the materialistic world were important aspects of a vocation. "Working with people" and "getting to know Jesus" were aspects of vocations that both groups thought important to about the same degree (Table 7.12, page 141).

The characteristics of serving God and man, helping people find meaning, and doing God's will are all rather traditional vocational goals and do not require an innovative role change for priests and religious. These are the characteristics which those who once considered a vocation see as being very important. Therefore, it does not seem as though a change in the definition or the tasks of the religious life would appeal to any "dormant" vocations in this group.

TABLE 7.12

Proportion of Respondents Who Feel the Following Aspects of a Religious Career are "Very Important" by Typology

(Percent)

	Marginal	Non-Vocation
To serve God and man	69*	53
Support from a religious community	28	25
Helping people find meaning	76*	64
Working with people	64	58
Leading a disciplined life	14	18
Mediating between God and man	28	25
Doing what God wants me to do	58*	45
Working with people I like—other priests and religious	15	17
Getting to know Jesus	57	50
Leaving the materialistic world	20	16
	(348)	(828)

* Significant at .05 level or better.

Explanatory Models for Vocational Aspirations

It is clear from the previous analysis that those who have thought about a vocation to the religious life are different from those who have never thought about it on a number of attitudinal and demographic characteristics. In this section we take the discussion a step further and attempt to explain the relationships between the factors which support and hinder vocational development. What are the particular combinations of forces and situations which influence someone to think about having a vocation at all? Once they have begun to think about it, what prompts them to think about the religious life in a serious fashion? In the beginning of this section we treat this first stage of vocational development: the initial question or interest—simply thinking about the religious life as a possibility. In the latter part of this section we examine the components of the second stage: serious reflection and inquiry—whether or not religious life is a serious career alternative. Before we proceed with the more substantive aspects of these data, however, some brief comment about the scales to be used is in order.

It is customary and usual in most social science analyses to develop from the questionnaire scales or clusters of items which measure the same attitude—this is a little bit like spreading your bets around at the horse races so that rather than putting all of your money on one horse you put a little bit of your money on several different horses, in the hope that one of them will come in. So too, sociologists put a little bit of their money on several different attitude measures so that we have a greater chance of measuring what is really going on.

In the diagrams which follow, different variable names appear, and some of these variable names are actually collections of items from the questionnaire.

Models for the Initial Thinking About a Vocation

One-third of the young Catholic adults in the United States say that they have at least thought about having a vocation to the religious life at some time. This is about equally split between men and women. The question to be answered in this part of the analysis, then, is what are the factors which influenced the one-third to think about having a vocation. Our hypothesis is that if one never thinks about having a vocation, he or she will never take the next step of actually doing anything about it. Therefore, this variable is an initial entrance gate into religious vocations. Many items from the questionnaire were examined to see if they had a relationship with "having thought seriously about a vocation," and from those items a series of variables were constructed. The correlations between these variables themselves and between the variables and vocational aspirations are presented in Table 7.13, page 143.

The correlation coefficients may be considered as indicative of the raw relationship between the variables. In other words, the strongest relationship with "vocational aspirations" is whether or not the respondent was encouraged by someone to think about a vocation (.36). The next strongest relationship is with one's attitudes toward the religious life (.24). All of the components of this correlation matrix have a significant relationship with vocational aspirations.

Using multiple regression techniques, we constructed a general model for the relationships between the variables that led up to a person thinking about a religious vocation. In Figure 7.1 (page 143), we can see a graphic presentation of the general model which shows that having received encouragement for a vocation is the strongest predictor of whether or not the respondent ever thought of having a vocation. The strength of this relationship is independent of the contribution of all the other factors is the model, and the model itself explains 18 percent of the variance in thinking about a vocation. This means that almost one-fifth of the difference between those who at least have thought about a vocation and those who never thought about a vocation can be explained by using this model.

TABLE 7.13

Correlations for Vocational Aspirations
(Coefficient = Pearson's r)

	Vocational Aspirations	Attitudes	Encouragement	Warm Images	(Altar Boy#)	Catholic Education	Family Religiosity
Attitudes	.24***						
Encouragement	.36***	.13**					
Warm Images	.10*	.25***	.13**				
(Altar Boy)#	(.25***)	(.09)	(.29***)	(.01)			
Catholic Education	.15***	.02	.21***	.02	(.34***)		
Family Religiosity	.15**	.01	.17***	.08	(.34***)	.35***	
Family Spirituality	.11*	.00	.17***	.21***	(.15*)	.04	.39***

Significance: *** = .001   ** = .01   * = .05
(# For Males Only)

FIGURE 7.1

General Model for Vocational Aspirations

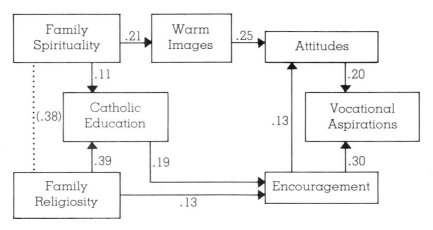

VARIANCE EXPLAINED = 18%
STATISTICS: R^2 = .18   F = 16.549
MULT. R = .42   SIG =   .000

Just to elaborate on the model for a moment, note that the influence of family religiosity and a Catholic education are channeled primarily through encouragement, while the power of family spirituality goes through religious imagery. (This is the same imagery measure which is used in Chapter Three.) A key question which arises when looking at this model is what would happen if attitudes toward the religious life were removed. This is important because attitudes are notoriously unresponsive to changes in policy. If the case is that attitudes are extremely important in predicting whether or not the respondent has ever thought of a vocation, there may be very little that can be done to improve the situation.

Figure 7.2 (page 145) consists of the general model with the attitudes removed. Note that the amount of variance explained goes down from 18 to 14 percent, which means that by removing the attitudes from the model, we have lost only about one-fifth of our explanatory power. The attitudes which make up this component of the model range from those having to do with the nature of the work in the religious life to more general attitudes about the Church. Four-fifths of the explanatory power which we originally had in the model is left in the model after the removal of the attitudes. This indicates that attitudes, while important for the general model, are not critically important for the support of religious vocations. Family background, Catholic education, and, especially, the encouragement of a vocation are the dominant forces in the general model.

Figure 7.3 (page 146) is an adaptation of the general model for males only, which includes the fact of being an altar boy. This model explains considerably more of the variance in the vocational aspirations, 28 percent. As in the general model, we see that having been encouraged is still a very important variable for whether or not one thinks of a vocation, and being an altar boy is quite strongly related to the encouragement factor. (Being an altar boy appears to be largely the result of Catholic education and family religiosity.)

Following the same procedure that we did for the general model, we removed the attitudes variable from our model for males (Figure 7.4, page 147). The amount of the variance explained goes from 28 to 24, a loss of about 14 percent, which is less than the loss suffered in the general model. In other words, the attitudes toward the religious life are even less important in predicting the males' thinking about a vocation. The model in Figure 7.4 explains almost a quarter of the variance in young Catholic males having ever thought about a religious vocation. The major factor was whether or not they were encouraged, and the secondary one was whether or not they were an altar boy. It is worth noting that having been an altar boy does have a direct path of .10 with vocational aspirations, which means that it has a relationship aside from the other elements in the model.

FIGURE 7.2

**General Model for Vocational Aspirations
with "Attitudes" Removed**

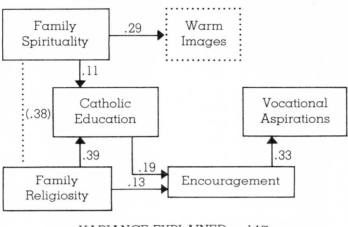

VARIANCE EXPLAINED = 14%
STATISTICS: MULT. R = .38   F = 5.699
R^2 = .14   SIG =   .000

In summing up this first set of models, then, we can see that encouragement is a major importance in determining whether or not an individual even thinks about having a vocation to the religious life. From the first section of this chapter, we know that the people most likely to offer encouragement are mothers, nuns or brothers, and priests. Even when all the attitudes which usually bear on religious topics were eliminated from the model, the explanatory power did not decrease very much. The next set of models explores the components which obstruct or support an individual's thinking more seriously about a vocation.

Models for Thinking Seriously About a Vocation
Almost one-fifth of young Catholic adults have thought seriously about a vocation to the religious life, and then either decided to pursue it or decided to pursue a lay vocation. With regard to these data presented in Table 7.14 (page 147), there is a difference between the sexes in that of those who thought seriously about a vocation, two-thirds of them were male. (Given the relatively low number of people who are actively pursuing a vocation to the

religious life, this stage of development of having given serious consideration to a vocation is as far as we can go with our present analyses.) The interrelationships between the components used in the analysis of whether or not respondents thought seriously about a vocation are presented in Table 7.15 (page 148). Attitudes toward the religious life and having been encouraged toward a vocation reverse their positions in this table. It should also be noted that "warm images" have a rather high correlation of .18 with having thought seriously about a vocation. This is almost twice as high as the correlation in the more general model presented previously. An added feature in this table is the variable called "celibacy," which is actually part of the vocation attitude variable, but will be treated separately in the analysis presented in this section.

FIGURE 7.3

General Model for Vocational Aspirations for Males

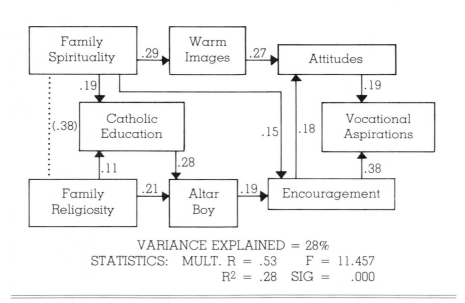

VARIANCE EXPLAINED = 28%
STATISTICS: MULT. R = .53   F = 11.457
R² = .28 SIG =   .000

Figure 7.5 (page 149) is a graphic presentation of the general model and accounts for one-quarter of the variance in thinking seriously about a vocation. The strongest path is from attitudes, and the second strongest path is from encouragement. This is a slightly different dynamic than we observed previously. Family spirituality and warm images are strongly related to vocational aspirations. The main differences, then, between this general model discussed before are the increased importance of attitudes towards the religious life and the direct path from family spirituality, and warm images. The encouragement variable is less important in this model.

FIGURE 7.4

Model for Males' Vocational Aspirations with "Attitudes" Removed

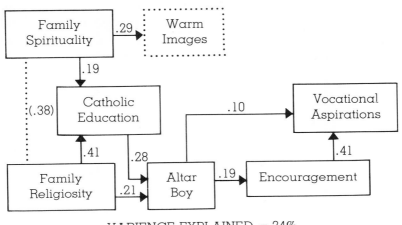

VARIENCE EXPLAINED = 24%
STATISTICS: MULT. R = .49   F = 11.400
R^2 = .24   SIG =   .000

TABLE 7.14

Serious Vocational Aspirations of Young Catholic Adults
(Percent)

At least thought of a vocation		81
Thought seriously of a vocation		19
		(N = 326)

	Males	Females	
At least thought of a vocation	41	59	(N = 263)
Thought seriously of a vocation	64	36	(N = 63)

The model presented in Figure 7.6 (page 150) is the same as Figure 7.5 with the attitudes removed. The first thing to note is that the r² decreases from .25 to .13, which means that attitudes are much more important at this stage of the process than they were in the previous stage of simply thinking about a vocation. The next thing to observe is that with the attitudes removed, encouragement, family spirituality, images, and Catholic education all begin to play a more direct role in encouraging people to consider seriously a vocation to the religious life. However, even for this group, of those with serious vocational aspirations, it is still true that half of the explainable variance is due to things other than attitudes about religious issues and the religious life. Encouragement, Catholic education, and the nature of the spirituality of the family are all very important factors in determining whether or not a person gives serious consideration to a religious vocation.

TABLE 7.15

Correlations for Serious Vocational Aspirations
(Coefficient = Pearson's r)

	Serious Vocational Aspirations	(Celibacy ##)	Attitudes	Encouragement	(Altar Boy#)	Warm Images	Catholic Education	Family Religiosity
(Celibacy ##)	(.28***)							
Attitudes	.38***	(.55***)						
Encouragement	.26***	(.04)	.00					
(Altar Boy#)	(.17**)	(.03)	(.07)	(.19**)				
Warm Images	.18**	(.21**)	.26***	.06	(.01)			
Catholic Education	.18**	(.08)	.02	.21***	(.50***)	.11		
Family Religiosity	.03	(.03)	.14*	.12*	(.06)	.05	.28**	
Family Spirituality	.06	(.21***)	.07	.13*	(.10)	.19**	.00	.36***

Significance: *** = .001   ** = .01   * = .05
(# for males only)
(## This is included in "Attitudes")

Just as we did in the first section, we have constructed models for the males in the sample, including the variable about whether or not they had ever been an altar boy. In Figure 7.7 we can see that over 36 percent of the variance is explained by a model which includes attitudes toward the vocation as well as having been an altar boy. Attitudes become quite important in this model as it did in the previous one. An obvious question to ask is whether or not any particular kinds of attitudes are more important than others.

One of the factors included is people's attitudes about celibacy and a married clergy. When we substitute "celibacy" for "attitudes" as we do in Figure 7.8, the proportion of the variance explained declines from 36 percent to 27 percent. An interesting point of contrast between Figure 7.7 and Figure 7.8 (pages 151–152) is that as long as general attitudes are in the model, the influence from warm images is channeled through it; however, as soon as "celibacy" is substituted for general attitudes, "warm images" creates its own direct path of .22 to thinking seriously about a vocation. It appears that images are articulated through some attitudes and not through others. Apparently, the warm religious imagery is not articulated very well through celibacy, but it is articulated through factors which relate to the nature of discipline and work in the religious life.

FIGURE 7.5

General Model for "Serious Vocational Aspirations"

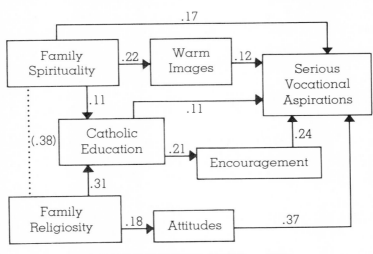

VARIANCE EXPLAINED = 25%
STATISTICS: MULT. R = .50   F = 10.486
R² = .25   SIG =   .000

This is a different set from those in previous models. See Appendix.

Finally, we have removed all of the attitude factors from the model and we find the r² or the ability to explain variance drops to .20, or 20 percent of the variance as opposed to 36 percent when we started this procedure. Another way of looking at this is that more than half of the explained variance is due to factors other than attitudes toward the religious life, including celibacy. It should be noted that celibacy has no role at all in the model presented earlier, which was whether or not people thought of a vocation at all. It only becomes important when we start to look at those who thought seriously about a vocation. It adds about a quarter to the explained variance. In other words, celibacy is a problem, but it is not *the* problem, for vocational development. The absence of encouragement is a more serious problem, and the absence of "warm" stories of God is as serious. The celibacy issue may be more important in distinguishing between those who "seriously consider a vocation" and those who finally persevere in one, but encouragement and warm images are more important for starting the process off (Figure 7.9, page 153).

FIGURE 7.6

**Model for Serious Vocational Aspirations
with "Attitudes" Removed**

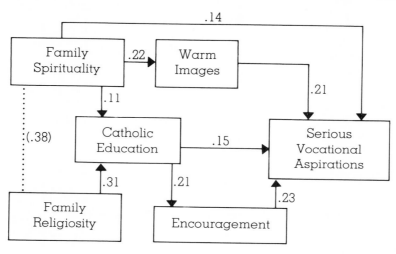

VARIANCE EXPLAINED = 13%
STATISTICS: MULT. R = .36   F = 5.699
R² = .13   SIG =   .000

It is always possible that explanations based on data from one source may apply only to that particular situation. By examining some of the data from our Canadian sample, we can see if the picture we have drawn of the vocational situation holds true for another neighboring country as well. Tables 7.16 and 7.17 (pages 151–152) consist of some descriptive statistics which indicate that vocations are going even less well in Canada. Three-quarters of the adult and the adolescent population have never even thought of a religious vocation, and the same proportion have never received any encouragement at all to do so. The list of those who are likely to encourage vocations is similar to the one for the U.S., with mothers, nuns or brothers, and priests in that order.

FIGURE 7.7

Model for Serious Vocational Aspirations for Males

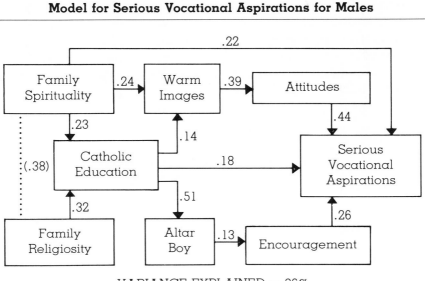

VARIANCE EXPLAINED = 36%
STATISTICS: MULT. R = .60   F = 6.239
R^2 = .36   SIG. =   .000

TABLE 7.16

Canadian Responses to Vocation Question
(Percent)

Adolescents:		Adults:	
In Training	1.9	In Training	0.2
Considering	3.7	Considering	0.4
Considered, but		Trained in the past	0.4
not seriously	17.6	Considered in the past	1.5
Never considered	76.9	Considered, but	
		not seriously	23.3
		Never considered	74.3
	N = 216		N = 541

In Figure 7.10 (page 153) we can see that the dynamic between the components in the general model is quite similar to that found in the U.S. data. Encouragement is a strong factor, and warm images are even stronger in Canada than they are in the U.S. The Canadian models behaved very much like the U.S. ones when

151

similar manipulations were performed, such as removing attitudes. The point of this comment is not to generalize to the Canadian Catholic population—that will take another report—but rather to demonstrate that the model holds for at least one other culture than our own. This does not seem to be a localized U.S. phenomenon but rather one which is quite likely the same in most of the western countries.

FIGURE 7.8

Model for Serious Vocational Aspirations for Males with "Celibacy" Substituted for "Attitudes"

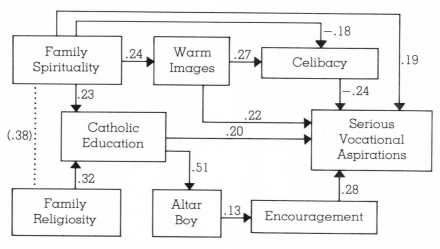

VARIANCE EXPLAINED = 27%
STATISTICS: MULT. R = .52   F = 4.35
R^2 = .27   SIG = .000

TABLE 7.17

Canadian Sample: People Who Encouraged Respondent to Think About a Religious Vocation

(Percent)

Mother	11
Father	6
Sibling	1
Grandparent	5
Relative	3
Priest	7
Nun or Brother	9
Friend	2
No one ever encouraged	75

N = 757

FIGURE 7.9

Model for Serious Vocational Aspirations
for Males with "Attitudes" Removed

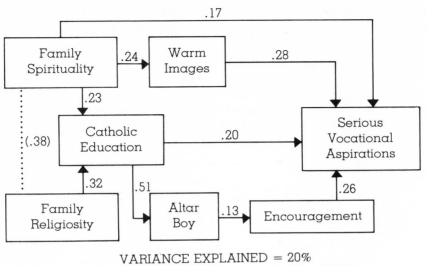

VARIANCE EXPLAINED = 20%
STATISTICS: MULT. R = .45   F = 3.275
R^2 = .20   SIG =   .006

FIGURE 7.10

Canadian General Model for
Vocational Aspirations

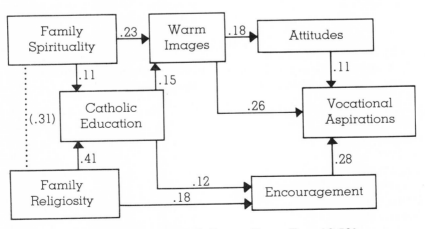

STATISTICS: MULT. R = .46   F = 16.561
R^2 = .21   SIG =   .000

Conclusions

If we project our figures out to the national Catholic population, we estimate that 2.8 million Catholic youths between the ages of 21 and 30 have at least thought about a religious vocation in some fashion, and that over a half million of them have given it some serious consideration. Three things emerge as being important elements in whether or not these vocational seeds take root and grow. The first is the extent to which the individual is encouraged to think about a vocation. In all of the analyses we have done, the encouragement factor is large and does not go away. Encouragement seems to come particularly from the family and from religious personnel such as priests, brothers, or nuns. Thus, much of the decline in vocations seems to be attributed to a decline in the levels of encouragement being offered to young people by religious personnel. Encouragement is more important at the first stage of the vocational process when the young person begins thinking about the possibility of the religious life, but it is also important in sustaining the process into that stage when a vocation is more seriously considered.

Second, the warmth of the religious imagery combines with Catholic education and, at least for the males, the fact of whether or not they were an altar boy, to provide a considerable impact on vocational aspirations. These variables are representative of the Catholic symbol system in a way that other variables are not. Previous research has indicated that Catholic schools influence people not so much by their curricula or by their hours of religious teaching, but rather by the symbolic milieu in which the students live. Being an altar boy is a relatively short-lived experience; if it has an impact as one moves into adulthood, it is because it is touching something deeper than just the experience of serving at Mass. Religious imagery, as has been observed elsewhere in this report, is a factor which is connected to one's self-identity and to one's most intimate relationships in the family. All of these, then, can be considered to be symbolic factors which are tied to the way in which an individual perceives the Catholic tradition.

Third, attitudes toward the religious life have a differential impact at different stages of the process. They have a relatively low impact on whether or not a person ever thinks of the vocational option, and they have a stronger impact on whether or not one continues to think seriously about it. However, even in those cases where attitudes have a strong impact, still half the variance is explained by other factors.

The respondents were asked if a series of changes would make them think more seriously about becoming priests. (Women were asked to answer these as if it might become possible for women to be ordained.) Among those who had considered a vocation but had rejected the idea, there was only one change which produced a significantly greater likelihood that they would reconsider a vocation, and that was allowing priests to marry. One-third of this group said that they would consider a vocation if this change were made. There was a moderate impact due to such proposed changes as shortening the term of commitment, allowing "weekend" priests, and having alternatives to living in rectories. However, overall, the importance of the lack of encouragement is much greater than the celibacy issue, because the former precludes people from even thinking about pursuing a vocation. For this reason, any discussion of future Church policy directions ought to at least begin with the problems surrounding the lack of encouragement for vocations to the religious life.

One relatively simple explanation of why we do not have as many vocations today as we might is that we have not encouraged them. Of particular importance is the fact that priests, brothers, and nuns have not encouraged vocations among young Catholics. We can probably do very little about people's symbolism in the short run. We can probably do even less about changing attitudes toward such things as celibacy and the nature of the religious life. But we can do a good deal more than we are doing in terms of encouraging young people to consider vocations to the religious life. We can probably do a good deal more than we are doing to teach, prepare, and encourage families to do the same. If we could begin to upgrade the encouragement that young people receive from religious professionals and from their families with regard to considering a religious vocation, we might easily have twice as many vocations in the near future as we currently have.

The vocational situation in the American Church is currently very bleak. To a great extent, we have no one but ourselves to blame since we have not encouraged people to pursue vocations very vigorously. The data and the analysis presented indicate that encouragement alone could vastly improve the vocational picture. Of greater importance for Church policy is the fact that vocational encouragement can be done at relatively little cost, since it does not require the change or the modification of any existing Church policies. In order to change people's attitudes, some rather drastic changes may have to occur. To get people to encourage young Catholic adults to think about a religious life, no change other than an examination and recommitment need occur.

The Knights of Columbus and Catholic Fraternal Groups

Highlights

1 *The overwhelming majority of teens and young adults had heard about the Knights of Columbus, but only a few had any detailed knowledge of the organization.*

2 *The most appealing aspect of fraternal groups to young adults and teens alike is the opportunity for "fellowship."*

3 *There is a "moderately strong" relationship between a person's religious behavior and practice and one's interest in fraternal groups.*

4 *Similar to the pattern that was found with respect to priestly and religious vocations, the persons who were attracted to the Knights of Columbus were the ones who had a greater exposure to such fraternal groups.*

5 *Young unmarried adults of Hispanic and Italian backgrounds were more likely to choose to join a fraternal organization than a parish organization.*

6 *Young people are seeking a better understanding of their faith by joining fraternal organizations rather than activities of their local parish.*

7 *The persons who are interested in Catholic fraternal groups have a greater interest in service than the average young Catholic.*

Chapter 8

The Knights of Columbus and Catholic Fraternal Groups

Our investigation of the relationship of Catholic (and former Catholic) young people to Catholic fraternal organizations covers four areas:

1. Exposure to and interest in fraternal groups, especially the Knights of Columbus.
2. Opinions on specific organizational issues (e.g., initiation rituals, organizational goals).
3. A portrait of the sort of person interested in fraternal organizations.
4. Analysis of the choice young people often make between fraternal organizations and parish organizations.

The investigation concludes with a discussion of the implications of the four sets of findings.

Exposure to and Interest in Fraternal Groups, Especially the Knights of Columbus

Preliminary analysis paints a far from bleak picture for the future of the Knights of Columbus. As shown in Table 8.1 (page 160), the Knights are the best known Catholic fraternal group represented in the questionnaire, with 90 percent of the young adult (18-29) population and 73 percent of the teen (14-17) population having heard of the organization. The Columbian Squires and the Daughters of Isabella, however, are much less well known.

Although the "Knights of Columbus" stir recognition in most young people, only a few know a great deal about the organization. As shown in Table 8.2 (page 160), 11 percent of both the teen and young adult population feel that they know "a lot" about the Knights. The most common response in both groups is "Heard of group (the Knights) but don't know much about it." However, half of the young people at least know a little about the group.

TABLE 8.1

**The Proportions of Young Catholics and Former Catholics
Who Have Heard of Various Fraternal Organizations**

(Percent)

Organization	Adults (aged 18–29) (N = 873)	Teens (aged 14–17) (N = 360)
Daughters of Isabella	17	10
Catholic Order of Forresters	15	11
Knights of St. Peter Claver	9	9
Columbian Squires	12	10
Catholics Daughters of America	34	28
Knights of Columbus	90	73

TABLE 8.2

**How Much Young Catholics and Former Catholics
Know About the Knights of Columbus**

(Percent)

Knowledge	Adults (aged 18–29) (N = 893)	Teens (aged 14–17) (N = 361)
Have not heard of Knights of Columbus.	10	27
Heard of group but don't know much about it.	41	37
Heard of group. Know a little about it.	39	25
Heard of group. Know quite a bit about it.	11	11

While young adults seem to have received more exposure to the Knights than have teens, Table 8.3 (page 161) shows that the two groups have learned about the organization in similar fashions. Most often, a young person has heard about the Knights through church bulletins or announcements. The second and third most common ways of learning about the Knights are through seeing members of the group engaged in an organizational activity and by viewing a Knights of Columbus publication or poster.

Teens and adults differ most in the exposure which they receive to the Knights through advertisements in magazines and newspapers. It appears that advertisements in the press are a less effective way to reach teens—with 23 percent of the adolescents (in contrast to 44 percent of young adults) having seen a Knights advertisement. It should be noted that, besides the channels of communication listed in Table 8.3, the Knights of Columbus halls offer an additional connecting link between the Knights and the public. The most common response in the "Other sources" category concerns a Knights of Columbus hall—either seeing a hall or attending a function in one. Tables 8.4 and 8.5 (page 162) deal with the question of actual membership in Catholic fraternal organizations (among 18 to 29 year olds) and also with interest in joining fraternal groups (among non-member young adults and teens). The tables show that about 3 percent of the young adult population consider themselves members of a Catholic fraternal or sisterly group, while more than double that proportion—another 7 to 9 percent—is interested in joining such an organization. Among young adults, the Knights of Columbus holds a larger proportion of members than any other Catholic fraternal group.

TABLE 8.3

The Ways By Which Young Catholics and Former Catholics Have Heard About the Knights of Columbus
(Percent)

Ways	Adults (Aged 18–29) (N = 736)	Teens (Aged 14–17) (N = 236)
Father or another family member belonged to Knights or told person about them	33	20
Friend told person about group	27	23
Person heard about K of C in church announcements or church bulletin	63	50
Person saw the members of the group in some public activity—like collecting money for a charity	52	40
Person saw a poster, pamphlet, or newspaper published by the Knights of Columbus	51	48
Person saw a K of C advertisement in a newspaper or magazine	44	23
Person read a story about the group in the general or religious press	22	14
Heard about the group through the Columbian Squires	2	3
Other sources	11	25

In the youthful population, however, the most common response to fraternal organizations is a lack of interest in joining. Table 8:6 (page 163) reveals that, in the 18-to 29-year-old group, the most common reason for not wanting to join a Catholic fraternal group is a lack of general religious interest. In contrast, teens are more likely to assert that they do not know enough about Catholic fraternal groups to be interested in joining. However, like the

younger teens, a rather large minority of 18-to 29-year olds do not
know enough about Catholic fraternal groups to be interested in
joining.

TABLE 8.4

Proportion of Young Adult Catholics and Former Catholics (Aged 18–29) Who Consider Themselves Members of a Catholic Fraternal or Sisterly Organization

(Percent)

Members of Organization	(N = 881)
Member of any Catholic fraternal or sisterly organization	2.9
Member of Knights of Columbus	0.9
Member of Daughters of Isabella	0.0
Member of Catholic Order of Forresters	0.2
Member of Knights of St. Peter Claver	0.0
Member of Columbian Squires	0.0
Member of Catholic Daughters of America	0.2
Member of other Catholic fraternal or sisterly organization	1.6 [a]

[a]Respondents listed the following organizations as "other" Catholic fraternal or sisterly groups; each group is represented by one respondent. (Although the groups are not all technically fraternal or sisterly organizations, all those mentioned by respondents are listed.) Ateitis—Lutheran Catholic Youth Association, Catholic Aid Association, CYO, Jednota, Knights of the Altar, League of Sacred Heart, Parish board, Phi Kappa Theta Fraternity, Rosary Society, Serra, St. Joseph's Society, Vallienne, West End Catholic Home and School Association.

TABLE 8.5

Interest Levels of Young Catholics and Former Catholics in Joining a Catholic Men's or Women's Fraternal Service Organization (If Not Currently a Member)

(Percent)

Interest Levels	Adults (Aged 18–29) (N = 850)	Teens (Aged 14–17) (N = 361)
Very interested	1	2
Somewhat interested	6	7
Neutral	18	17
Not very interested	22	28
Not at all interested	53	46

Opinions on Specific Organizational Issues

This section presents the opinions of teens and young adults
concerning initiation rites, the potential effectiveness of life
insurance as a drawing card for fraternal groups, and those
aspects of fraternal organizations which the young people

personally find most and least attractive. Since the respondents with an active interest in fraternal groups may hold different opinions on fraternal matters from the rest of the youthful population, we will first examine the views of the general group and then will compare the views of "fraternal sympathizers" with the non-sympathizers. In this analysis, a fraternal sympathizer is (1) a young adult who considers himself or herself to be a member of a fraternal group, or (2) a teen or young adult who had indicated interest in joining a Catholic men's or women's fraternal service organization. In both the teen and the young adult populations, 9 percent of the respondents are fraternal sympathizers and 91 percent are non-sympathizers. Males and females are equally likely to fall into the sympathizer group.

TABLE 8.6

The Main Reason Young Catholics and Former Catholics Do Not Wish to Join a Catholic Fraternal or Sisterly Organization

(Percent)

Main Reason	Adults (Aged 18–29) (N = 786)	Teens (Aged 14–17) (N = 320)
No longer a strong Catholic	36	15
Not a "joiner"	27	14
Doesn't enjoy the company of the sort of person in fraternal service organizations	4	5
Doesn't feel would be welcome in local chapter	0	1
Never asked to join	4	5
Doesn't care for secret initiation ceremonies and fancy titles	1	3
Doesn't know enough about the groups to be interested	26	56
Cannot afford a dues-paying organization	2	2

Table 8.7 (page 164) concerns the aspect of fraternal membership which the youthful population finds most appealing. The greatest proportion of both adolescents and young adults find the possibility of "fellowship" the most attractive aspect of fraternal organizations. Community service is a fairly strong runner-up among the young adult group. Table 8.8 (page 164) reveals that the goals of fraternal sympathizers and non-sympathizers do not vary drastically. Sympathizers are more likely to find attractive the

religious aspects of Catholic fraternal groups and seem somewhat less likely to seek group services from fraternal organizations.

TABLE 8.7

The Proportion of Young Adults and Teens Who Indicate That a Particular Aspect of Catholic Fraternal Organizations Best Fits Their Interests

(Percent)

Interests	Adults (Aged 18–29) (N = 601)	Teens (Aged 14–17) (N = 243)
Community service	21	12
Helping respondent to understand or to practice religion more fully	17	14
Opportunities for recreation	14	15
Fellowship, friends, place to gather	27	34
Group action to achieve a common goal	13	11
Opportunities for inexpensive travel or other group services	8	13

TABLE 8.8

The Proportion of Fraternal Sympathizers and Non-Sympathizers (Young Adults and Teens Together) Who Indicate That a Particular Aspect of Catholic Fraternal Organizations Best Fits Their Interests

(Percent)

Interests	Sympathizers (N = 70)	Non-Sympathizers (N = 774)
Community service	24	18
Helping respondent to understand or to practice religion more fully	29	15
Opportunities for recreation	9	15
Fellowship, friends, place to gather	26	29
Group action to achieve a common goal	11	12
Opportunities for inexpensive travel or other group services	1	10

Tables 8.9 and 8.10 (page 165) turn the question of organizational goals around—illustrating those aspects of Catholic fraternal organizations which are least attractive to young people. Table 8.9

notes the lack of importance which the average young person attaches to the group services and religious aspects of fraternal organizations. Table 8.10 reveals a fairly strong tendency for the fraternal sympathizers to attach even less importance to group services than do the non-sympathizers and to value religious factors more.

TABLE 8.9

The Proportion of Young Adults and Teens Who Indicate That a Particular Aspect of Catholic Fraternal Organizations Least Fits Their Interests

(Percent)

Interests	Adults (Aged 18–29) (N = 613)	(Teens) (Aged 14–17) (N = 250)
Community service	8	12
Helping respondent to understand or to practice religion more fully	25	29
Opportunities for recreation	7	8
Fellowship, friends, place to gather	6	4
Group action to achieve a common goal	7	16
Opportunities for inexpensive travel or other group services	48	31

TABLE 8.10

The Proportion of Fraternal Sympathizers and Non-Sympathizers (Young Adults and Teens Together) Who Indicate That a Particular Aspect of Catholic Fraternal Organizations Least Fits Their Interests

(Percent)

Interests	Sympathizers (N = 77)	Non- Sympathizers (N = 786)
Community service	9	9
Helping respondent to understand or to practice religion more fully	8	28
Opportunities for recreation	6	7
Fellowship, friends, place to gather	3	6
Group action to achieve a common goal	6	10
Opportunities for inexpensive travel or other group services	68	40

Our final organizational question concerns life insurance and initiation ceremonies. When asked whether life insurance at group rates would make them more likely to join a fraternal organization, teens interestingly answer more affirmatively than do young adults. As shown in Table 8.11, 23 percent of teens answer "yes" or "maybe" to the insurance incentive question, while 10 percent of the young adults respond in the affirmative. Teens may be answering the question from a less-informed perspective concerning the availability of life insurance, or, alternatively, may experience fewer opportunities to qualify for group insurance.

TABLE 8.11

Whether or Not Life Insurance Would Make Teens and Young Adults More Likely to Join a Fraternal Organization
(Percent)

	Adults (Aged 18–29) (N = 788)	Teens (Aged 14–17) (N = 266)
Yes	1	5
Maybe	9	18
No	89	77

When, as in Table 8.12, the views of fraternal sympathizers are compared to those of non-sympathizers, the sympathizers are more drawn by the insurance incentive. While 29 percent of the sympathizers answer "yes" or "maybe" to the likelihood question, the comparable figure for the non-sympathizers is 13 percent. Apparently, once a person leans toward fraternal membership, life insurance offers him or her more of an incentive for joining.

TABLE 8.12

Whether or Not Life Insurance Would Make Fraternal Sympathizers and Non-Sympathizers More Likely to Join a Fraternal Organization
(Percent)

	Sympathizers (N = 100)	Non-Sympathizers (N = 954)
Yes	7	2
Maybe	22	11
No	71	88

The initiation issue reflects a pattern similar to the insurance question. The questionnaire asked respondents to express their opinion of secret initiation rituals by choosing from the following two alternatives: "I feel that an initiation ritual, known only to members, brings the members of a group closer together," or "The idea of initiation rituals makes me uncomfortable; it seems artificial and unnecessary." Table 8.13 shows that teens are more likely than adults to express a favorable opinion of secret initiation rituals.

TABLE 8.13

Teen and Young Adult Opinions of Secret Initiation Ceremonies
(Percent)

	Adults (Aged 18–29) (N = 856)	Teens (Aged 14–17) (N = 355)
Brings group closer	27	39
Artificial and unnecessary	73	61

And as in the life insurance case, Table 8.14 reflects the fact that fraternal sympathizers are the most favorable of all, with nearly half approving of the secret rituals. On the other side, a full half of those who hold a favorable view of fraternal organizations feel uncomfortable with the idea of secret initiation rituals.

TABLE 8.14

Fraternal Sympathizer and Non-Sympathizer Opinions of Secret Initiation Ceremonies
(Percent)

	Sympathizers (N = 114)	Non-sympathizers (N = 1097)
Bring group closer	49	19
Artificial and unnecessary	51	81

A Portrait of Those Most Likely to Join Fraternal Organizations

Those who study organizations inform us that individuals join an organization because the group fits their needs. Barnard (1938) in his classic organizational work, *The Functions of the Executive*, notes that "The net satisfactions which induce a man to contribute his efforts to an organization result from the positive advantages against the disadvantages which are entailed." Theorists variously divide the sorts of incentives which attract people to organizations into the three categories of material, emotional, and ideological incentives (e.g., Weber, 1964) or simply into two incentive categories—material and psychological (e.g., Etzioni, 1965).

Although fraternal organizations do offer some material rewards (i.e., group insurance), the rewards are usually more intangible—opportunities for leadership, fellowship, understanding religion, serving the community. This section of the chapter develops a portrait of the young person most likely to join a fraternal organization. Based on the notion that people join organizations which foster their goals, we look at five different areas which might distinguish those attracted to religious fraternal groups from those who are not.

1. *Religion*. The last section of the chapter revealed that those who are interested in a religious fraternal organization are more likely than is the average young Catholic to turn to organizations for a better understanding of their religion. This ideological incentive which attracts young Catholics would lead us to expect that young people interested in joining fraternal organizations are more religious than average. We test this expectation using the five dimensions of religiosity developed in Chapter Two.

2. *Personal goals*. Besides differing in their religiosity, these young people probably differ in their personal goals. Fraternal groups like the Knights of Columbus emphasize traditional goals—fellowship, family, community. The groups also offer an opportunity for service to others. We might expect the fraternally-interested to endorse traditional other-oriented goals as opposed to material or "me-oriented" objectives.

3. *Attitudes*. In the same vein, differences in goals might express themselves in differences in attitudes on issues. We examine two sorts of attitudes—attitudes toward the Church and attitudes on social issues. We would expect a person attracted to a religious fraternal group to take a traditional stand on Church policy and on social issues like abortion and working mothers. However, because of their service motivation, we would expect from these respondents a lack of prejudice against minorities and a feeling of sympathy for the poor.

4. *Exposure to fraternal groups*. In more practical terms, those interested in fraternal groups have probably received more exposure to such groups, and a higher quality of exposure. They might well have heard of the Knights of Columbus, for example, in more ways than other young people, and from family and friends rather than through less personal sources. Thus, they might become more aware that the fraternal organizations could help implement their goals.

5. *Demographic characteristics.* Finally, these young Catholics may differ in demographic characteristics from those who are less interested in fraternal organizations. They may come from subcultures whose needs are better served by fraternal groups, i.e., newly arrived ethnic groups.

For this particular analysis, we include the "neutrals" in with the actively interested, as well as those who currently belong to a fraternal organization. The population of those interested in fraternal groups, by this definition, equals 25 percent of our sample of young Catholics.

As we see in Table 8.15, our first hypothesis that, on the average, the fraternally-interested young person is more religious than the average young adult, is true across all five of the religious dimensions developed in Chapter Two. These young Catholics are more likely to participate at Mass, to receive communion, to feel close to their parishes, to express orthodox views on doctrinal and sexual issues, to feel close to God, and to have had a mystical experience, than are the average young Catholics. The relationship between religiosity and interest in a religious fraternal group is moderately strong, as indicated by the coefficient of .28 for "general religiosity."

TABLE 8.15

Correlations Between Religious Dimensions and Attraction to the Fraternal Groups
(Coefficient = Pearson's r)

General religiosity**	.28*
Ritual/Parish dimension	.17*
Sexual orthodoxy	.16*
Doctrinal orthodoxy	.21*
Personal relationship to God	.14*
Mystical experience	.11*

*Significant at .05 or better.
**The five dimensions combined.

In addition to exhibiting a higher than average religiosity, these young people also differ in their personal goals from those who are less interested in fraternal organizations. Table 8.16 shows that the young adult who feels an attraction to fraternal membership (or at least is neutral on the subject) is somewhat more likely to indicate as important goals the following: "serving God in a church career," "living up to strict moral standards," and "having children." "Job security" and "helping solve social problems" are a little more important to them, and "having a lot of free time" and "have nice material possessions" are less important personal goals.

TABLE 8.16

Correlation Between Personal Goals and Attraction to Fraternal Groups Among Young Adults

(Coefficient = Pearson's r)

1. Having a lot of friends	ns
2. Living up to strict moral standards	.15*
3. Having children	.14*
4. Job security	.09*
5. Having a lot of free time	−.08*
6. Becoming famous	.01
7. Having a beautiful home, a new car, and other nice things	−.06*
8. Spending a lot of time getting to know inner self	.03
9. Having a high paying job	−.03
10. Helping solve social problems such as poverty, air pollution	.08*
11. Serving God in a Church career	.24*
12. Traditional goals (summary of #2, #3, #11)	.26*

*Significant at .05 or better.

The goal which best distinguishes the two groups is "serving God in a Church career." A summary of traditional goals which combines answers on "serving God" with answers on "living up to strict moral standards" and "having children" only strengthens the association by 2 points over the simple "serving-God" variable. Table 8.16, then, confirms the hypothesis that those interested in fraternal organizations will express different personal goals from those who are less interested and that their goals will be of a traditional nature.

On the chance that respondents interested in fraternal organizations express their different goals through stands on issues, we examine two sets of attitudes—those on Church policy and those on social issues. Church policy issues have been reduced to three scales as described in Chapter 10. The Progressive scale reflects attitudes toward improving leadership and sermon quality, democratizing the Church, objecting to current birth control and divorce teachings, and endorsing certain social action issues. The Traditional scale includes opinions on imposing more order and discipline in the Church and on returning to the Latin Mass and Friday abstinence. The Clerical Change scale measures disapproval of clerical celibacy and endorsement of the ordination of women (Table 8.17, page 171).

Interestingly, those attracted to fraternal organizations are no more likely than the average young Catholic to take a positive or negative stand on the progressive issues. However, they are more likely to score high on the Traditional scale, indicating they are more likely than the average young adult to favor a return to pre-Vatican II practices. Finally, they are slightly less likely than the average young Catholic to advocate changes regarding priesthood.

TABLE 8.17

Correlation Between Being Interested In a Fraternal Organization and Two Sets of Attitudes: Church Policy and Social Issues

(Coefficient = Pearson's r)

Church Policy	
Progressive	.02
Traditional	.25*
Clerical change	−.06*
Social Issues	
Opposed to abortion on demand	.19*
Responsible for aiding poor	.11*
A working mother emotionally injures her preschool child	.02
Jewish businessmen are honest	−.05
There is an obligation to work to end segregation	.05*

*Significant at .05 or better.

The social issues represent an interesting complement to Church policy issues in reflecting the goals of these young Catholics attracted to fraternal groups. Although they are slightly less likely to approve the ordination of women, they are not different with regard to their attitudes toward working mothers of preschoolers, nor are they significantly less tolerant of Jews than are the less interested. They more strongly oppose abortion on demand, and they are slightly more sympathetic to the poor and toward integration.

To summarize, then: those interested in religious fraternal organizations conform to many of our expectations concerning their attitudes. They are somewhat more traditional than the average young person concerning Church practices, abortion, and clerical change. On the other hand, they are slightly more concerned with working for integration and with aiding the poor than are the average young Catholics, and this may be a reflection of their greater "service orientation" observed back in Table 8.7.

As we can see in Table 8.18 (page 172), those interested in fraternal organizations are likely to have heard about the Knights of Columbus in more ways than those who are less interested. They have heard of the Knights of Columbus in more personal or parochial ways—through friends or family, by seeing members engaged in some activity, and through announcements in church or parish bulletins, as opposed to newspapers or pamphlets. The Personal-Parochial scale shows that when exposure to the Knights in these personal ways is taken into account, those young people with greater exposure are a good deal more likely to feel attracted to fraternal groups. In the case of fraternal organizations, then, familiarity breeds attraction, not contempt.

TABLE 8.18

Correlation Between Ways of Hearing About the Knights of Columbus and Attraction to Fraternal Groups Among Young Adults
(Coefficient = Pearson's r)

1. Told by father or family member	.14*
2. Told by friend	.14*
3. Church announcements or bulletins	.12*
4. Saw members in some activity	.14*
5. Saw K of C poster, pamphlet or newspaper	.02
6. Saw K of C advertisement	.07*
7. Read about group in press	.03
8. Heard through Columbian Squires	.09*
9. Other	−.05
10. Personal Parochial Scale Summary Score (Combination of #1, #2, #3, and #4)	.23*

*Significant at .05 or better.

Finally, we can compare those interested in fraternal organizations with those less interested according to their demographic characteristics. As we can see in Table 8.19 (page 173), the best predictor of interest in fraternalism is being a member of a minority. Table 8.20 (page 173) separates young people into four different groups, according to the part of the world from which their ancestors came. (If the ancestors came from more than one place, the respondent chooses the place to which he feels closest.) Those with ancestors from Mexico and Puerto Rico are a good deal more likely to express interest in joining a fraternal organization than those with Eastern or Western European heritage. Members of other non-European cultures are also somewhat more likely than those of European backgrounds to seek membership in a fraternal group. However, interest in membership does not seem to correlate with a family's time of arrival in the U.S. The number of a person's grandparents who were born in the U.S. does not predict interest in fraternal membership.

Another demographic characteristic which predicts attraction to fraternalism is the number of brothers and sisters a respondent has. Those young people who come from large families are likely to favor fraternal membership. People from larger families are differentially attracted to fraternalism in three out of the four ethnic divisions, the Eastern European group being the exception.

TABLE 8.19

Correlations Between Demographic Characteristics and Attraction to Fraternal Groups
(Coefficient = Pearson's r)

Number of years Catholic education	.00
Expected maximum educational level	.06*
Current educational level	−.04
Sex (Female high)	−.03
Number of siblings in family	.11*
Presently married	−.00
Expected number of children	.01
Number of grandparents born in U.S.	.05
Member of minority group	.12*

*Significant at .05 level or better.

TABLE 8.20

Young Adults Attracted to Fraternal Membership by Ethnic Group
(Percent)

East European	24
West European/Canadian	24
Mexican, Puerto Rican	45
African, Asian, Other	33
N = 752	

The other demographic factors bear little relationship to fraternal interest. Those who aspire to higher levels of education are slightly more likely to be interested in fraternalism. Marital status has no effect. Age, as we can see in Table 8.21 (page 174), has a bi-modal relationship to fraternal attraction and the two ages in which youth appear most interested are the college years, 18–20, and the mid-20s, 25–27.

We conclude with a final model of fraternal attraction (Table 8.22, page 174) in which the critical—and nearly equally important—characteristics turn out to be a traditional stand on Church policy (a fondness for the old ways), having heard about the Knights of Columbus in many personalized ways, traditional personal goals of family, morality, and religiosity. These four factors together explain 15 percent of the variance in fraternal attraction. When these four factors have been taken into account, the size of a young person's family of origin and the ethnic group from which the person comes no longer bear a statistically significant relationship to fraternal attraction.

TABLE 8.21

The Relationship Between Age and Fraternal Attraction Among Young Adults*
(Percent interested)

Age	Those Attracted To Fraternal Organizations	N
14–17	25	(331)
18–20	32	(246)
21–24	20	(286)
25–27	30	(235)
28–30	18	(249)
		(1347)

* Significant at .05.

TABLE 8.22

Model of Fraternal Attractiveness Among Young Adults

	r	B
Religiosity	.28*	.12*
Traditional Church policy stand	.25*	.16*
Traditional personal goals	.26*	.15*
Summary heard-of KC score	.23*	.16*
Minority ethnic group (Hispanic, Asian, African)	.12*	.00
Number of siblings	.11*	.06

Multiple R = .38   F = 11.4
R² = .15   Sig = .000

* Significant at .05 or better.

Parish Organizations and Fraternal Groups: Making a Choice

In the previous section we proposed the question of why some young men and women might be interested in joining a fraternal organization. In this section we address a somewhat different question. Given that a young person is predisposed to organizational activity in the Church, and given that he/she is prepared to choose either parish or fraternal, but not both, what are the factors which predispose him/her to make the choice one way or the other?

One could suggest a number of explanatory models:
• The reasons might be "demographic"—age, marital status,

ethnic background, educational attainment. Hispanic and Italian Catholics seem to have less parish loyalties than do Irish, Polish, or German Catholics. The young and the unmarried might be less tied into the neighborhood parish because they have fewer roots in such a community. The better educated might well be put off by the style of the fraternal organization, which would appear to them to be a throwback to immigrant days; or alternatively, the better educated would prefer greater independence from the "parochial" parish community provided them.

• Young Catholic adults might turn to fraternal organizations instead of parochial ones for reasons having to do with the organizational structure of their own parish: the poor quality of clerical service, hostile attitudes toward the local clergy, or the absence of parish organizations.

• The young Catholic may choose a fraternal organization in preference to the parish for *functional* reasons. It may well be that there are activities which he/she may engage in with a fraternal organization which are simply not available to him/her, or at least are not perceived as available in the parish structure.

• Finally, there may be *religious* reasons for his/her choice. It could be that a young person wishes affiliation with the Catholic religious heritage, but does not aspire to devotional involvement that accompanies parish activism. Thus, he/she can be perceived, and indeed he/she may perceive himself/herself, as a good Catholic, and yet not have to maintain a level of personal piety that accompanies the role of an "active parishioner."

The analysis of this section uses a "multi-step" or "layered model," investigating first how much of the variance in activism option can be accounted for by demographic background, then adding situations in the respondent's parish, next bringing into the model the reasons one might consider a fraternal organization membership, and finally adding religious devotion.

As noted in the previous section, the questionnaire asked respondents whether they currently belong to a Catholic fraternal organization, and if they do not belong, how interested they are in joining such an organization. The questionnaire also asked respondents whether they belong to any parish organizations. Twenty-eight respondents indicated that they were active in both fraternal and parish organizations. Another 1,194 respondents stated that they were not active in either. One hundred twenty-five respondents were active in their parish but were not interested in fraternal organizations, while seventy-nine were either active in, or at least interested in, fraternal organization membership but were not active in their parish. It is these two latter groups of 204 respondents who have exercised an option, or at least have made themselves ready to exercise an option, between one of the two types of affiliations that this section will concern. Why would some young Catholic adults choose geographical, parochial organizations, and why do others choose non-geographical, functional or fraternal organizations?

The unmarried, those who have not attended college, and those with Latin backgrounds are substantially more likely to choose fraternal organizations over parish organizations than are those who attended college, who do not have Latin backgrounds, and who are married (Table 8.23). All of the differences are statistically significant at the .05 level or better. There seems to be an inverted "U"-curve in popularity of fraternal organizations according to age. Those under eighteen and over twenty-five are less likely to choose the fraternal organization in preference to the parochial, while those between nineteen and twenty-eight are more likely to choose the fraternal organization.

TABLE 8.23

Activism Option by Demographic Background
(Percent choosing fraternal organizations)

College	
Attended	44*
Not Attended	60*
Ethnic Background	
Latin	58*
Non-Latin	32*
Marital Status	
Married	46*
Not Married	55*
Age	
Under 18	26*
19 − 22	61*
23 − 25	54*
26 − 28	50*
29 − 30	33*

*Significant at .05 level.

This choice parallels the "mini life cycle" phenomenon which has been reported in Chapter Five. There is a considerable decline in religious activity for Catholics in their middle 20s, and then an upsurge in devotional activities (in parochial affiliation, if not activism) at the end of their 20s. Much of this rebound effect can be attributed to a reintegration into society, which accompanies marriage (and from which, incidentally, studies show the Democratic Party benefits as well as the Catholic Church). However (Table 8.24, page 177), while the numbers are all too small, it does appear that decline in the fraternal option is a function of age and not of marital status. It may be toward the end of their 20s even when an unmarried young adult is prepared to settle down geographically in terms of religious activism. It may also be that those who have exercised the fraternal option would not give it up even after they have married.

TABLE 8.24

Activism Option By Age and Marital Status
(Percent choosing fraternal organizations)

Age	Married	Not Married
19–22	50	64
	(6)	(33)
23–25	57	52
	(7)	(17)
26–30	41	42
	(24)	(9)

Thus, the expectations of a demographic explanation are confirmed by the data. Latin younger people (though over eighteen) and the less well educated are more prone to exercise the fraternal option. There is, incidentally, no difference between men and women in the propensity to choose non-geographic organizational activism.

It is also true that, as we speculated earlier, as compared to parish activists, fraternal activists are disproportionately recruited from those who are less devout (Table 8.25, page 178). Only three out of ten of the weekly Mass attenders choose the fraternal option; whereas five out of ten of the less than weekly Mass attenders prefer the fraternal to the parochial organizations. Nevertheless, personal, private devotion as measured by daily prayer does not distinguish between the two groups. Thirty-nine percent of those who pray nearly every day and thirty-nine percent of those who pray less often exercise the fraternal as opposed to the parochial option. Thus, we know from the previous section that the fraternally interested are more devout than average. We now discover that those active in parish organizations are even more devout than the fraternally interested in terms of external behavior, but that the two do not differ in personal, private behavior.

(There is also a .15—statistically significant—correlation between years of Catholic education and the choice of parochial as opposed to fraternal activism. This variable is omitted from the model because it seems to be a function of the fact that those who have gone to parochial schools are more likely to attend college.)

TABLE 8.25

Activism Option By Religious Devotion
(Percent choosing fraternal organizations)

Mass	
Almost weekly	31
Less	53
Communion	
Almost weekly	31
Less	56
Prayer	
Nearly every day	39
Less	39

Many of the circumstances of a respondent's parish which we thought might be related to a choice of a fraternal affiliation do not, in fact, seem to have any effect. It does not matter if the respondent rates the quality of sermons as excellent, or whether he or she has spoken to a priest recently, or whether he or she finds the priest sympathetic to his or her problems, or whether he or she approves of the pastor's parochial performance, or whether he or she perceives that lay people have a great deal of influence in this parish. What does matter, however, and significantly and substantially, is whether there are a lot of activities in the parish. Close to a third of those respondents say there are a lot of activities in their parish, but nonetheless they chose a non-geographic affiliation. But more than half of those who say there are not a lot of activities in their parish opt for the fraternal affiliation (Table 8.26, page 179). One joins fraternal organizations, in other words, because there is nothing to join in the parish.

Finally (Table 8.27, page 179), those who are most likely to accept or exercise the non-geographic option are those who are seeking a better understanding of religional—most three-fifths of those respondents chose the fraternal as opposed to the parochial membership. We would have anticipated beforehand that fellowship and group action motivations would be the most powerful for fraternal affiliation and that those who wish to improve their religious knowledge would go to the parish to do so. In fact, it may well be that parishes are not perceived as sources of adult religious education and, therefore, those interested in such a service turn to fraternal organizations, hoping that they would find some such education. We find evidence, then, that the fraternal organizations would be well advised to emphasize their religious education function.

We are now prepared (Table 8.28, page 180) to consider the multi-layered model described earlier. The first two columns represent the simple and the standardized correlations between each variable and the fraternal option. The second two columns represent a series of regression equations in which each variable is added one by one, which might be considered a mixture of the chronological and the logical.

TABLE 8.26

Option by Parish Situation
(Percent choosing fraternal organizations)

Spoken to a priest recently	
Yes	39
No	39
Sermon quality	
Excellent	43
Not excellent	36
Priest's ability to understand problems	
Excellent	34
Not excellent	37
Lay influence in parish	
A great deal	38
Not a great deal	43
Approval of pastor's performance	
Yes	36
No	39
A lot of parish activities	32
Not a lot of parish activities	54

TABLE 8.27

Option by Reason for Considering a Fraternal Organization
(Percent choosing fraternal organizations)

Community service	42
Better understanding of religion	58
Recreation	23
Fellowship	32
Group action	40
Group services	8

First of all, the betas are not by and large substantially diminished from the "r's," suggesting that each of the variables makes a relatively independent contribution to the activism decision. Each of the different layers, in other words, seems to make its own contribution to the choice.

TABLE 8.28

Correlations With Activism Option and Layered Model

Variable	r	beta	R	R²
Age	−.17*	−.21	.17	.03
Latin	.23*	.16	.29	.08
College	−.16*	−.17	.34	.12
Active parish	−.22*	−.23	.42	.17
Reason for considering Fraternal Organization				
more religious knowledge	.24*	.23	.48	.23
Frequent reception of communion	.22*	.15	.50	.25

* Significant at .05 or better.

Secondly, as each new variable is added to the model the variance explained goes up four, or five, or even six percentage points until the very last variable, frequent reception of communion, is added. Age accounts for three percent of the variance; age and Latin background for eight percent of the variance; age, ethnic background and college attendance for twelve percent; age, ethnic background, college attendance and an inactive parish for seventeen percent of the variance. The religious educational motivation adds six percent more to the explanation of the variance, and finally, frequent reception of communion contributes an additional three percentage points. The explanatory model accounts for a quarter of the variance in organizational choice, a not totally unsatisfactory performance in our problematic discipline.

Summary and Implications

The Young Catholics Study depicts the opinions of young people regarding Catholic fraternal service organizations. It appears that, among youth, the organizations are not for everyone. In fact, 75 percent of young Catholics and former Catholic Americans express disinterest in joining a Catholic fraternal service organization, and another 16 percent feel neutral toward the organizations.

However, the picture is not all gloomy, particularly for the Knights of Columbus. The Knights is the best known of the fraternal service organizations and has attracted more youthful members than any other group. Their potential is even greater. While about one percent of the youthful population currently holds a membership in the Knights, another eight percent is either somewhat or very interested in joining a fraternal group. Considering that roughly half of these fraternal sympathizers are female, that still leaves the Knights with a recruiting base about four times larger than its current youthful membership. If those young people who are neutral about joining fraternal groups are considered recruitable, the male recruiting base jumps to more than twelve times the current youthful membership.

The "fraternal sympathizers" seek different things from a fraternal organization than the average young Catholic. They wish roughly equal doses of religious enrichment, fellowship, and community service. The non-sympathizers, in contrast, would place fellowship at the top of their list, de-emphasizing religion. Because of their high religious motivation, the sympathizers could probably be most efficiently reached through recruitment drives in parishes and campus religious centers. Colleges should be especially effective places for recruitment since the college years, ages 18-20, are years marked by openness to fraternal organization.

Demographically, the Hispanics offer the largest recruitment potential. While 25 percent of the youthful population feels interested or at least neutral toward fraternal groups, this figure is 45 percent for Hispanic Americans. And among Hispanics who come from families with more than two children, the figure is even larger—50 percent sympathetic to Catholic fraternal groups. Young Hispanics and other minorities—blacks and Asians— offer a recruitment base more open to religious fraternal organizations than are those young people of Eastern or Western European heritage.

In terms of basic philosophy, those young people who express interest or neutrality toward fraternal groups mirror many of the same concerns as the Knights. They are religious, favor traditional goals of family and leading a moral life, oppose abortion, and are interested in serving the community. Thus, it does not appear that the Knights of Columbus would have to change or expand its organizational goals in order to attract youthful recruits. The organization need only make potential members aware of the opportunities available through the Knights.

Our study indicates that about half of the fraternal sympathizers would be interested in fraternal organizations which incorporate secret initiation ceremonies. The other half of the group, however, is critical of such ceremonies. Given the large number of young people who, even though they are positively inclined toward fraternal groups, are not drawn toward secret ceremonies, the Knights may want to discuss modifications in initiation procedures.

The possibility of group life insurance rates appears to be less of an incentive to join fraternal groups than it probably has been in the past. However, a fair-sized minority—roughly 30 percent of the fraternal sympathizers—feel that the group insurance rate might make them more likely to join a fraternal group. While religious enrichment, fellowship, and community service should receive more emphasis in a recruiting drive, the insurance benefit adds to a fraternal group's attractiveness.

A somewhat different picture emerges of the fraternally active and interested when they are compared to parish activists as opposed to the general youthful population. Compared to those active in parish organizations, they are less likely to have attended college, are more likely to be of Italian or Hispanic background, and are less likely to be married. The fraternal sympathizers are less likely to attend Mass and communion regularly. In comparison with the general youthful population, the fraternally interested are more likely to be of college age or in their mid-20s. In contrast, parish activity is greater in the high school years and the late 20s. The fraternally active, then, form a middle ground in many respects. They are less religious than those active in the parish, but more religious than the average young person. They are less likely to have attended college than the parish activists, but are more likely than the average young person to aspire to higher education. They are more likely than the parish activists to be either Italian or Hispanic, and more likely than the average to be Hispanic. They are more likely than those active in the parish to be single, but are not more likely than the average young person to be single.

In the area of religious education, however, the fraternally active occupy no middle ground. They are more likely than the average person and more likely than the parish activists to seek a better understanding of their religion. They seek this better understanding regardless of the quality of their parish sermons and priests. In fact, when two religiously motivated groups—the fraternal activists and the parish activists—are compared, and even when age, ethnic background, college attendance, and lack of parish organizations are considered, the desire for more religious knowledge still adds six percentage points to the explanation of variance in fraternal interest.

In conclusion, about one-quarter of Catholic and former Catholic young adults feel attracted or at least neutral toward religious fraternal groups. Not coincidentally, the goals and philosophy of the Knights of Columbus. Also, these young people are more likely to have received more exposure to the Knights and more personalized forms of exposure. To increase membership, then, the solution seems to be a personal membership campaign among Catholic young people. The campaign would probably reap the highest benefits among Hispanic and minority youth who show a higher initial attraction to fraternal membership.

The decision of the young person as to what his or her style of organizational affiliation will be in the Catholic Church, if any, is likely to be a rather complicated affair. It will be influenced by a considerable number of relatively independent factors, perhaps manifesting the operation of many different levels of his or her personality and world views. However, given the mesh between the goals of the Knights of Columbus and the needs of young people, the organization should be able to appeal to youth—and appeal to them on more than one level.

Family and Fertility

Highlights

1 Contrary to popular stereotypes, the size of Catholic families today is not significantly larger than other American families.

2 The majority of young married Catholics believe that they were married at a younger age than the age they would identify as "ideal."

3 Among young Catholics, there is no trend toward living together. Marriage is still highly valued as an institution.

4 One quarter of the young Catholics indicate that they expect to have less than the ideal number of children for their family.

5 Contrary to popular stereotypes, the presence of children in a family does not lower the level of marital satisfaction.

6 Lower levels of marital satisfaction are reported by those in religiously mixed marriages and by those who belong to a minority group.

7 The experience of children with divorced parents affects their own marital satisfaction when they are older. Ten percent of the 27 to 30-year olds reported that they were already divorced.

Chapter 9

Family and Fertility

The sample used in this study is doubly interesting to demographers. They are interesting, first of all, because they are Catholics, and Catholic fertility has been of persistent demographic interest. Secondly, they are interesting because they are a particular group of Catholics, the young people born during the post-World War II baby boom. Moreover, the young adult years are an especially interesting time to study them, for it is during these years that they will be leaving their parents, completing their educations, beginning their careers, and starting their own families. Demographically and sociologically, our respondents are an important group that has been interviewed at an important time in their lives.

In the early decades of the twentieth century, Catholic fertility appears to have been consistently and significantly higher than the fertility of non-Catholics (Robinson, 1936; Stouffer, 1935). During the 1920s and the early 1940s, there appears to have been a convergence of Catholic with non-Catholic fertility (Freedman et. al., 1959). Then with the beginning of the baby boom in about 1946, Catholic fertility began once again to diverge from the non-Catholic trends. Although fertility rose for the entire population in 1950s, it rose even faster for Catholics, with an especially large differential from 1955 to 1962 (Westoff, 1979; Burch, 1966; Kirk, 1965; Westoff et. al., 1966). More recently, Catholic fertility has again declined to the generally low levels now experienced by the rest of the population. Westoff and Jones (1979) look for a continued convergence of Catholic and non-Catholic fertility. Our sample provides a group of young Catholics on whom to test the convergence hypothesis.

Within the U.S. population the effects of the baby boom have been tremendous. Because fertility dropped after the baby boom (the "baby bust"), the baby boom birth cohorts form the largest age groups in the population. This has had implications in terms of their relative resources and influences on the market and other institutions. Just as they caused overcrowded schools in the 1950s, they influenced a housing crunch in the 1970s when they began to look for their first homes. They are potentially a significant voting bloc, and eventually, they will become the largest group ever to receive Social Security benefits. Moreover, if they have a large number of children or even if they bear a few children but all within a short span of time, they may produce rapid population growth and a "baby boomlet" or "echo effect."

Because the Catholic baby boom was even larger than that of the general population, young Catholics might have an even greater impact on their Church. In 1978, when people aged 18–29 accounted for 21 percent of the U.S. population, they were 28 percent of the Catholic population (data from the 1978 General Social Survey and U.S. Census, 1979). Our sample also includes 14–17-year olds, and so it seems likely that our respondents represent about one-third of the U.S. Church. Just what their effect will be is not yet possible to judge, but it seems significant that they are the first group to have been familiar with the post-conciliar Church since their youth. They also grew up with the civil rights movement, the Vietnam War and its protests, the "sexual revolution" of the 1960s, and the women's liberation movement. All of these events may color their attitudes and perceptions. And just as the baby boom represents the potential for rapid population growth for the country as a whole, the Catholic baby boom might produce significant natural increase within the Church.

This chapter explores some of these issues by looking first at the family of origin, the family in which our respondents grew up. Next we look at "ideal" families as they describe them, and from there we turn to a description of their marriages, their expected and actual number of children, and their satisfaction with their marriages.

Family of Origin

The popular stereotype of the large Catholic family, together with the knowledge that the Catholic fertility rate did rise after World War II, suggest that our respondents might have come from larger-than-average families. And the large families, in turn, might have become their model for what a "normal" family is. If this were the case, we might expect our young Catholics to bear somewhat larger numbers of children themselves to reproduce the family conditions in which they grew up.

In fact, Catholics did not grow up with significantly more brothers and sisters than did other Americans. Table 9.1 (page 189) shows the mean number of brothers and sisters of the respondents in our sample. For majority whites (that is, white respondents who are not of Spanish origin), there are sufficiently large case bases to permit an analysis of birth cohorts. A birth cohort is made up of persons who were born in the same year or group of years and who are, thus, of approximately the same age. Comparative data are presented from the General Social Surveys (GSS) for 1972–1978 and the OCG–II data, which are based on a special questionnaire attached to the March 1973 Current Population Survey of the U.S. Census Bureau.

TABLE 9.1

Mean Number of Siblings in Family of Origin: A Comparison of Surveys[a]

Ancestry, Sex, Birth Cohorts	Catholics and Former Catholics, 1979			General Social Survey, 1972–78			OCG–II 1973	
	Mean	Standard Deviation	N	Mean	Standard Deviation	N	Mean	Standard Deviation
Majority White Males								
1948–52	3.26	2.05	121	3.03	2.77	384	3.05	2.16
1953–57	3.36	2.13	139	3.61	2.65	254		
1958–62	3.32	2.12	155					
1963–67	3.02	1.69	94					
Majority White Females								
1948–52	3.51	3.12	151	3.26	2.33	446		
1953–57	3.52	2.34	155	3.67	3.28	254		
1958–62	3.39	2.17	172	3.18	1.89	38		
1963–67	3.17	1.86	83					
Hispanic Males								
1948–57	5.21	3.18	29	6.45	4.40	20	4.94[b]	2.73[b]
1958–67	4.12	2.69	25	6.47	4.18	30		
Hispanic Females								
1948–57	5.43	2.89	31	6.10	4.16	29		
1858–67	3.82	3.20	23					
Black Males and Females								
1948–67	4.18	2.98	35	5.29	3.73	226		
Black Males								
1948–52				4.96	3.35	51	4.87	2.79

Source: OGC–II data from Hogan (1976)
[a] Categories have been collapsed where necessary to provide N ≥ 20.
[b] Refers to data from 1948–52 cohort.

As the table shows, there are no aggregate differences between Catholics and the GSS respondents in mean number of siblings with two exceptions. Black Catholics have significantly fewer siblings than all blacks (based on a t-test of difference; $p < .05$). This finding might be due to the fact that both Catholicism and lower birth rates have been associated with upward mobility among blacks. But our case base is too small to permit detailed analysis of this question. The second exception is Hispanics; for both males and females there was a significant *decline* in the mean number of siblings between the two cohorts that is not reflected in GSS data. Sibling size in the GSS is larger by more than one for Hispanic males and by .7 for females born 1948–1957. However, these differences among Hispanics must be cautiously interpreted because of the small case bases.

It is possible for fertility rates to rise and yet for the mean number of siblings to increase only modestly, as it did for majority whites between the 1948–52 and 1953–57 cohorts. This is true because changes in the fertility per woman do not ncessarily translate into similar changes in siblings per child. For example, fertility rates could rise whether childless women were having one child or whether women with seven children were having their eighth child. But these two circumstances would have different effects on the mean number of siblings in the entire population. However, as we shall see below, the number of siblings does have a modest and usually positive effect on the number of children an *individual* Catholic actually has.

About 50 percent of the sample were the eldest child in their homes, and 4 percent were only children. Another 21 percent were the younger of two or the youngest of several. And 25 percent were "middle" children. The baby boom contained a disproportionate number of first children because many women delayed bearing their first child during the Depression and war years. Most of the respondents reported that they had had happy childhoods. Over 36 percent said that they were "very happy," 52 percent were "happy," and 11 percent were "not too happy" or "not happy at all." There was a highly significant association (chi square = 67.4, V = .23) between living with both one's parents at age 14 and being happy; 39 percent of those who lived with both parents were very happy versus 21 percent of those who did not. The relationship between being happy and having parents who got along well together was even higher and significant; 61 percent of those whose parents got along were very happy. About 15 percent of the sample did not live with both parents; of this group, 58 percent lost a parent through separation or divorce, 19 percent lost a parent through death, and 8 percent were adopted or orphaned.

Ideal Family

Respondents were asked a number of questions about "ideal" aspects of families, including ideal age at marriage and ideal number of children. The ideal age at marriage for women was thought to be 24.4 years, and 26.2 years for men, and two years after the marriage was considered the ideal time for the arrival of the first baby. The ideal number of children was 2.6. For both men and women, there was a significant negative correlation between the number of ideal children and the ideal time for the first baby to arrive—that is, the higher the ideal number of children, the shorter the "ideal" interval between the marriage and the first born.

There were a number of variations in the patterns of ideal number of children. Some of these are displayed in the first column of Table 9.2 (page 191). Women's ideal number of children was slightly higher than that of men, but their ideal time for first birth came somewhat later in the marriage than did men's. A woman's actual age at marriage, although not a man's, was significantly correlated with her ideal number of children. The younger she had been when married, the more likely she is to have a large ideal number of children.

TABLE 9.2

Ideal Number of Children by Selected Attributes: A Comparison of Surveys

Attribute	Catholics and former Catholics 1979			Catholics and former Catholics* 1978 GSS			Non-Catholics* 1978 GSS		
	Mean	S.D.	N	Mean	S.D.	N	Mean	S.D.	N
Total Sample	2.62	1.00	866	2.67	0.93	127	2.52	0.98	262
Men	2.54	0.92	402	2.60	0.92	47	2.44	0.95	112
Women	2.68	1.05	464	2.71	0.93	80	2.59	1.00	150
Ethnic Group									
Majority White	2.58	0.99	732	2.63	0.91	92	2.36	0.76	141
Black	3.08	1.26	25				2.81	0.95	36
Hispanic	2.77	0.95	84						
Other	2.68	1.06	19						
Birth Cohort									
1949−52	2.46	0.85	306	2.46	0.77	48	2.41	0.85	107
1953−57	2.57	0.95	341	2.65	0.92	60	2.53	1.03	117
1958−62	2.91	1.19	219	3.25	1.10	19	2.82	1.11	38
Marital Status									
Married now	2.54	0.90	375	2.55	0.83	65	2.47	0.86	135
Once married, not married now	2.29	0.80	58				2.56	0.90	23
Single	2.74	1.09	428	2.83	1.04	54	2.59	1.13	104

* Persons aged 18 −29 in 1978 in GSS, persons aged 18 −30 in 1929 in Young Catholic Study.

There is also a pattern of variation by birth cohort. The youngest respondents have a significantly higher ideal number of children, and their ideal time for the first birth is significantly earlier than that of the oldest birth cohort. Blacks, Hispanics, and others have higher ideal family sizes than minority whites: in the case of the black/majority white comparison, the difference is statistically significant. The other notable ethnic group difference is in the timing of the first birth. Hispanics report that the first birth should come 1.75 years after the marriage, and blacks and majority whites are more likley to report that it should come a little more than two years after the marriage. About 10 percent of majority whites say that their ideal time is "whenever it comes"; Hispanics are 1 1/2 times as likely to give this response, and blacks twice as likely to give this response.

One of the most interesting aspects of the "ideal" family issues is how far many of the respondents see themselves from their ideal. Only 13 percent of the married respondents were married at the age they themselves reported as ideal or at an older age; all the others married at an age that they considered below the ideal age. About two-thirds of the sample expect to have the number of children that they say is the ideal number of children. The respondents who do not expect to have as many children as the ideal were disproportionately those who married at ages below their ideal age; 52 percent of the women who married young, compared to their own ideal, do not expect to have as many children as the ideal, versus 36 percent of the males.

Moreover, among the married respondents there is a significant association between lower marital satisfaction and expecting fewer than the ideal number of children. There is also a significant association between lower marital satisfaction and being married at less than the ideal age. Only 36 percent of the women who married earlier than their "ideal age" are "very satisfied" compared with 64 percent of the total sample; conversely, 6 percent of them are not satisfied with their marriage compared with 3.7 percent of the sample. This relationship is stronger for the women in the sample than for the men.

Columns 2 and 3 of Table 9.2 show that there are few differences between our sample and the young Catholics interviewed in the 1978 General Social Survey in terms of ideal number of children; furthermore, there are few differences between Catholics and non-Catholics. What differences there are, such as those between black Catholics and non-Catholics, are not significant. However, with the single exception of once-married Catholics, in every comparison the Catholic group has a slightly larger ideal number of children than the non-Catholic group.

The multiple regression analysis in Table 9.3 represents an attempt to predict the ideal number of children among Catholics on the basis of certain background variables. In Table 9.2 the younger respondents reported a higher mean ideal number of children; on this basis, we expect a negative coefficient for age. In general, higher education tends to be associated with lower fertility, so we also expected a negative coefficient for education. Minority status, judging from Table 9.2, has a positive influence on the number of children thought ideal. We reasoned that being happy as a child and having lots of brothers and sisters might also be positively associated with ideal family size. We hypothesized that "pro-life" attitudes would be associated with a higher ideal number of children. It was here defined as disagreement with birth control (if a family has as many children as it wants) and disagreement with abortion (if a woman has as many children as she wants). Frequency of communion was also included as a measure of general level of devotion.

The model in Table 9.3 explains about 13 percent of the variance in ideal number of children. All of the coefficients are in the expected direction. The older you are and the more education you have, the lower your ideal number of children: being a member of a minority group, having a large number of siblings, having been happy as a child, being a frequent communicant, and having pro-life attitudes are all associated with higher family sizes. The constant, 2.01, indicates a "baseline" ideal number of two children.

TABLE 9.3

Regression of Expected Number of Children on Background Variables and Attitude Variables

Variable	b	Beta
Age	−.03	−.09**
Minority group (1=yes, 0=no)	.21	.07**
No. of siblings	.01	.07**
Childhood happy	.13	.09**
Education in 1979	−.04	−.06*
Against birth control	.18	.10**
Against abortion as birth control	.29	.15**
Frequent communion	.08	.14***
Constant	2.01	
R²	.13	
N	697	

* $.05 < p \leq .10$
** $.04 < p \leq .05$
*** $p \leq .01$

Comments

The "ideal" family is not necessarily an ideal that is formed in childhood. Indeed, it may be a reaction that is formed by later unhappy experiences. Thus, it may be the case that women with unhappy marriages reason that their marriages would be happier if they had waited. Thus, their ideal age at marriage might rise as the marriage deteriorates. But a similar rationalization that would increase the ideal number of children seems unlikely; and the ideal number of children is larger for women who marry "early." It is particularly interesting that the respondents who married "too early" expect to have fewer than the ideal number of children. This might result from the poorer economic conditions often faced by younger couples who did not have a chance to earn a "nest egg" before marriage. One explanation for the large postwar Catholic baby boom was that Catholics, more than other groups, had been affected by the Depression and so could not have as many children as they would have liked. When prosperity returned after the war, their fertility boomed. In the same fashion, it appears that there may be some deferred childbearing among the young Catholics. The discrepancy between ideal number of children and expected number of children suggests the possibility of a "baby boomlet" that might be realized only with much stronger economic conditions.

Marital Status

Table 9.4 (page 195) shows the current marital status of the sample. Over 43 percent of the entire sample are married, but only 13 percent of the youngest group are married. (Questions about marital status were not asked of the 14–17-year olds in the sample.) The percentages of sample members who are widowed, divorced, separated, or living together are based on such small case bases that they might not be reliable. The data suggest that living together, either before marriage or after divorce, is not a sweeping trend among young Catholics. Since comparable national population data are based on couples under the age of 45, it is not possible to make a meaningful comparison to other young adults.

The data on mean age at marriage show the usual one-to-two-year age gap between the average bride and groom except for the very youngest group. However, because only 13 percent of this group are married, the mean age at marriage for them is not meaningful and should not be interpreted as showing a trend. Despite the fairly young age at marriage for those in our sample who are married, many others have delayed marriage. For example, The National Center for Health Statistics data show that 24 percent of all young women at age 24 are still single, versus

44 percent of our female respondents at the same age. Similarly, although 38 percent of all young men are single at age 24, 51 percent of young Catholic men are single at that age. It is interesting to note that, even for the oldest group, the ideal age at marriage is so much higher than the actual age at marriage for those of our sample who have married. The ideal age at marriage preserves an age gap between the sexes that is similar to the gap actually observed.

TABLE 9.4

Marital Status and Mean Age at Marriage, by Birth Cohorts (Percent)				
	All Cohorts (N=884)	1949–52 (N=334)	1953–57 (N=341)	1958–61 (N=229)
Marital Status				
Married	44	69	41	13
Widowed, divorced, separated[a]	5	10	4	0
Living together, never married	3	2	5	2
Living together, past married	2	3	1	0
Single	46	17	48	84
Mean Age at Marriage[b]				
Total, both sexes	20.7 (2.5)	21.2 (2.7)	20.4 (2.0)	18.5 (1.3)
Males	21.6 (2.3)	22.0 (2.3)	21.2 (1.8)	18.3 (1.9)
Females	20.2 (2.5)	20.7 (2.8)	19.8 (2.0)	18.5 (1.2)
Reported "Ideal" Age at Marriage				
For males	26.2 (9.8)	26.3 (7.7)	27.0 (12.0)	25.0 (8.8)
For females	24.4 (9.9)	24.2 (7.7)	25.3 (12.1)	20.5 (8.8)

[a] 3 widowed, 28 divorced, 17 separated.
[b] Standard deviation in percentages.

The delayed age at marriage is not attributable to a continuation of the traditional Irish custom of late marriage. About 18 percent of the sample are Irish, and 21 percent of those who are single are Irish. However, the delayed marriage does argue for continued lower fertility. Older age at marriage means that the woman has not been exposed to the risk of childbearing for so long a time as her sister who marries younger. The young Catholic who delays marriage may do so to complete an education, and we have seen both that more education and greater age are independently associated with lower ideal number of children. The woman's age at marriage, apart from her chronological age at the time of the interview, is inversely related to her ideal number of children: the older she is, the fewer children she thinks ideal.

Expected Number of Children

As we have seen, for about one-quarter of our sample the expected number of children is less than the ideal number of children. Nevertheless, our respondents expect more children than those in one national sample:

	CPS: Results	Sample of Catholics
	(Number of children expected per 1,000 women)	
Age 18–24		
All women	2,033	2,684
Majority white	2,040	2,679
Hispanics	2,196	2,818
Age 25–29		
All women	2,060	2,229
Majority white	2,021	2,191
Hispanics	2,305	2,300

*CPS: Current Population Survey published in:
Current Population Report.

There is a notable convergence among the older women; indeed, there is no difference between the samples of 25–29-year-old Hispanic women. But even the 25–29-year-old majority white, Catholic women expect an additional 170 children per thousand. Among the 18–24-year-old women, the difference for majority white Catholics amounts to 639 more children per 1,000 women.

Table 9.5 (page 197) presents additional detail on the mean number of children expected. Looking at Catholics only, we say that as with ideal number of children, women and younger respondents expected more children than men and older respondents. But there are some surprises. The ideal number of children for black Catholics was larger than that for majority whites; the expected number is smaller. The expected number of children for "other" ethnic groups was larger than the ideal number. The expected number of children for single Catholics is very close to the number for married Catholics, although the ideal number for singles had been .20 higher than that for the married.

Compared with non-Catholics from the 1978 GSS, Catholics in every category expected more children, with one exception: black Catholics expect fewer children than black non-Catholics, even though their ideal number of children is higher than that for black non-Catholics. As Table 9.1 showed, black Catholics also had fewer siblings than black non-Catholics. This is an unusual pattern that suggests that black Catholics are restricting themselves even more than other Catholics and more than other blacks from having their ideal number of children.

TABLE 9.5

Expected Number of Children by Selected Attributes: A Comparison of Surveys

Attribute	Catholics and former Catholics, 1979			Catholics and former Catholics, 1978 GSS*			Non-Catholics, 1978**		
	Mean	S.D.	N	Mean	S.D.	N	Mean	S.D.	N
Total sample	2.40	1.35	955	2.45	1.45	132	2.26	1.40	271
Men	2.34	1.26	442	2.35	1.44	49	2.19	1.32	115
Women	2.45	1.42	513	2.51	1.47	83	2.30	1.46	156
Ethnic group									
Majoity white	2.35	1.34	813	2.50	1.38	94	2.04	1.06	146
Black	2.29	1.56	28				2.67	1.39	36
Hispanic	2.66	1.08	86						
Other	3.09	2.09	22						
Birth cohort									
1949–52	2.27	1.28	341	2.26	1.41	51	2.27	1.39	111
1953–57	2.26	1.16	375	2.45	1.50	62	2.22	1.22	120
1958–62	2.79	1.62	239	2.95	1.35	19	2.32	1.89	40
Marital status									
Married now	2.41	1.15	416	2.60	1.24	68	2.41	1.25	143
Once married, not married now	2.22	1.67	65						
Single	2.42	1.53	474	2.36	1.65	55	2.06	1.55	104

* Catholics and former Catholics aged 18–20 in 1978.
** Persons who were not Catholic at the time of the interviews nor at age 16 but who were aged 18–29 in 1978.

Table 9.6 (page 198) displays the Pearson correlation coefficients for expected number of children with number of siblings, with number of children actually born, and with number of children the spouse expects. Most of these correlations are significant, indicating the continuing influence of the family of origin and the very strong influence of the spouse. For the sample as a whole, the respondents expected 2.40 children and the spouses expected 2.41.

TABLE 9.6

Mean Number of Children Expected by Selected Attributes, with Pearson Correlation Coefficients and Related Variables

Attribute (N in Parentheses)	Mean Number of Children Expected	Pearson Correlation Coefficients (r)		
		With Number of Siblings	With Number Children Born	With Number Children Spouse Expects[a]
Total Sample (893)	2.40	.14*		
Men (413)	2.34	.09*		
Women (480)	2.45	.17*		
Ethnic Group				
Majority white (813)	2.35	.12*		
Hispanics (86)	2.66	.11		
Birth Cohort				
1949–52 (341)	2.27	.21*		
1953–57 (375)	2.26	.08		
1958–62 (251)	2.79	.12*		
Marital Status				
Married now (416)	2.41	.18*	.39*	.63*
Unmarried now (539)	2.39	.12*	.10*	
Single (474)	2.42	.13*		
Ever-married men (403)	2.34	.02	.32*	.69*
Ever-married women (635)	2.38	.25*	.44*	.63*

[a] Computed only for 337 matched spouses.
* Significant at $p \leq .05$.

The correlation between expected and ideal number of children is highly significant ($r = .65$), so this suggests that similar variables affect them. Table 9.7 combines the number of siblings with the other variables used above in Table 9.3, but this time to predict expected number of children. Despite the correlations in Table 9.6, the number of siblings is not significant and neither is education, although the signs of the coefficients are in the expected direction. Compared with Table 9.3, age and attitudes toward abortion and birth control have become more important predictors of expected number of children. However, neither the model in Table 9.3, nor the one in Table 9.7 (page 199) explains much of the variance.

TABLE 9.7

Regression of Expected Number of Children on Background Variables and Attitude Variables

Variable	b	Beta
Age	−.04	−.11*
Minority group (1=yes, 0=no)	.34	.08*
No. of siblings	.01	.05
Childhood happy	.12	.06*
Education in 1979	−.03	−.04
Against birth control	.25	.11*
Against abortion as birth control	.44	.16*
Frequent communion	.03	.12*
Constant	1.88	
R²	.12	
N	764	

* Significant at .05 level or better.

Actual Number of Children

Because of the youth of our sample, and because so many of them are not yet married, most of their childbearing will be done in the future. But, there are clear ethnic group differences in fertility; majority whites report .50 children on the average, compared with .70 for blacks and .91 for Hispanics. In Table 9.8 (page 200) are three separate regression equations, one for each ethnic group, using background variables plus expected number of children as predictors. An additional background factor that was added was closeness to father, on the assumption that relationship with one's parents was an encouragment to having children, not only because of one's own positive feelings about childhood but also because the parents would like to be grandparents. (Closeness to mother was not significant.) As in the previous equations, we expected education to be negatively related to children, and closeness to father, number of siblings and expected number of children to be positively related. Age was also expected to be positively related because an older person has had more time in which to become an adult.

The equation for blacks explained about two-thirds of the variance, and that for Hispanics explained about one-half of the variance. Only one-third was explained for majority whites. But several of the variables worked in an opposite direction from that predicted. For all three groups, education had the expected negative coefficient. But, for majority whites and Hispanics, closeness to father was negatively related to the number of children and this was significant for the majority whites. Number of siblings was not significant for any group.

TABLE 9.8

Regression of Number of Children on Background Variables, by Ethnic Group

	MAJORITY WHITES		BLACKS		HISPANICS	
	b	Beta	b	Beta	b	Beta
Expected no. of children	.15	.24***	.26	.41***	.20	.19***
No. of siblings	.01	.05	−.01	−.18	.00	.05
Close to father	−.05	−.06*	−.11	−.16	.04	.04
Age in 1979	.14	.55***	−.11	.36**	.20	.67***
Education in 1979	−.15	−.30***	−.38	−.54***	−.22	−.30***
Constant	−2.84***		−1.28		−3.90***	
R²	.32		.66		.48	
N	797		27		77	
Expected no. of children	.30	.34***				
No. of siblings	.01	.06*				
Close to father	.10	−.10*				
Duration of marriage	.17	.52***				
Education in 1979	−.08	−.13***				
Constant	−.66					
R²	.45					
N	400					

*.05<p≤.10
**.01<p≤.05
***p≤.01

The second panel of Table 9.8 uses duration of marriage in place of age; this is a better proxy for exposure to pregnancy, but it cuts the sample size by eliminating those who have never been married. For the black and Hispanic groups, the sample sizes became too small to use. In this new model for majority whites, duration of marriage becomes the most important predictor and number of siblings becomes significant.

This suggests the importance not only of birth cohorts but also of marriage cohorts. Jones and Westoff (1979) analyzed cumulative fertility by marriage cohorts as part of the supporting data for their hypothesis of converging Catholic fertility. Table 9.9 presents marriage cohort data from the 1972–1978 General Social Surveys, and compares the findings with those of Jones and Westoff.

There are two important differences between Table 9.9 (page 201) and the comparable table used by Jones and Westoff. Table 9.9 uses a kind of "moving average" of marriage cohorts, while Westoff and Jones use non-overlapping marriage cohorts. The

Jones–Westoff data mask a good bit of variation in the data. If you read the first column down, for 2.5 average years of marriage duration, the numbers in parentheses (Jones and Westoff's numbers) become progressively smaller. In the "moving average" marriage cohorts, there is considerably more fluctuation. Substantial fluctuations may be noted in the other columns as well. However, the data in Table 9.9 are based on much slimmer case bases than are the Jones–Westoff data. One result is unreliability, such as that seen in the marriage cohort of 1959–63, whose cumulative fertility *declines* between 12.5 and 17.5 years (an impossibility).

TABLE 9.9

Number of Children by Marriage Cohort and Average Duration of Marriage, White Catholic Ever-Married Women, General Social Surveys, 1972–78

(Data in parentheses are from Jones and Westoff [1979] and are further limited to women married only once, and married before age 25)

Marriage Cohort	2.5	7.5	Average 12.5	Duration 17.5
1954–58				3.59
1955–59				3.59
1956–60	(1.15)	(2.82)	(3.36)	3.23 (3.57)
1957–61				2.86
1958–62				2.86
1959–63			3.38	3.12
1960–64			2.39	
1961–65	(1.06)	(2.32)	2.15 (2.86)	
1962–66			1.96	
1963–67			2.44	
1964–68		1.86	2.66	
1965–69		1.68		
1966–70	(0.92)	1.48 (2.00)	(2.86)	
1967–71		1.61		
1968–72		1.61		
1969–73	0.40			
1970–74	0.72			
1971–75	0.58 (0.62)			
1972–76	0.54			
1973–77	0.50			
1974–78	0.50			

A second difference in Table 9.9 is that it is not limited to women whose marriage was contracted before age 25. As our data show, to limit Catholic data in this way is somewhat misleading, because so many Catholics marry later than the national average. Those who marry earlier have higher ideal numbers of children. Table 9.10 shows that even for women in the same marriage cohort, those whose age is lower (and who therefore must have married earlier) have higher fertility than those who married later. It is possible, then, that Jones and Westoff have "selected" for the higher fertility Catholics by their age at marriage limitation. Perhaps the convergence of Catholic/non-Catholic fertility will proceed even more rapidly than Jones and Westoff predict because of variations in the age at marriage.

TABLE 9.10

Fertility of Young Catholic Women by Marriage Cohort and Age in 1979 (Ever-Married Women 18 Years and Older), with a Comparison to Jones & Westoff

MARRIAGE COHORT	AGE			
	All Ages	20 – 24	25 – 27	30
before 1970	2.19	—	2.16	1.88
1971 – 73	1.29	1.54	1.17	1.38
1974 – 76	0.75	0.90	0.54	1.00
1977 – 79	0.41	0.46	0.33	—

MARRIAGE COHORT	AVERAGE MARRIAGE DURATION	
	2.5 Yrs.	7.5 Yrs.
1966 – 70[a]	0.92	2.00
1971 – 75[a]	0.62	
1969 – 73	—	1.55
1974 – 79	0.60	

[a] Data from Jones and Westoff (1979) refer to ever-married white women who are Catholic. Data from the Young Catholic study include a small number of black women.

Fertility Conclusions

In looking at ideal and expected number of children, one finds little evidence of an immediate convergence of Catholic fertility except, perhaps, among the oldest women. But actual fertility data show a strong convergence, and perhaps even a stronger convergence is occurring than Jones and Westoff found. This convergence is affected by the fact that 25 percent of our respondents expect to have fewer children than their ideal. Among the women who married young, there tends to be higher ideal number of children, but many of them feel that they cannot expect this ideal for themselves. This is also true of black Catholics, whose ideal family size is 3 children, but who expect only a little over 2 children. In the case of women in particular, not having as many children as one considers ideal is associated with marital unhappiness, although it is not necessarily caused by an unhappy marriage.

In every comparison the youngest women expected more children or had higher ideal numbers of children. Those women who were already married, the youngest women actually had more children. It is possible that this is a genuine cohort effect—that is, that the younger members or the members of the Catholic baby boom have higher fertility goals than the older members. It seems more likely, however, that this is an age effect, and as these young people mature and get married, they will adopt a more "realistic" view of how many children they should have. This is an issue that cannot be resolved until the youngest members of the cohort are married.

Marital Satisfaction

If our respondents' reports about their childhoods are correct, how one's parents get along is an important determinant of childhood happiness. And so marital satisfaction is an important topic to consider not only for the sake of the spouses themselves but also in terms of the environment their children experience. Our questionnaire asked about ten areas of marital satisfaction and also asked an overall question about marital satisfaction. The questions about the ten areas of satisfaction were answered on a five item scale ranging from "poor" to "excellent." Two overall indexes of satisfaction, SAT1 and SAT2, were made by summing the scores for the first nine and the first eight areas, respectively. (The tenth area, agreement of childrearing, applied only to those married couples with children.) SAT1 and SAT2 correlated highly and positively with the answers to the overall questions about satisfaction.

Over 65 percent of the principal respondents are "very satisfied" with their marriage, compared with 72 percent of their spouses. The summary on page 204 contrasts the percentage of the "very satisfied" respondents who nevertheless rated their marriage "poor" on some areas of the relationship, with the "unsatisfied" respondents who nevertheless rated their marriage "excellent" on the specific area of the relationship.

Several things seem to be surprising. One is the surprising number of "unsatisfied" respondents who can nevertheless report that sexual fulfillment, opportunity to express love and affection, and agreement on financial issues are "excellent." For these unsatisfied spouses, emotional satisfaction (exclusive of the opportunity to express love and affection) and the ability to express disagreement without threatening the relationship are least likely to be excellent. Also surprising is that even for those who report themselves "very satisfied," there can apparently be poor agreement on religious issues without endangering the level of satisfaction. It is interesting to note that no other aspect of the relationship is so often reported "poor" by those respondents who consider themselves to be very satisfied in their marital relationship.

Aspect of relationship	Percentage of "very" satisfied who consider this aspect "poor"	Percentage of "unsatisfied" who consider this aspect "Excellent"
Ability to talk about problems with spouse	1	14
Emotional satisfaction	0	8
Confidence in stability of marriage	0	13
Agreement on financial issues	1	15
Opportunity to express love and affection	0	20
Agreement on basic values	0	17
Ability to express disagreement	1	10
Agreement on religious values	6	11
Agreement on how to raise children	0	11

Table 9.11 (page 205) shows the percentage of "very satisfied" respondents by a variety of variables. Male respondents tend to be more satisfied than female respondents, and majority white respondents more than Hispanics or other minority groups. Marriages in which both spouses have the same

religion—whether that religion is Catholic or not—appear to have higher levels of satisfaction than mixed marriages. There is, however, still a high level of satisfaction in mixed marriages in which our principal respondent is Catholic. For other forms of mixed marriages, the case bases are too small to be relied on.

TABLE 9.11

Percentage of Respondents "Very Satisfied" with Marriage, by Selected Attributes with N on Which Percentage Is Based

Selected Attributes	Percent	N
Total Sample	65.4	407
Male	72	155
Female	61	252
Majority white	67	356
Hispanic	60	35
Other minority	47	15
Current Religion		
Both Catholic	68	207
Both, non-Catholic	67	61
Mixed	61	137
R Catholic	64	114
R not Catholic	48	23
Not same as spouse,		
R not Catholic	33	6
R not Catholic		
same as spouse	53	17
Married by Priest		
Yes	70	250
No	59	149
Age Cohort		
1949–2	64	221
1953–57	64	153
1958–61	79	33
Duration of Marriage		
(For First Marriages)		
1–2 years	76	79
3–4 years	68	71
5–6 years	63	68
7+ years	63	149
Presence of Children		
R has none	65	172
R has children	66	234

Respondents married by a priest are more likely to report that they are "very satisfied." Several reasons could be offered for this. One that could be cited is that being married in the Church is less likely to involve conflict with the family of origin and may represent an integration of several areas of the respondent's life. Satisfaction tends to be highest among the newly-wed and among the youngest birth cohort—there is, of course, considerable overlap between these two groups.

Contrary to evidence in some of the recent literature on marital satisfaction, the presence of children does not seem to lower the satisfaction of our respondents. In fact, the satisfaction of respondents with children is marginally (not significantly) higher than that of respondents without children.

TABLE 9.12

Percentage of Couples with Both Spouses "Very Satisfied" With Marriage, by Selected Attributes

Selected Attributes	Percent	N
Sample	53	314
Marriage Duration		
1−3 years	62	107
4−5 years	53	49
6−7 years	53	68
8+ years	57	62
Race of R		
Majority white	60	277
Hispanic	35	26
Other minority	40	10
Religious Orientation		
Not mixed	60	209
Mixed	54	84
Number of Own Children (No Stepchildren)		
None	61	121
One	55	75
Two	59	63
Three-plus	55	20
Stepchildren		
None	58	279
Some	44	34
Previous Marriages		
None	60	242
Spouse divorced	46	39
R divorced	42	12
Both divorced	50	14

Table 9.12 presents similar data, except that the data are the percentage of marriages in which both spouses agree that they are "very satisfied." This is a little over half of the entire sample. Some findings of Table 9.11 confirmed: joint marital satisfaction

tends to be lower for minority groups and for religiously mixed marriages, and it tends to decline with the duration of the marriage, although the joint satisfaction measure rises again for those married eight or more years.

There are some important modifications to the findings from Table 9.11 well. The first concerns the presence of children. Unlike the measure reported in Table 9.11, joint marital satisfaction declines a bit for those with one or three children, compared with those with no children (although it is still above the mean). But there is a pronounced decline in joint satisfaction for those couples in which either the husband or the wife has children by a previous marriage.

The issue of stepchildren may be related to the depressing effect that previous marriages have on joint satisfaction in the current marriage. Where either the respondent or the spouse has been previously divorced, the joint satisfaction is quite low. (Here again the reader should be warned that some case bases are very small.)

Multiple regression enables us to "predict" statistically the value that a person or couple will have for a given variable. The variables predicted will be satisfaction scores—SAT1 and SAT2, discussed above, and JTSAT1 and JTSAT2. JTSAT1 is the sum of the responses of both husband and wife on the five-point scale for aspects 1−9 of their marital relationship (see the listing of the aspects above). JTSAT2 is the same kind of scale, but it includes only aspects 1−8. Table 9.13 presents four regression equations. None of the sets of predictive variables is very "good" in the sense of explaining a great deal of the variance. The values of r^2 indicate that only 5 to 8 percent of the variance is being explained.

Considering the relative unimportance of agreement of religious values to the very satisfied, it is surprising to find how important mixed marriages are in explaining SAT1 and JTSAT1. For the individual respondent, a mixed marriage subtracts 2.3 points from the satisfaction score; for the couple, it subtracts .05. But the scale being used here includes agreement on religious values as one aspect of the relationship. The other two variables, SAT2 and JTSAT2, eliminate this variable. When this is done, we see that a mixed marriage subtracts only 1.6 points from the individual's satisfaction score, although it still subtracts .05 points from the couple's score.

A higher score, it should be recalled, means more satisfaction. Being in a mixed marriage, being a member of a minority group (or having either partner in the marriage a member of a minority group), a previous divorce by either the respondent or the spouse, and older age and marriage duration are all associated with lower scores. For SAT1, 2.5 points are subtracted from one's score by being a member of a minority group; 2.2 points are subtracted for being previously divorced; and 1 point is subtracted for every five years of additional age. On the other hand, additional levels of education for the spouse and for the respondent raise the satisfaction score. The more educated you are, the more satisfied you are likely to be.

TABLE 9.13

Regression Equations for Predicting Marital Satisfaction for Married Catholics

INDEPENDENT VARIABLES	B	B
	SAT2	JTSAT1
Mixed marriage	−2.27**	− .05*
Race[a]	−2.46**	−3.89*
Education—Spouse		+1.41**
Marriage duration		− .53*
Education—R	+0.57*	
Divorce—R	−2.24*	
Age—R	−0.22	
(Constant)	14.05**	39.47**
R	.24	.26
R^2	.06	.07
F	4.12**	4.92**
N	347	267

	SAT2	JTSAT2
Mixed marriage	−1.56**	−.047*
Age—R	−0.24*	
Race[a]	−2.22**	−3.07
Divorce—R	−2.37*	
Education—R	+0.50**	
Divorce—JT		−6.05*
Education—Spouse		+1.26**
Marriage duration		−0.56**
(Constant)	10.84**	33.48**
R	.23	.28
R^2	.05	.08
F	3.78**	4.41**
N	342	267

[a] For joint satisfaction variables, a dummy variable = 0 if both spouses are Majority white.
* Significant $.10 < p < .05$
** Significant $p < .05$

The equations in Table 9.13 do not "explain" or predict satisfaction scores very well. It appears that many things matter a little in marital satisfaction and nothing matters a lot. But Table 9.14 presents an equation that explains a good deal of the variance in satisfaction scores—40 percent for SAT1 and 39 percent for SAT2. The population used in Table 9.14 are those respondents who did not grow up with both parents.

TABLE 9.14

**Predicting Marital Satisfaction for Married Catholics
Who Did Not Grow up With Both Parents Present**

VARIABLE	SAT1		SAT2
	B		B
Parents divorced	−3.63		−3.45*
Divorce—R	−6.79**		−6.40**
Mixed marriage	−7.30**		−6.41**
Expected children	−1.92**		−1.67**
Current level of education—R	+1.90**		+1.57**
(Constant)	16.30	21.03**	13.46
R	.63		.62
R²	.40		.39
F	6.00**		5.76**
N	51		51

** $p < .05$
* $.10 < p < .05$

As we saw earlier, 58 percent of these respondents had parents who were divorced. The divorce of parents, their own previous history of divorce, and the existence of a mixed marriage were all highly significant in increasing dissatisfaction. Parents' divorce subtracted 3.6 points, one's own divorce subtracted 6.8 points, and a mixed marriage subtracted 7.3 points. Every additional child expected subtracted 2 points, and this is an exception to the previous comment that number of children does not appear to affect marital satisfaction. For this group as well as for the larger group of respondents, level of education served to raise the satisfaction scores—that is, to increase the levels of satisfaction. Every additional level of education raised the satisfaction score by 2 points.

Summary

The data discussed in this chapter show that, in general, young Catholics look back on fairly happy childhoods in which they had about as many siblings as other children their age. They are marrying at slightly later ages than other Americans, and there is no pronounced trend toward living together instead of marrying. They expect more children than other Americans their age report expecting. Over 60 percent are "very satisfied" with their marriage, with higher education and religiously homogeneous marriages associated with higher levels of marital satisfaction. One is tempted to say that this is a group of young people that likes children, that does not see children as lowering the level of satisfaction in their marriage, and that finds considerable emotional satisfaction and sexual fulfillment in marriage. On the other hand, the pervasive effects of divorce must also be noted—on the children as they grow up, on the current satisfaction of the once-divorced, and through the effects of parental divorce on the marriage satisfaction of the young Catholics. The fact that almost 10 percent of the 27 to 30-year olds in the sample are already divorced must be a matter of some concern.

TABLE 9.15

Mean Number of Siblings: Canada			
Ancestry, Sex, Birth Cohorts	Mean	Standard Deviation	N
French Males			
1948−52	5.16	3.74	44
1953−57	4.41	2.90	64
1958−62	3.38	2.90	63
1963−67	2.42	2.79	38
French Females			
1948−52	5.67	4.01	60
1953−57	4.89	3.01	79
1958−62	3.94	3.10	84
1963−67	2.77	2.42	65
Other Males			
1948−57	4.17	2.99	46
1958−67	2.69	1.73	51
Other Females			
1948−57	4.90	3.57	58
1958−62	3.27	2.50	62
Number of siblings by "other" mother tongue			
English	3.93		
Italian	3.30		
Other	3.85		

TABLE 9.16

Mean Number of Children Expected by Selected Attributes, with Pearson Correlation Coefficients and Related Variables: Canada

ATTRIBUTE (N IN PARENTHESES)	MEAN NUMBER OF CHILDREN EXPECTED	PEARSON CORRELATION COEFFICIENTS (R)	
		With Number of Siblings	With Number Children Born
Total Sample (514)	2.40	.11*	
Men (216)	2.34	.15*	
Women (216)	2.43	.08	
Ethnic Group			
French (339)	2.30	.06	
Other (170)	2.61	.22*	
Birth Cohort			
1949–52 (148)	2.23	.13	
1953–57 (206)	2.27	.22*	
1958–62 (157)	2.74	.11	
Marital Status			
Married no(216)	2.42	.21*	.07
Unmarried now (301)	2.38	.06	.08
Single (248)	2.40	.06	
Ever-married men (82)	2.23	.29*	−.05
Ever-married women (155)	2.44	.17*	.33*

* Significant at $p \leq .05$

Canadian Data

Table 9.15 (page 210) shows a quite remarkable drop in sibship size from the oldest cohort to the youngest one. This appears to have been a part of a general decline in Catholic fertility in Canada, one shared by French and others as well. Among the non-French speakers, the Italian speakers have the lowest sibship sizes, possibly because they are recent immigrants and are urbanized.

Table 9.16 (page 211) indicates that fertility among Canadian Catholics is likely to remain low. Although French-Canadian fertility was historically higher than that of English Canadians, among Catholics the expected French fertility is lower. The pattern of expectation is similar to that in the United States, and the levels of fertility are strikingly similar. However, the correlation with number of siblings is significant for fewer demographic groups—a finding that might be expected, given the apparently rapid decline in Catholic fertility. The insignificant correlation coefficients with number of children actually born suggests that some Catholic fertility in Canada will be delayed, just as it has been in the United States.

A Note on Data Quality

Table 9.17 presents the percentage distribution of our sample and of the United States population aged 14–29 as estimated for July 1, 1978. The differences between these two distributions may be due to three influences. First, they may be due to sampling error or response bias. For example, the small number of 14-year olds in the sample probably reflects the fact that by chance, fewer 14-year olds were located for the sample; or it may indicate that 14-year olds were somewhat less likely than other age groups to complete the questionnaire. Second, some difference is due to the aging of the population between July 1, the date to which the percentages in column 2 refer, and Spring of 1979, when our data were collected. Third, the data may reflect genuine differences between the two populations. Because we know that Catholics had higher fertility during the baby boom we may expect somewhat larger proportions of younger Catholics than in the population as a whole; and that is, indeed, what we find.

TABLE 9.17

Age of the Sample of Young Catholics Compared with
U.S. National Population Estimate
(Percent)

Age	Catholics and Former Catholics	U.S. Population July 1, 1978
Total aged 14–30	100.0	100.0
N	1398	
14	1.9	6.0
15	7.2	6.1
16	7.9	6.2
17	6.9	6.3
18	6.9	6.2
19	5.9	6.3
20	5.3	6.4
21	5.0	6.2
22	4.7	5.9
23	4.7	5.7
24	7.1	5.8
25	5.6	5.6
26	5.7	5.4
27	6.4	5.3
28	7.0	5.1
29	6.6	5.1
30	5.1	5.4

Source: U.S. Census, 1979: 1.

Religion and Politics

Highlights

1   *A person's religious behavior and practices point to either a liberal or conservative approach to politics, rather than to a particular political party.*

2   *Those young Catholics who feel a sense of closeness to God and who hold an orthodox position on religious doctrine are slightly more likely to identify with the Democratic Party.*

3   *In their attitudes towards Jews and Blacks, those young Catholics who are religious show more tolerance to both groups. This is in contrast to earlier studies of the general Catholic population.*

4   *Those young Catholics who report mystical experiences are more likely to engage in all kinds of political activity, except voting.*

5   *Young Catholics who score high on a Progressivism scale are more liberal on political and Church issues.*

6   *When young Catholics score high on a Traditional scale, they also had a more conservative stance on secular and political matters.*

Chapter 10

Religion and Politics

The relationship between religion and politics remains a lightly studied phenomenon. Those studies which do exist (e.g., Verba and Nie, 1972; Knoke, 1974; Greeley, 1974; Hanna, 1979) mostly relate religious denomination, and occasionally amount of church attendance, to political variables. The assumption seems to be that religious denominations represent different subcultures within the U.S. population (see Davis, 1979). Church attendance may represent a degree of involvement in a particular subculture. These subcultures, because of their differing histories, social patterns, and needs might seek different things from the political system.

Although little is known about the actual connections between religious and political beliefs, there are a number of possibilities:

1. Religious and political beliefs may not be connected. Religion may represent a spurious correlate with political attitudes, standing for a collection of other variables. For example, in the U.S., Catholicism is linked to certain later-arriving ethnic groups, to certain educational patterns, and to certain historical experiences, which may relate to attitudes and behavior. Catholics may identify with the Democratic Party, for example, not because they are Catholic, but because they generally arrived later to this country than Protestants, and the Democratic Party made an effort to attract new immigrants. (Indeed, this is partially the case. See Fee, 1976.)

2. Religious and political beliefs may relate only occasionally when the two meet in direct, policy-oriented ways. For example, a Catholic priest might suggest support for certain political candidates who oppose abortion. A politician might profess to a Jewish audience his positive attitude toward the State of Israel. Or, as in 1960, a candidate's religion might become a campaign issue. (Converse, 1966, documented the added support that John Kennedy received from fellow Catholics in 1960 and the support that his religion lost for him from non-Catholic Democrats.)

3. Alternatively, religion may represent for people a particular meaning system by which they guide their lives. Religious and political attitudes may relate to each other because they compose different components of an integrated, ongoing philosophy. Wuthnow (1976) has made a pioneering effort in relating systems to attitudes toward social experimentation. His meaning-systems are an attempt to define the guiding force in a person's life—whether it be God, social science, individualism, or mysticism.

Two questions, thus, arise:
1. To what degree are religion and politics related?
2. When we say that religion and politics are related, what aspect of religion is being considered—religion as an ascriptive denomination, religion as a belief system, or religion as a social system?

This chapter seeks to shed light on the two questions by examining within one particular denomination how religion relates to political views. By restricting analysis to a single denomination (or subculture), we reduce the chances of religion representing a spurious correlate. By further restricting the analysis to one age group (18 to 29 year olds), the chapter concerns itself with people who have the same historical experience and who should roughly represent the same stages of religious and political development.

As shown in Chapter One, there is considerable variation within the young Catholic population in the intensity with which they practice and profess various dimensions of their religion—church going and parish involvement, doctrinal orthodoxy, sexual orthodoxy, their personal relationship to God, and mystical experience. Furthermore, Catholics vary in the policy directions which they wish their Church to take. This chapter studies the relationship between these different dimensions of religion and three sorts of political items:
1. the respondent's political label (his/her party identification and self-perception as a liberal or conservative)
2. the respondent's stand on a number of issues
3. the degree to which the respondent participates in the political world.

Religion and Political Labels

American Catholics continue differentially to identify as Democrats. (Greeley, 1977; Fee, 1976; Hanna, 1979). There have been conflicting findings on the relationship between regular church attendance among Catholics and likelihood to assume a Democratic party identification (Lenski, 1961: Knoke, 1974). In addition, regular church attenders of all denominations are known for their conservatism (Stouffer, 1955). The analysis will test whether or not, among young people, the more religious Catholics tend toward Democratic identification and toward conservatism. If so, the analysis will reveal which *aspects* of religiosity are linked to political self-perceptions.

Table 10.1 depicts the relationship between two political labels—party identification and self-perception as a liberal or conservative—and different dimensions of religiosity. The religiosity dimensions are those developed in Chapter One. There is also a general religiosity variable which represents the sum of the respondents' scores across dimensions. Both political party and liberalism/conservatism are arrayed on seven-point scales. The liberal/conservative dimension ranges from extreme liberal through moderates to extreme conservatives. The party continuum begins with strong Republicans through Independents to strong Democrats.

TABLE 10.1

The Relationship Between Various Dimensions of Religiosity and Political Labels Among Young Adults

	General religiosity	Ritual/Parish	Sexual morality	Doctrinal views	Personal relationship with God	Mystical experience
Political Party (High = Democratic)	.07	−.03	−.02	.10*	.08*	−.01
Liberalism/Conservatism (High = Conservatism)	.20*	.32*	.26*	.15*	.11*	−.00

* Significant at .05 level or lower.

The table reveals that among Catholics all dimensions of religiosity, except mystical experience, are more closely aligned to self-definition as a liberal or conservative than they are to choice of party. Those who feel they are more religious—in the sense of regular church attendance, a close personal relationship to God, and orthodox views on sexual and doctrinal issues—are more likely to perceive themselves as conservative than are the less religious of their generation. Involvement in church and parish and views on sexual issues best predict liberal/conservative bent.

The only two qualities which predict a more Democratic party affiliation are the young adult's sense of personal relationship to God and his or her doctrinal orthodoxy. Among young Catholics, those who feel closer to God and who take orthodox positions on doctrine are slightly more likely to hold a Democratic Party identification. The fact that religiosity and party identification are not strongly related among young Catholics supports the view that a Democratic identification seems more closely tied to ethnicity and historical experience among Catholics than to religion as a philosophy (see Lipset, 1964; Fee, 1976). It should be noted, however, that Greeley in Chapter Five finds a life cycle effect among young Catholics concerning party identification. When young adults at the end of their 20s begin to become more religious, they also show signs of becoming more Democrat in party affiliation.

Attitudes and Religiosity

Stouffer (1955) made one of the first attempts to link religiosity and attitudes by studying the varying amounts of tolerance of non-conformists shown by regular church attenders versus less regular attenders. Perhaps surprisingly, he found that those who attended church more regularly showed less tolerance than the less frequent attenders or the non-attenders. Hanna (1979) duplicated Stouffer's results in the Catholic population with both 1950 and 1970 data, but found that among Catholics the differences between frequent and non-frequent attenders diminshed over the two decades and in neither decade equalled the Protestant differences between attenders. However, in the area of racial issues, Hanna discovered that frequent Protestant church attenders showed less prejudice, whereas frequent Catholic attenders showed more or an equal amount of prejudice than less frequent Catholic attenders. On the question of abortion, Hanna noted that the more frequent Catholic attenders were more likely to favor the Church's position—opposing legalized abortion.

The Young Catholics Study data allows comparisons to be made of the attitudes not only of frequent and infrequent church attenders but also of those who espouse orthodox church doctrine, those who do not, those who feel close to God, those who feel less close, the mystics, the non-mystics. Although the Stouffer non-conformist items were not replicated here, there are discrimination items concerning blacks and Jews, attitudes toward aiding the poor, feminist attitudes, and attitudes toward abortion.

Table 10.2 (page 221) reports the correlations between the religious dimensions and social attitudes. A glance at the summary religiosity measure indicates that the more religious Catholics are generally more likely to support the Church's view—to oppose abortion, but to favor aid to the poor and to hold a positive attitude toward blacks and Jews. Religious Catholics also hold a traditional view of motherhood, believing that a pre-school child will suffer emotional damage if the child's mother works. Religiosity exerts the strongest impact on the issue of abortion, with which every dimension of religiosity correlates. Although religiosity correlates both with the issue of abortion when the fetus may have a serious defect and abortion on demand, it correlates most strongly with the more extreme abortion on demand issue. Next to abortion, religiosity correlates most strongly with the idea that those who have a hard time making ends meet still have a responsibility for aiding the poor.

TABLE 10.2

The Relationship Between Various Dimensions of Religiosity and Attitudes On Issues Among Young Adults

(Coefficient = Pearson's r)

	General religiosity	Ritual/ Parish	Sexual morality	Doctrinal views	Personal relationship with God	Mystical experience
Abortion,[a] serious defect	.29*	.20*	.28*	.10*	.21*	.11*
Abortion, wants no children	.41*	.34*	.36*	.25*	.28*	.08*
Whites have right to keep blacks out of neighborhood	.07*	.04	.05	.03	.01	.04
Blacks shouldn't push where not wanted	.10*	.08*	.04	.00	.02	.07*
Obligation to work for end of racial segregation	.09*	.04	.04	−.03	.04	.16*
Jews have too much power in U.S.	.11*	.10*	.07*	.00	−.00	.00
Jewish businessmen as honest as others	.10*	.07*	.09*	−.06*	.02	.05
Pre-school child likely to suffer emotional damage if mother works	.09*	.07*	.17*	.08*	.10*	.01
Even though person has hard time making ends meet, should aid poor	.26*	.13*	.16*	.12*	.21*	.19*
Good Christian ought to think about next life and not worry about fighting poverty and injustice	.03	−.03	.05	.10*	.07*	.03

* Significant at .05 or lower.
[a] The issue answers are coded so that a high response reflects the Church's position—anti-abortion, pro-racial justice and human rights. Although the Church's stand on feminism is unclear, it appears to take more of a traditional than non-traditional stance. A high response represents a traditional attitude.

For the discrimination question, the more religious Catholic adults show slightly more tolerance toward both Jews and blacks than the less religious. (However, one religious dimension, doctrinal orthodoxy, shows a small but significant correlation with lack of tolerance to Jews.) This trend contradicts that found by Hanna, who found the opposite when she used just church attendance as a measure of religiosity.

Participation and Religiosity

There is the notion that more religious people are, especially Catholics, the more they are concerned with the next world than with this world and, thus, would be less likely to participate in politics. Wuthnow (1978) outlines in detail the theories which argue for and against the idea that *mysticism*, certainly an aspect of the Catholic religion, is linked to reduced political activity. Weber and Troeltsch, he notes, point to mysticism's inner-worldly orientation, its "acosmic love," its privacy, its intimacy, its quest of ultimate meaning, and its need for peace rather than violence, as reasons for its apolitical nature. Other scholars, he asserts, take an opposite view and link mysticism with political action because of the mystic's need for tolerance and liberalism—his or her concern with building a better society. Whereas Wuthnow studied the relationship between political action and mysticism in the general population, here we examine the link between different dimensions of Catholicism and political activity, taking special note of the mysticism dimension.

Table 10.3 (page 223) notes the connection between religiosity and 1) interest in politics, 2) having participated in six different sorts of political activities, and 3) a summary measure, having participated in *any* of the six listed types of political activity. As can be seen from the summary religiosity and political participation measures, among young Catholic adults, religiosity is related to an increased likelihood of participation. More dramatic, however, is the consistent relationship of mysticism to all political acts except voting. Those who have felt close to a powerful spiritual force that seemed to lift them out of themselves, have sensed that their life has a purpose beyond the limitations of their present existence, have felt in direct contact with "the Sacred" or "the Holy," are consistently more likely to have participated in politics. If these characteristics can be viewed as an interest in "other worldliness," it appears that those most directly touched by other worlds also take more interest in the world in which they live. This mysticism finding confirms for the young Catholic population Wuthnow's results for the general American population.

In terms of specific political acts, religiosity most strongly relates to having canvassed, distributed leaflets, or collected signatures for petitions in support of a cause. Generally, however, religiosity shows a weak but persistent relationship to the political activity of young Catholics.

TABLE 10.3

The Relationship Between Dimensions of Religiosity and Political Participation Among Catholic Young Adults
(Coefficient = Pearson's r)

	General Religiosity	Ritual/ Parish	Sexual morality	Doctrinal views	Personal relationship with God	Mystical experience
Any participation	.12*	12*	.00	.03	.01	.08*
Voted	.06*	.09*	.00	.04	−.02	.10
Contributed money	.02	−.01	−.00	.00	−.05*	.06*
Attended meetings or rallies	.00	.01	−.02	−.03	−.7*	.12*
Campaigned	.07*	.05	.03	.02	−.04	.13*
Canvassed, leafleted, distributed petitions	.12*	.09*	.06*	−.04	.00	.16*
Contacted public official	.03	.02	.01	−.05	−.02	.15*
General interest in politics	−.03	.01	−.06*	−.04	−.05	.14*

* Significant at .05 level or lower.

Religious and Political Styles

Ten different Church policy issues, ranging from the need to impose more order and discipline on the Church to the need for women priests, were entered into the analysis. The respondents had rated each of these issues on a scale of 1 to 4 according to their importance. Table 10.4 (page 224) summarizes the results of the analysis.

When a principal axis factor analysis had been followed by a varimax rotation, three orthogonal (unrelated) factors emerged—a Progressive factor, a Traditional factor, and a Clerical Change factor. The Progressive factor stresses the need for better leadership, a more democratic church structure, improved sermon quality. To a lesser extent, it emphasizes involving the Church less in secular politics, bringing the birth control and divorce teachings more in line with current social practice, and involving the Church more in social action. The Traditional factor stresses returning to Friday abstinence and to more traditional worship, and the need to impose more order and discipline on the Church. The Clerical Change factor consists of attitude toward the possibility of female priests and toward allowing married priests.

TABLE 10.4

Three Policy-Related Factors, Factor Loadings*

Progressives	
Improve quality of leadership	.74
Structure more democratic, more lay input	.55
Improve quality of sermons	.53
Involve Church less in secular politics	.42
Bring birth control and divorce teachings in line with social practice	.42
Involve Church more in social action, e.g. integration, human rights	.36
Clerical Change	
Allow women to become priests	.73
Allow priests to marry	.57
Traditionals	
Return to Friday abstinence	.75
Impose more order and discipline	.68
Return to more traditional worship, e.g. Latin mass	.50

*Rotated Factors

Perhaps most interesting is the structure of the factors. Rather than constituting a single dimension which represents Traditionalism/Progressivism, the policy attitudes occupy three distinct dimensions. This means that those young Catholics who are progressive are not necessarily anti-traditional concerning worship, and vice versa. It also means that, among Catholic young adults, opinions on the importance of permitting female or married priests are not systematically related to a person's general progressive or traditional orientation to other issues.

Having noted the three different factors which characterize political styles on Church policy, in Table 10.5 (page 225) we compare them to political self-perceptions and attitudes on issues. A person's score on Progressivism most consistently predicts political self-perceptions and attitudes. A high score on Progressivism is linked to slightly higher than average political

interest, a slightly greater likelihood to consider oneself a
Democrat and perceiving of oneself as more liberal than the
average Catholic young adult. In terms of issues, those who
advocate a progressive policy stance for the Church also favor
working to end segregation, fighting poverty and injustice in this
life, and are slightly more likely to favor aiding the poor than is the
average Catholic young adult. They express a bit less prejudice
toward Jews and are slightly less likely to oppose abortion on
demand than is the average Catholic young adult. Finally, they
are probably a bit more likely to take a feminist stand than is the
average young Catholic. This issue was of borderline statistical
significance.

TABLE 10.5

**Relationship Between Views on Church Policy and Political
Self Perception and Views on Selected Issues**
(Coefficient = Pearson's r)

	Progressive	Traditional	Clerical Change
Political Self-Perception			
Political Interest	.07*	−10*	.08*
Party (High-Democrat)	.06*	.04	.00
Liberalism/Conservatism			
(Liberalism High)	.17*	−.20*	.19*
Issues [a]			
Abortion, want no more			
children	−.10*	.22*	−.24*
Individual obligation to aid			
poor	.06*	.14*	−.02
Obligation to work to end			
segregation	.18	−.04	.14*
Fight poverty and injustice	.13*	−.13*	.11*
Jewish businessmen as			
honest as others	.11*	−.13*	.05
Preschool child suffers			
emotional damage if			
mother works	−.05	.19*	−.12*

[a] A high score equals acceptance of the Church's stand—anti-abortion, anti-discrimination,
pro-human rights. As in Table 2, a high score on the feminist item represents a traditional view.
* Significant at .05 level or lower.

Traditionalism significantly predicts all political characteristics
except political party and views on integration. In contrast to those
who score high on progressivism, the traditionalists show less
political interest than the average Catholic young adult and are
more likely to perceive themselves as politically conservative.

225

They show more prejudice toward Jews and are less likely to favor fighting poverty and injustice in this life. They are even more likely than the Progressives to favor aiding the poor, but are much less likely to condone abortion on demand, or the mother of a young child working.

The Clerical Change factor least effectively predicts political views, since knowing people's score on clerical change will not offer clues to their political party or their attitude toward Jews or aiding the poor. Where clerical change is linked to political views, it shows the same pattern as Progressivism. However, those who score high on clerical change are more likely than those who score high on progressivism to oppose the Church's stand on abortion and to believe that a mother's working will not emotionally injure her young child. That feminist issue stances accompanying the Clerical Change factor is not surprising since many advocates of clerical change support the ordination of female priests.

Summary and Conclusions

The findings of this chapter can be summarized as follows:

1. There are persistent low to moderate correlations between religiosity and political views even when age and religious denomination are controlled.
2. The more religious Catholic young adults across four dimensions—church attendance and parish involvement, sense of personal relationship to God, sexual and doctrinal orthodoxy—are more likely to perceive themselves as politically conservative than is the average young adult in the group.
3. Among Catholic young adults, religiosity and party identification are not closely related.
4. Religiosity correlates with opposition to legalized abortion, with a reduced likelihood of prejudice against Jews and blacks, and with a sense of responsibility for aiding the poor. However, all dimensions of religiosity correlate most strongly with the abortion items.
5. Among Catholic young adults, religiosity correlates with increased political participation. The religious dimension which most consistently predicts political participation is mystical experience.
6. When attitudes toward Church policy are analyzed, three styles emerge: a Progressive style, a Traditional style, and a Clerical Change style which favors changes in the priesthood.
7. Although a person's scores on Church progressivism best predict political label and attitudes on issues, a high score on any of the styles carries with it certain political expectations—the Progressives and Clerical Change types taking more liberal views on issues, the Traditional types espousing more conservative

positions. The advocates of Clerical Change differ from the Progressives in their stronger stand on feminist issues.

In conclusion, the analysis contained within this chapter points to a relationship between religiosity and politics. The relationship is a low to moderate one. Having controlled for religious denomination and age, of course, has substantially reduced the within-population variance and would reduce the size of the correlations.

Although religiosity achieves its highest potential as a predictor of political views when a summary score across religious dimensions is used as the predictive variable, the Ritual/Parish dimension is not a bad substitute for the summary measure. In other words, when a researcher has access to only limited information on religiosity, church attendance *can* serve as a good rough and ready substitute for religiosity (at least among young Catholics, and most probably among Catholics generally).

Although church attendance serves as a fair substitute for general religiosity, it cannot rival mystical experience as a consistent predictor of political interest and participation. Besides its success with political activity, mystical experience is also about the only dimension of religiosity which aids in predicting attitudes toward blacks.

Thus, two dimensions of religiosity which best predict political attitudes and behavior are mainly "action" dimensions. The Ritual/Parish dimension consists of Mass attendance, communion reception, participation in parish activities and a sense of closeness to the parish. The mystical experience dimension consists of having out of body experiences, sensing a purpose beyond present experience, and feeling in direct contact with "the Sacred" or "Holy." These two dimensions correlate stronger with both political activity and attitudes than do doctrinal beliefs, sexual attitudes, or a person feeling that there is a personal relationship with God.

The linking of religious activity with political attitudes and behavior and also the linking of religious style (in the Catholic case—Progressive, Traditional, and Clerical Change) with political style both suggest a real connection between religious and political behavior. Yet, as this chapter is written, a national study has yet to be done of the connection between the political and religious behavior of Americans. The field remains a ripe one for inquiry.

Chapter 11

Implications and Policy Recommendations Based on the Findings

This volume has been written by a number of different authors, each bringing to his or her assigned topic his or her own particular skills and analytic techniques. We have not sought to homogenize the perspectives or the approaches of the different authors because we believe that this would diminish the richness of the book. In this chapter one of the authors has been mandated by the Principal Investigator to summarize the findings, discuss the implications, and offer policy recommendations. The statement of the findings has been checked with the other writers whose findings are summarized. The commentary on implications and the recommendations are the responsibility of the author of this chapter.

Commentary and recommendations are necessarily tentative because they represent interpretative exercises which go beyond the data themselves. Different social scientists might find other implications and make different recommendations. No policy recommendation can ever be *proven* by sociological analysis. The best that one can say is that the recommendation seems to follow more or less clearly from the data.

Findings

The following are the principal findings of this report:

1. Young Catholics do not accept many of the formal doctrinal propositions of the Church, nor most of its sexual teachings. The majority of them do not go to church every week, and some have left the Church.

2. The factors which affect their religious behavior are, however, parallel to those which affect the religious behavior of older Catholics. The most important dynamisms at work are the religiousness of the spouse (if a young person is married) and the

229

strength and effectiveness of the local parish community, especially the local parish priest, and especially, the quality of his preaching. One's spouse and one's priest are the major religious influences in the life of the young married adult.

3. Whatever is to be said about their doctrinal and ethical convictions, the religious imagination of young Catholics is still powerfully and profoundly Catholic, and its importance should not be underestimated. It is a more important force for the continuation of personal prayer, social commitment, world view, and marital adjustment than is doctrinal orthodoxy.

4. Furthermore, there is a tendency for those who have drifted away from regular religious practice in their early and middle 20s to drift back again during their late 20s. The drift away is a part of a general alienation from all social institutions, and the drift back is part of a reintegration which occurs at the time of marriage.

5. The return is especially likely to occur among those who are happily married to other Catholics and who share warm religious images and a sexually fulfilling marriage with such spouses.

6. Catholic schools continue to be more important to the work of the Church than they were during the pre-conciliar years. Their major effectiveness seems to consist in the closer integration of a young person into the Catholic community. Those who have had Catholic education are especially likely to return to the Church toward the end of their 20s.

7. The Church is doing a moderately effective job of reaching a high proportion of its grammar school population with some kind of religious education. It is much less successful with its high school population, but there is little reason to think that such success is possible for the salient factors are beyond the control of the educational institutions.

8. Other than the spouse (for those who are married), the next most important influences on the religious behavior of young Catholics are the quality of preaching they hear and the pastoral empathy expressed by priests they know. Even so, the clergy still get very poor grades from young people on the quality of their ministerial skills.

9. The strength of the Mary image is enormous. It not only persists, but it also has a powerful impact on young people's lives, however "preconscious" or "preconceptual" that influence might be. The strength of the Mary symbol is quite independent of any formal education and is linked to childhood experiences.

10. There is a cycle of decline and rebound in sexual fulfillment during the first ten years of marriage. If charted, the decline takes place between the second and the eighth year, and the rebound occurs during the ninth and tenth year. This rebound is accompanied by a dramatic change in the quality of the religious images shared by the couple and is greatly facilitated if both pray frequently.

11. "Passionate" religious imagery—for example, God as a "lover" or heaven as a "paradise of delight"correlates positively with sexual fulfillment in marriage, but negatively with sexual permissiveness. Respondents with such images have more fulfilling relationships in marriage, but are less likely to approve of promiscuity.

12. Finally, approximately 2.8 million Catholics between 15 and 30 have thought of a religious vocation, and half a million of those have thought about it seriously.

Implications

The social researcher is often faced with the "everyone knew that all along" reaction. Whatever the findings may be, some will say that these things were so self-evident that no project was needed to establish their truth. Before we turn to a discussion of the implications of our findings, we will compare some assertions of the "conventional wisdom," which one can find in many Catholic journals, with the findings we have presented. I doubt that our conclusions will shatter the conventional wisdom, but the comparison may persuade a few readers that not everything reported in this volume is self-evident to everyone.

Wisdom 1: Young Catholics turn away from the Church because of their concern about feminism, racism, and the Third World.

In fact, social relevance has little to do with religiousness. Those correlations which do exist run in the opposite direction. The religious young people are more socially concerned than the non-religious. The sermons in one's parish, the religiousness of one's spouse, and the nature of one's sexual relationship with the spouse are far more important elements in why young people are or are not close to their Church than is the Third World.

Wisdom 2: Sexual and doctrinal orthodoxy are the foundations of a Catholic life. The inconsistency between doctrinal unorthodoxy and religious commitment will cause a strain that will drive young people out of the Church.

In fact, the religious imagination is far more important in its impact on life than is doctrinal orthodoxy. Many young Catholics seem to experience no strain or inconsistency at all in being devout and dedicated Catholics (from their own viewpoint), while at the same time rejecting certain Catholic teachings. It may well be that they should experience strain; however, they do not.

Wisdom 3: The ordination of women, birth control, divorce, and abortion are the really important issues on the minds of young Catholics.

In fact, all of these issues put together are not a fraction as important in affecting the religious practice of young Catholics as is the quality of the Sunday sermon which is offered them.

Wisdom 4: In an ecumenical age after the Second Vatican Council, the Mary Symbol is of little importance in the life of young Catholics.

In fact, it is hard to find a symbol of their religion which is more important.

Wisdom 5: Celibacy is the main reason for the vocation crisis.

In fact, while celibacy is an important factor, the absence of encouragement from priests and from one's family is at least as crucial.

Wisdom 6: Young Catholics are hardly likely to be interested in fraternal organizations like the Knights of Columbus.

In fact, a substantial number are, especially those with Hispanic or Italian backgrounds.

Wisdom 7: This is the age of the laity.

Maybe it is. But, in fact, the ministry of the priest is as important for young people as it is for older people. In other words, the influence of an empathetic priest is a most powerful factor in their religious lives; second to their spouse, if they are married.

Wisdom 8: The big issues which preoccupy journalists—authority, sexual teaching, freedom to dissent—also are critical for the ordinary young Catholic.

In fact, the family and the local religious community dwarf all other factors.

Wisdom 9: One's picture of Jesus, Mary, and God can hardly be expected to affect one's sexual fulfillment.

On the contrary, such images are more important for sexual fulfillment than attitudes of "sexual liberation" or "permissiveness." One's imagery of Mary in particular correlates with sexual fulfillment.

Far from being obvious, our findings are not likely to find acceptance in many Catholic quarters precisely because they are the *opposite* of "what everyone knows is true." Indeed, our findings are likely to be rather unpopular because they constitute in many instances positions "which everyone knows can't be true."

What, then, are the implications of our work for the Church? Before listing some of them, we must remember that this interpretative exercise goes beyond the data and is an attempt to fit into a coherent pattern of commentary the findings reported in this book.

Commentary

1. The American Church must contend with a number of serious weaknesses in its work with young people. Doctrinal and ethical orthodoxy is not highly valued; teaching authority enjoys very little credibility; devotional obligations are not taken seriously; mixed marriages and invalid marriages are entered into frequently.

2. On the other hand, the Church enjoys some extremely important assets. The commitment of most young Catholics persists in spite of the problems cited in the previous paragraph. It is rooted in tenacious religious images and in powerful and demanding human relationships. It takes its strength from the local religious community and an ultimate commitment to the fundamentals of the Catholic world view: God's love for us, life after death.

3. The combination of commitment and laxity is made possible by a "selective" or "compartmentalized" Catholicism. Young Catholics do not so much *wall off* separate segments of their religious life, as they do *wall out* those aspects of the Church which might trouble them if they listened. The Pope is not an unimportant figure; but the religious stance of the spouse and the quality of Sunday preaching are things they listen to and are affected by, far more than any Roman decisions.

4. Such a "selective" Catholicism is possible in turn—and this may be the most critical of the implications of our work—because much of one's religious stance is shaped by the family of origin, the family of procreation, and the local religious community quite independently of formal teaching—whether it be in school, in the content of Sunday sermons, in papal encyclicals, or in episcopal pastoral letters. The Catholic "community"—the informal network of human relationships among the faithful—is able to exercise its religious influence while disregarding what the Church as a formal institution does or says. It also has a much greater impact than does the Church as a formal institution. The religious commitment passed on by the Catholic "community" is remarkably tenacious and persists despite the alienation period of young adulthood and the rejection of certain doctrinal and ethical propositions. Because it is encoded in religious "stories," memories, experiences, and needs, formal institutions and doctrinal propositions have little power over it.

It is beyond the scope of this book to say whether "community Catholicism"—the Catholicism of image, picture, story, memory, family, parish priest, and local community—ought to be forced into harmony with formal structural norms and propositons. It is not beyond the scope of this book, however, to observe that such attempts, should they be made in the name of responsibility and obligation on which the leadership must act, are going to have little effectiveness. The Church will ultimately be mediated to one through one's spouse, and through the Sunday sermon, and through one's religious imagination (with its stored up memories of past experiences) *regardless of what the formal institution tries to force one to do.*

5. In particular, we do not think that the young people who return to the Church at the end of their 20s and the beginning of their 30s could be driven out of it. Their return is the result of deliberate and conscious choice, made with awareness of the problems involved, and the frustrations to be encountered. They will complain; but more often about the quality of preaching, the performance of the liturgy, the inadequacy of pastoral sympathy, and the absence of effective work with young people, than they will about papal encyclicals or social or sexual teachings.

It may well be that some Church leaders will think that this is not the way things ought to be. It is, in fact, the way things are, and the way they are likely to continue to be.

6. Thus, the Church in the United States is likely to survive the rest of this century and millennium without catastrophic losses. The reasons which produce losses are not those one reads about in the papers or the magazines. While many young people offer the opinion that women ought to be ordained, there is no evidence that this issue is salient enough in the lives of our young adults to make much difference to them religiously one way or another. Again, one may want to argue that this is not the way things ought to be. We must reply to these advocates just as we replied to ecclesiastical leaders: it is, however, the way things are, and the way they are likely to continue to be. Discussion of the issue ought to take place in a context where no one is predicting mass defection, because that simply is not going to happen.

7. When we said it looked as if Catholicism could survive the rest of the millennium in the United States without major losses, one of our associates remarked, "if only we could find some more good priests." While we would add "and more religious spouses," we must note that there is rather less the Church can do about the quality of marital intimacy than it can about the quality of pastoral ministry. Undoubtedly, the most important task for the Church in the next two decades is to upgrade the quality of pastoral ministry.

8. Just as the reasons for affiliating with or returning to the Church are, to a considerable extent, outside of the control of the formal institution, so are the reasons for not affiliating with it or disaffiliating with it. Evangelization and re-evangelization are part of the mission of the Church, but they must contend with deep and serious difficulties—rooted in the life, the experiences, and the relationships (particularly familial) of the individual. Shallow and superficial approaches to these problems are surely a waste of time and may do more harm than good. Affiliating or disaffiliating is the result of complex cultural, psychological, biographical, and interpersonal factors over which the institution can expect at most to have modest control. This is not meant to be an excuse for inaction, but a reason for serious, sophisticated, and realistic efforts.

Recommendations

We divide the recommendations into three groups—action recommendations, policy reassessment recommendations, and study and experimentation recommendations.

Action Recommendations

Under this heading we subsume a number of recommendations which seem to follow from the data, if not inevitably, at least with such clarity that most social scientists would make them if they agreed to make any recommendations at all.

1. Every Catholic parish in the country should have a program aimed at its teenagers and young adults. The failure to have such a program for whatever excuse comes close to irresponsible pastoral leadership. Youth programs are not activities which the clergy grudgingly concede to the laity as a privilege to be taken back when windows are broken, but a strict and essential part of the ministry of the Church and an obligation to the people of the parish. Refusal to establish such a program ought to be considered grounds for dismissal for a parish priest. However important in such work the new profession of youth minister might be, young people should still have a chance to know and be close to their parish priest.

2. The quality of the professional performance of the clergy needs to be improved dramatically—particularly in the areas of preaching and sympathetic understanding. If the Church were to do only one thing in the two decades which remain in this second millennium, that one thing should be to improve the quality of Sunday preaching.

3. Vocational recruitment activities ought to focus on the parish priest and the mother. Their encouragement seems to be of primary importance; the lack of it at least seems as much to do with the vocation shortage as the obligation of celibacy. In future research the reason for the decline in encouragement from the principal vocational recruiters should be assessed.

4. All organized evangelization efforts which do not aim at the family unit should be abandoned.

235

5. The Church should stop neglecting the Mary image, one of the most powerful resources available to it. However, the Marian revival which our data seem to mandate will only bear fruit if it is supported by an intelligent understanding of the role the Mary "story" plays. It is not clear, however, that Church teachers and preachers understand this "Mary function" today; nor will the repetition of the saccharine clichés of the past be of any help. Marian images can survive such abuse, a fact which is clearly established by this study, but they are certainly not helped by it.

Policy Reassessment Recommendations

Under this heading we place a series of recommendations which indicate the need for a reconsideration of some of the policies which are presently widespread in the Church.

1. *Catholic Schools.* The policy of not constructing new Catholic schools ought to be reappraised. It is clear that no adequate substitute for the school exists and that they are more important to the work of the Church in times of fluidity and transition than they were in times of stability. Doubtless there are situations where it is no longer practical to build Catholic schools. Our evidence indicates, however, that the Church ought to consider the possibility of reestablishing the policy of viewing the presumption as being in favor of Catholic schools instead of being against them.

2. *Marriage Education.* We urge a reconsideration of the strategies of marriage education in the absence of any data of which we are aware indicating impact or absence of impact of pre-marriage education. However, on theoretical grounds we wonder if limited resources ought not better be expended on the years after a marriage (particularly the middle years of the first decade) than on the weeks and months immediately before a marriage. The decline/rebound phenomenon of the first decade seems to pressent a superb opportunity for religious education and support—at a time when the young family is getting precious little support from anyone.

3. *Mixed Marriages.* Some readers of The *Young Catholic Family* misinterpreted the finding reported there (as well as in this volume) about the problems of mixed marriages. If there is anything which ought to be clear from the present research, it is that new restrictions are a waste of time. However, the general acceptance of religiously mixed marriage in the years since Second Vatican Council (as demonstrated in *Catholic Schools in a Declining Church*) has obscured what appear to be serious religious and human problems. Neither the religious nor marital rebounds observed in these data occur in religiously mixed marriages (or they have not occurred yet, at any rate). A good deal more attention ought to be paid to these problems by both the clergy and the laity as they strive to establish an environment in which marital choices are made.

4. *Fraternal Organizations as Religious Educators.* Surely, the fraternal organizations are aware that they are, in part, in the religious education business, although, perhaps, they themselves do not perceive how important their appeal as religious educators is. Those responsible for adult education in the Church should consider whether the religious education potential of the fraternal groups ought not be much more comprehensively and enthusiastically used than it is presently.

5. *Guidelines for Those Who Return.* The presently popular "guideline movement" is legalistic in its application, if not in its intent. Those who are drifting back to the Church at the time of marriage or baptism are presented with what is in effect a checklist of obligations they have to fulfill before they are back. The evidence gathered in this study should raise the question of whether such a policy is not a major tactical and strategic blunder. The "returners" will be more effectively helped by a joyous and welcoming celebration. Intelligent explanation and courteous and attractive liturgical performance from a warm, friendly, and sympathetic priest are likely to have a much greater impact than a series of legalistic rules laid down by an authoritarian priest. Certainly, the preparation for a sacrament ought to include instruction and motivation. However, this should be done, it seems to us, subtly, delicately, charmingly, as something intrinsic to the ceremony itself, rather than "steamrollering" people with pages of formal regulations. Our analysis does not indicate that the steamroller drives people away (though in some cases it might). At a certain age in life many young people want their religion back no matter what the cost in legalistic obstacles that has to be paid. We doubt, however, that their religious and spiritual maturation is helped by such tactics. The Church leadership should ask itself whether the strategy of the father of the prodigal son might not be the best model for educational pedagogy at this time in a person's life.

Study and Experimentation Recommendations

Three relatively new perspectives were introduced in this study—religious imagination, marital rebound, and religious life cycle. Responsible researchers do not urge policy actions on the basis of a single survey testing a new approach. However, when there seems to be empirical payoffs in these approaches, they should, at least, recommend further study, discussion, and preliminary experimentation. Thus, we propose the following:

1. The effectiveness of the religious imagination needs to be explored in greater detail, as do methods for enhancing its development. Superficial and faddish efforts to educate the religious imagination would be counterproductive. Yet, the religious imagination is what keeps many young people in the Church. It is a much more decisive force in their lives than formal doctrines. Catechetics, homiletics, and apologetics should pay much more attention to the picture, images, and "stories" of God which flourish in the human imagination.

2. The close connection between religion and intimacy reported in this work suggests that a "spirituality of human intimacy" ought to be developed out of the Church's rich resources in the region of "The Two Loves." Whereas there is little credibility left for the Church's role as a teacher of sexual ethics, there is no competition in the formulation of such a spirituality. It is not a question of establishing a linkage between human love and divine love. Rather, the challenge is to make that connection explicit and to aid people in illuminating their lives with it.

3. The unmarried years of the early and middle 20s are a relatively new phenomenon in American society—at least insofar as they have become a time of alienation from social institutions and norms. We have little understanding of the reasons for this period of religious and human crisis, though there is evidence that for many it is a time of great personal loneliness and pain. Any youth ministry in the United States must understand the roots of alienation and experiment with new methods of responding to its deep and frequently poignant human needs—needs which for many young adults are met, it would appear, only by the "singles" bars.

Conclusions

The recommendations in the first two categories seem quite traditional—youth organizations, better pastoral ministry, better sermons, vocational recruitment in the home and parish, devotion to Mary, Catholic schools, doubts about mixed marriages, kindness to those who are returning, the importance of fraternal organizations. Indeed, they could have been made, one suspects, thirty years ago and create less stir than they do now. That a policy recommendation is traditional and obvious does not mean that it need not be made. Many of the actions urged in previous paragraphs are not being taken now, were not being taken thirty years ago, and are not likely to be taken in the years immediately ahead. The obviousness of recommendations does not guarantee their being followed.

It is useful, nonetheless, to have a mass of empirical evidence in one's possession when one urges the obvious—especially, to paraphrase Chesterton, when the obvious has not been tried and found wanting, but found hard and not tried. It is helpful to be able to demonstrate how important the Sunday sermon is, even if one does not expect that such a demonstration will lead to an instant improvement in the quality of preaching.

Furthermore, the recommendations may be less conventional than they first seem. Much of the conventional wisdom of current pastoral practice is questioned—marriage education, mixed marriages guidelines, the reluctance to build Catholic schools.

They may also be controversial in what they do not say. We cannot urge on the basis of the data many of those social and egalitarian programs which are so fashionable today—minority rights, women's rights, concern for the Third World. We can and do urge them on other grounds: justice, charity, equity. The Church must be concerned about social problems. But there ought not to be a need to reinforce concern by the pragmatic argument that the absence of concern will lead to the "loss" of the young. Somehow it has always seemed to us that such a selfish argument demeans the cause of justice and charity. We should be socially concerned even if it is not necessary for our survival. Whatever one may think of the propriety of the argument for a "concerned" Church, we could find no evidence to support its validity.

Finally, the most unconventional dimensions of the recommendations and the report are twin assumptions about the nature of human religion. They present the context against which the recommendations are made and a perspective of the world in which the recommendations will be implemented—if, indeed, they are.

First, we contend on the basis of the evidence that religious behavior is a "primary group" phenomenon, influenced most powerfully by one's intimate relationships in the family of origin, and family of procreation, as well as in the local religious community. A papal encyclical on human sexuality or social justice has much less religious impact than does the quality of the Sunday sermon, the dedication of one's spouse, and the memories of one's childhood religious experiences that have been encoded in one's personal stories of God. For most people, the farther away a religious factor is from the place where they live (physically as well as psychologically), the less important it is likely to be.

Secondly, we also contend that the images, pictures, and stories which exist in the religious imagination provide much of the raw power of religion in people's lives. Furthermore, these facets of religious imagination are responsible for the tenacity with which many young people maintain their Catholic commitment despite inconsistencies in their propositional beliefs and their frustrations and dissatisfactions with the ecclesiastical institution. Theological systems, catechetical formulations, and creedal propositions are not unimportant. But, when it comes to how often a person prays, or how a person reacts to death, or how committed he or she is to the search for social justice, or how he or she relates to a marriage partner, religious images—stories of God—are far more important.

These two assumptions may also be old fashioned. Before modern transportation and communication were developed and before literacy and education were commonplace, the Catholic tradition was handed on by stories told in religious primary groups—the family and parish. What we may be saying is that, appearances to the contrary, that still seems to be the case.

In its work with young people the Church has two powerful forces on its side. First of all, the passionate faith of young people in a loving God, as revealed by the stories of God, persists in their religious imaginations. Secondly, their passionate commitment to one another in human love is, indeed, empirically linked to God's love.

Those are not bad cards to begin with.

Appendix I

Respondent Comments

Catholic youth speak with many voices—some soft, some strident, some enthusiastic, some alienated. This report reflects the tone and direction of those voices on religion and fraternal organizations, on family relationships and religious education. Within the body of the report, the respondents have spoken as a group, with their opinions recorded in tabular form. Statistical presentation offers the most accurate picture of youthful opinion as a whole. It allows the researcher to record the proportions of a population who take a particular stance or who behave in a particular way, and offers the opportunity statistically to explain variations in opinion or behavior using a number of possible models. The researcher may test which explanations are most effective for a population, which less so. Research at the population level is often termed *macro-level research*.

A fuller understanding of motivations, however, may often be obtained by also conducting micro-level research, by talking in depth with individuals. In the case of the Young Catholics Study, as with much survey research, a number of these individual interviews preceded construction of the survey questionnaire. The results of the interviews are reflected in the printed responses available to respondents.

However, the final questionnaire also offered an opportunity for individual comment. At the end of each the study's protocol, the following general question appeared: "Do you have any additional comments?" About 25 percent of the respondents took this opportunity to comment on their feelings about their relationship with God, the Catholic Church, or their opinions on the questionnaire itself. For the most part, the respondents offered positive comments concerning the study, more critical ones on the Church.

This appendix represents a sampling of the responses given. While the comments flesh out the data and may enrich our understanding, the caveat stands that they may not be typical of the whole group, especially since the average person offered no comment. The quotations presented here, however, do attempt to portray the range of respondent reactions. (They under-represent a great number of the "I enjoyed participating in the study" sentiments.)

A number of young people expressed their desire for a personal relationship with God which they felt could be fulfilled outside of Catholicism.

> I felt that you were searching the wrong areas as to why Catholics leave the Church. It, I feel, has little to do with the pope, Latin Mass, Church structure, etc., but rather it barricades people from God through a series of roadblocks to perpetuate Church structure with priests, confessionals, and rituals, all far from biblical, to insulate the individual from a personal relationship with God, which is the very reason for Christ's death, which they try to nullify with these roadblocks, to widen the gap between God and man. Those who wish to find God cannot find him in the Catholic Church.

> I really don't like the way you refer to religion; I like people, I accept people, I don't ask them what church they go to, I just tell them about the wonderful thing God has done in my life. Time after time God has shown me it is not the religion or church you go to that's going to save you, but in your own personal relationship you have with him through his son Jesus Christ. You ask him to come into your heart and make himself more real in your life and he will, if you are sincere.

Some respondents turned away from Catholicism permanently or temporarily because it did not meet their needs in a time of personal crisis or because of difficulties with certain clergymen and congregations.

> I'm not very fond of the Catholic Church, in my times of need—they were never there. When I asked for help or guidance, it was denied. I associate my Catholic religion with pain, disgust, and disappointment. Thank goodness I found an honest warm Methodist minister. . . My answers have been different than I normally would have put, but since the death of my fiance, I have questioned religious aspects a lot.

> I used to feel very close to my religion, but due to tragic deaths of three of my immediate family members it took me a long time to accept God's love again. Now I've also had experience in dealing with eight different priests of different parishes, and they are not very willing to cooperate with the people as well as I think they should. They do need more help in running the parishes, but I think it should be from a parish council made up of lay people.

I am about to be married and was very disappointed in a certain church that I attended and had belonged to Catholic youth activities. We had new priests, and they were very cold and inconsiderate towards me when I went to talk to them about it. I resigned from this church and didn't have much faith until I joined another church which was better. I now happen to think the church is the one who decides whether you'll be a good Catholic or not.

The questions I feel did not completely encompass reasoning for turning away from the church. I personally feel that I've not lost my religion at all. My disappointment stems from the people within the church with whom I have had dealings. During my high school and beginning college years I was quite active within my church. The closer I got to the people within the church, the more it seemed I did not want to become like these people because of the separate standards for people with the church.

Thank you for allowing me to express my opinion.

I am not a U.S. citizen. I have lived only nine years in this country. I received all my education in Spain. I feel the Catholic church in U.S. is more cold and farther from people than in my country. I had became very dissatisfied with Catholic church and, in particular, our parish in our community. Catholics in U.S. do not work to help people as much as they do in other countries.

Both the religiously strong and the weak questioned a Catholic emphasis on rules or questioned the rules themselves.

The reason I have drifted away from the Catholic Church is that I feel this church dwells too much on its own rules instead of the basic Bible truths—much like the Jews did before Jesus Christ came into the world.

Catholic Church does not provide spiritual guidance, and therefore, I do not feel closely related, and its rules and regulations are without relevance. Catholic Church does provide opportunity to hear Jesus' word, so I attend for that only.

I really hope that the Catholic Church changes their rules on birth control and divorce. We could not marry in church because my husband was married in church before. It didn't last a year, but it knocked us out of being married in church or receiving the sacraments.

My most basic disagreement with the church is the position it takes towards divorced people. My girl friend has been divorced, but I see no reason for us not to be able to be remarried in a church if it is what we want. I see no sin in being divorced and then remarried.

The reason why my family and myself denounced the Catholic religion is the rules are too harsh. God is a loving God, but the Catholics make it seem that we were put on earth to suffer and pay dues, when in fact, he meant for us to live happily, providing we live by the laws of man, God, and the universe—truth, honesty, and love for one another.

The Catholic religion is the original after Christ and, they are always trying to improve. I would never change my faith, regardless of rules or regulations I dislike or don't follow.

When I was attending religious classes for public elementary school children, the thing I remember most about them was how they kept making me feel afraid of going to hell. I know we are suppose to have some fear of God, but that's all they kept preaching. I used to breakdown and cry sometimes before going to confession because I was so scared. I didn't like the strong paranoia they set in me. I only hope now that they are teaching a little more of the Love and positive things a young Christian should know.

When I attended Catholic elementary school and had catechism classes, the teaching involved was so scary for children in that age group. Stories about—if you bit the host, it will bleed. I can remember having nightmares about some of the teachings. I began to question Catholicism when I was told it was a "sin" to attend another church. I felt as long as you worshiped "God" what difference did it make where you did such (i.e., home, synagogue, etc.).

I hope that this questionnaire helps, somewhat, to improve the religious education, particularly in schools like the one I attended. I'm somewhat biased since this school was for all girls administered by Spanish nuns in Puerto Rico (they are usually very strict and old-fashioned).

One respondent reacted more positively to her Catholic religious education.

I enjoyed answering the survey because it made me think about my childhood religious education which I sometimes feel have taken for granted. Some questions also brought new ideas to me such as life after death, images of God, and Jesus.

Younger teens (14-17) were likely to question the relevance of the Catholic Church in their own lives.

I think the Catholic religion would be more interesting if it was brought up to date. I go to church every week and learn about the Bible which is in the past. I think the Bible is extremely important, but it would help with getting the younger generation more interested if the sermons had a little to do with the present. The priest who gives the sermons at our Masses puts us teenagers asleep when it's (the sermon) supposed to enlighten us.

I think that today's younger generation demands more, therefore we need to find new ways to teach and help people understand more about religion. Suggestions: nowadays you probably have to come to us. Have more "rap" sessions in school, something to get to the problems of the people.

I feel that many changes should be made in the Catholic doctrine; while I can see that tradition is important I can't see teaching what was taught in the 15th century! Times and values have changed!!!

Then there were the perennial reactions to fundraising.

The Catholic Church puts too much time into charities and bingo. Rather than assist teens with organizations, it complains about rising costs of heating a building for a function.

. . . The Catholic Church is too money oriented.

I used to get pleasure from attending Mass as a child. However, too many things began to seem terribly unrealistic (some of the beliefs I was expected to have). Church now seems to me to be a fundraising affair, not only Catholic churches, but the others I have tried. The closest I have come to something acceptable to me is Emmett Fox's works. They mostly make sense to me.

A few respondents offered critical comments on the questionnaire.

Questionnaire should be a little bit shorter.

Too long!

The questions were pretty general, easy to answer. But I think that for a more thorough survey, there should possibly be a space to include extraordinary circumstances.

Some questions need to be answered with an explanation rather than yes-no-maybe. I did find your questions interesting—Quite a few really made me think about my answer.

However, most respondents enjoyed the opportunity to make their opinions known or to have their thoughts focused on religious questions.

I think it is a really good thing. I want to thank you for giving me the chance to answer these questions. Thanks for being so concerned about teenagers. Thank you for the two dollars also.

I appreciate the time you people have taken in realizing that teenagers do like to air their opinion.

I think this questionnaire not only helps NORC but it has helped me to think more about my opinions of some of these questions that otherwise I would not have considered thoughtfully. It has also gotten me to get more active in religious or spiritual activities. Thanks. I thought it was fun and I wouldn't mind doing some more like this.

This was an excellent questionnaire! Being in the field of medical research, I have an interest in gathering data. It proved to be rather thought provoking and if possible, I would like to have a copy of the final results.

Enjoyed doing survey, covered some real issues and concerns I've had for a long time. Made me think about what I'm doing. Bravo!

Enjoyed filling out this questionnaire. Took my time, pondered and stopped to reflect on several areas, to search within myself to reevaluate as to just what are my beliefs and feelings about the subject matter. This would be good for premarital guidance and training for future spouses to help understand each other.

I think this questionnaire explored deeply into most peoples lives. And I would like to see this carried out on a higher level to get people to think about themselves and the things around because we need a lot of this in today's struggling often untouched world!

One respondent suggested a follow-up study.

I enjoyed this very much. I would like to do this again in five years.

Another respondent echoed a question which the staff would like to have answered.

I would like to know what influence these questionnaires have on the Church.

And finally, a simple entreaty.

God help us all.

Appendix II

Guide to Statistical Terms

The Mean: The mean, which is symbolized by $\bar{X}$ or M, represents an average score. It is the sum of all scores divided by the number of scores.

Median: The middle observation of a series—the observation or response which divides the series into two equal parts. In the following series of numbers: 1, 3, 7, 8, 11, the median would be 7. If there is an even number of observations or responses, the median will fall halfway between the two middle observations. In the following series: 2, 4, 6, 8, the median is 5.

Mode: The response or observation which occurs most frequently. For example, in the following series: 10, 11, 11, 12, 13, 13, 13, the modal response is 13, which occurred three times.

Standard Deviation: The standard deviation is a measure of dispersion; that is, the spread of scores around the mean. By definition, the standard deviation (s) is the "square root of the arithmetic mean of the squared deviations from the mean."[1] If the scores form a normal distribution, or a normal curve, 68 percent of the scores will fall within one standard deviation above and below the mean; and 95 percent of the scores will fall within two standard deviations above and below the mean.

Z-score: A standardized score. A raw score from which the mean is subtracted. This is then divided by the standard deviation.

Correlation Coefficient: A correlation coefficient measures the degree to which two items are related. The Pearson product-moment correlation used in this paper is symbolized by the letter "r." Pearson correlations (r's) range between 0 (which indicates that two items are not associated in any regular way) and 1.0 (which indicates that as one item increases or decreases, the other will also increase or decrease in a perfectly related fashion).

A positive correlation shows movement in the same direction. Income and education provide an example of positive correlation. **247**

In the U.S. population, those members who have received a higher number of years of education, on the average, receive higher salaries. The correlation between education and income does not approach 1.0, however, since some people with a high school education make more money than those with undergraduate or graduate degrees. As might be expected, negative correlation occurs when two items are related in opposite ways; as one increases, the other decreases. Among U.S. adults, age and educational attainment show a negative correlation. Senior citizens are less likely to have received as many years of education as have younger adults.

In order to calculate a correlation coefficient, the items under study must be arranged in some sort of order, with numbers attached to each category. Many statisticians demand equal intervals between categories. Age, for example, leads itself to correlation—with a natural ascending order and one year between each unit. In contrast, even if a researcher assigned a number to each hair color (1 = brown, 2 = black, 3 = blond, 4 = red, 5 grey), hair color could not be correlated with other items. Brown is no "more" or "less" than grey. An exception is an item with only two categories. If a researcher wanted to discover whether being blond or brunette was associated with having more dates per month, he could arbitrarily assign blonds into one group—say 1's—and brunettes into another—2's. With only two groups, one high and one low, it is possible to determine whether membership in a particular group is associated with another item which is arranged on an interval scale (here number of dates per month).

Regression: While correlation is associated more with the *degree* of a relationship (whether it is strong or weak), regression is concerned with its *form*. The researcher produces a regression equation ($\bar{Y} = a + b\bar{X}$) which states exactly how much a dependent item will change for each unit of change in the first item (independent). A regression equation, for example, might show that, on the average, for each year of schooling that a person gets, his or her yearly income increases by $2,000. Likewise, an equation might show that for each year older a person gets, he attends church two more times per year.

Regression may also be used to calculate the *relative* importance of one independent item (variable) versus another in predicting a third (dependent) item. In this situation, which is termed a multiple regression equation, all of the predictor items (independent variables) are often converted to standard units (z scores), based on the degree to which the population varies on any one item, so that they may be compared. Using multiple regression, for example, a researcher could discover whether a person's age or his income better predicted how often he attended church.

Similarly, regression also shows how much variance in the dependent variable has been "explained." In the example above, when the researcher predicted church attendance using age and income, he or she would specify through the r^2 statistic exactly how much of a population's variation in church attendance is explained by age and income combined.

Path Analysis: A method of illustrating the relationships among a set of (linear) variables by assuming causal order among the variables. In the fictitious example below, it is assumed that parents' religiosity will directly affect whether or not their children attend Catholic schools and also how often the children attend Mass. It is also assumed that the parents' religiosity will affect a child's Mass attendance indirectly by the parents' decision whether or not to send the child to a Catholic school. The "E" represents the error component—that proportion of the variance in a child's Mass attendance which is not accounted for either by parents' religiosity or by Catholic education.

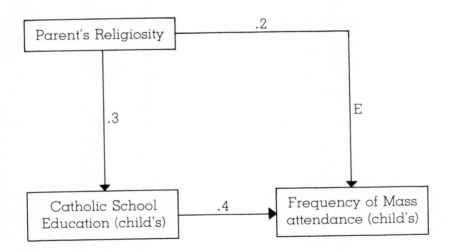

The numbers which appear along the paths illustrate the amount of impact which one variable has on the other. This impact is determined through regression equations. If, for example, parents' religiosity had no statistically significant effect on the frequency of a child's Mass attendance, the paths between the two variables would be zero or close to it and could be dropped from the model.

Path analysis is especially useful for showing *how* one variable affects another. In the above example, if Catholic school education were not taken into account, religiosity would relate to frequency of Mass attendance at .32 (.2 + .3 x .4). The model reveals that .12 points of the relationship is due to the impact of Catholic schools.

249

Factor Analysis: Factor analysis is a statistical technique based on regression, which reduces a large number of items to a smaller number of underlying *factors* or dimensions. In the Young Catholics Study questionnaire, for example, respondents indicate how often they engage in eleven methods of private prayer. Based on the correlations between the prayer items, a factor analysis reduces the eleven items to three underlying factors—or three categories of prayer. Of course, if the eleven methods of prayer were unrelated, it would be impossible to produce from them a smaller number of factors. Factor analysis, then, groups items together based on their intercorrelations. The researcher, however, must deduce the link that holds the items together.

Multiple Classification Analysis: A statistical technique used to estimate the effects of a nominal predictor variable on an interval or ratio level dependent variable. Nominal variables assume no natural order. An example of a nominal variable is religion. People may be Catholic, Baptist, Jewish, or of another denomination or "name." Unlike characteristics like age, the religions do not naturally arrange themselves from lowest to highest. Multiple classification analysis could be used to determine the effects of religion on variables like income or number of children. (A variable achieves the "interval" level of measurement when there are equal intervals between categories; a variable is considered at the "ratio" level when there are not only equal intervals between categories of the variable, but the variable also has a zero point. Intelligence quotients are an example of an interval level variable. Number of children in a family illustrates a ratio level variable.) The eta statistic measures the association between the variables in multiple classification analysis.

Eta: A measure of association used when the predictor variable is nominal and the dependent variable is interval or ratio. Eta, like Pearson's r, ranges from 0 to 1. Like r^2, eta squared measures the proportion of variance in the dependent variable accounted for by the independent variable. In the religion example above, eta squared would show the amount of variance in income or number of children accounted for by religion.

Chi-Square: Symbolized by X^2, chi-square constitutes a test to determine whether the *observed* frequency of occurrences in a table differs from that which would have been *expected* to occur by chance. For example, a researcher may wish to test the hypothesis that young female Catholics are more likely to attend church frequently than young male Catholics. If females constitute 51 percent of the youthful Catholic population and males 49 percent, then by chance one would expect females to represent around 51 percent of the frequent church attenders and males about 49 percent. The researcher could test this hypothesis by

250

producing the table below and using the chi-square statistic to determine whether a, b, c, and d constitute a statistically significant deviation from normal expectations.

	Males	Females
Frequent church attenders	a	b
Infrequent church attenders	c	d

T-Test: The t-test is a test of significance more powerful than the chi-square test—one used mainly on interval level data. Like the chi-square test, researchers use the t-test for hypothesis testing to determine, within certain confidence limits, whether an observed situation deviates from that which would be expected by chance. In social research the confidence level is usually set at either .05 or .01—that is, odds of 95 out of 100 or 99 out of 100 that the observed difference are real and did not occur by chance.

NOTES

[1]From Hubert M. Blalock's *Social Statistics* (New York, 1960), a readable introduction to the use of statistics in social research. Another slightly less technical guide is Hans Zeisel's *Say It With Figures*, 5th edition (New York, 1968). For an introduction to factor analysis, see Jae-On Kim and Charles W. Mueller, *Factor Analysis: Statistical Methods and Practical Issues* (Beverly Hills, California, 1978).

References

Allport, Gordon and J. Ross
1967 "Personal Orientation and Prejudice." *Journal of Personality and Social Psychology* 5: 432-443.

Barnard, Chester I.
1938 *The Functions of the Executive.* Cambridge, Massachusetts: Harvard University Press.

Burch, Thomas K.
1966 "The Fertility of North American Catholics: A Comparative Overview." *Demography* 3: 174-87.

Coale, Ansley J. and Paul Demeny
1966 *Regional Model Life Tables and Stable Populations.* Princeton, N.J.: Princeton University Press.

Converse, Philip E.
1966 "Religion and Politics: 1960 Election," in Angus Campbell, Philip E. Converse, Warren E. Miller, Donald E. Stokes, *Elections and the Political Order.* New York: Wiley.

Davis, James A.
1979 "Background variables and opinions in the 1972-1977 NORC General Social Surveys: Ten Generalizations about Age, Education, Occupational Prestige, Race, Religion, and Sex and Forty-Nine Opinion Items." *General Social Survey Technical Report* 18. Chicago: National Opinion Research Center.

DeJong, Gordon E., Joseph E. Faulkner and Rex H. Warland
1976 "Dimensions of Religiosity Reconsidered; Evidence from a Cross-Cultural Study." *Social Forces.* 54: 866-899.

Etzione, Amitai
1965 "Organizational Control Structure," in James G. March (ed.), *Handbook of Organizations.* Chicago: Rand McNally, 650-677.

Fee, Joan L.
1976 "Party Identification among American Catholics, 1972, 1973." *Ethnicity* 3: 53-69.

Freedman, Ronald, P.K. Welpton and Arthur A. Campbell
1959 *Family Planning, Sterility and Population Growth.* New York: McGraw-Hill.

Greeley, Andrew M.
1979 *Crisis in the Church.* Chicago: The Thomas More Association.

― ― ―

 1977   *The American Catholic.* New York: Basic Books, Inc.

― ― ―

 1974   "Political Participation among Ethnic Groups in the
         United States: A Preliminary Reconnaissance."
         American Journal of Sociology 80: 170-204.
― ― ― and Peter H. Rossi
 1966   *The Education of Catholic Americans.* Chicago: Aldine.
― ― ―, William C. McCready and Kathleen McCourt
 1976   *Catholic Schools in a Declining Church.* Kansas City:
         Sheed and Ward.

― ― ―

 1981   *The Religious Imagination.* New York: William H.
         Sadlier, Inc.
Hanna, Mary T.
 1979   *Catholics and American Politics.* Cambridge,
         Massachusetts: Harvard University Press.
Hogan, Dennis P.
 1976   "Differentials and Trends in Structure of Family of
         Origin." Paper read at the 71st Annual Meeting,
         American Socioligical Association, New York.
Jones, Elise F. and Charles F. Westoff
 1979   "The End of 'Catholic' Fertility." *Demography* 16:
         209-217.
King, Morton B. and Richard A. Hunt
 1975   "Measuring the Religious Variable." *Journal for the
         Scientific Study of Religion* 14: 13-22.
Kirk, Dudley
 1955   "Recent Trends of Catholic Fertility in the United
         States." *Current Research in Human Fertility.* Milbank
         Memorial Fund: 93-105.
Knoke, David
 1974   "Religious Involvement and Political Behavior: A
         Log-linear Analyses of White Americans, 1952-1968."
         The Sociological Quarterly 15: 51-64.
Krump, John M.
 1979   *Youth and the Church.* Chicago: The Thomas More
         Association.
Lenski, Gerhard
 1951   *The Religious Factor.* Garden City, N.Y.: Doubleday.
Lipset, Seymour M.
 1964   "Religion and Politics in the American Past and
         Present," in Robert Lee and Martin E. Marty, *Religion
         and Social Conflict.* New York: Oxford University Press.
O'Connell, Brian J.
 1975   "Dimensions of Religiosity Among Catholics." *Review
         of Religious Research* 16: 198-207.

Potvin, Raymond H., Dean R. Hoge and Hart M. Nelsen
    1976   *Religion and American Youth.* Washington, D.C.: U.S.
            Catholic Conference.
Robinson, Gilbert K.
    1936   "The Catholic Birth Rate: Further Facts and
            Implications." *American Journal of Sociology* 41:
            757-766.
Stark, Rodney and Charles Glock
    1968   *American Piety: The Nature of Religious Commitment.*
            Berkeley, California: University of California Press.
Stouffer, Samuel A.
    1955   *Communism, Conformity and Civil Liberties.* Garden
            City: N.Y.: Doubleday.

———

    1935   "Trends in the Fertility of Catholics and Non-Catholics."
            American Journal of Sociology 41: 143-166.
U.S. Bureau of the Census
    1979   Current Population Reports. "Estimates of the
            Population of the United States by Age, Sex, and Race:
            1976 to 1978." Series P-25, No. 800.

———

    1978   Current Population Reports. "Fertility of American
            Women: June 1978 (Advance Report)." Series P-20, No.
            330 (Rev.).
U.S. National Center for Health Statistics
    1979   Vital Statistics of the United States, 1975. *Vol. III:
            Marriage and Divorce.* Hyattsville, MD.: The Center.
Verba, Sidney and Norman H. Nie
    1972   *Participation in America.* New York: Harper & Row.
Weber, Max
    1964   *The Theory of Social and Economic Organization,* A.M.
            Henderson and Talcott Parsons (translators). New York:
            The Free Press.
Warren, Bruce
    1970   "Socioeconomic Achievement and Religion," in E.O.
            Laumann (ed.), *Social Stratification: Research and
            Theory for the 1970's.* New York: Bobbs-Merrill: 130-155.
Westoff, Charles F. et. al.
    1961   *Family Growth in Metropolitan America.* Princeton
            University Press.

———

    1979   "The Blending of Catholic Reproductive Behavior," in
            Robert Wuthnow (ed.), *The Religious Dimension.* New
            York: Academic: 231-40.
Whelpton, P.K., A.A. Campbell and J.E. Patterson
    1966   *Fertility and Family Planning in the United States.*
            Princeton, N.J.: Princeton University Press.

Wuthnow, Robert

    1976   *The Consciousness Reformation.* Berkeley, California: University of California Press.

  — — —

    1978   *Experimentation in American Religion.* Berkeley, California: University of California Press.